MAKING
SENSE OF
the Bible

MAKING SENSE OF the Bible

Difficult Texts and Modern Faith

Antony F. Campbell, SJ

PAULIST PRESS
New York · Mahwah, NJ

Cover design by Lynn Else
Book design by John Eagleson

Library of Congress Cataloging-in-Publication Data

Campbell, Antony F.
   Making sense of the Bible : difficult texts and modern faith / Antony F. Campbell.
      p. cm.
   Includes bibliographical references.
   ISBN 978-0-8091-4634-5 (alk. paper)
   1. Bible. O.T.–Criticism, interpretation, etc. I. Title.
   BS1171.3.C36 2010
   221.6–dc22   2009047352

Published by Paulist Press
997 Macarthur Boulevard
Mahwah, New Jersey 07430

www.paulistpress.com

Printed and bound in the
United States of America

Dedicated to my mother and father
in gratitude for the wisdom
that comes with age

*The greatest force opposing our acquiring knowledge
is the knowledge we already have for sure —
but that ain't so.*

— Mark Twain —

*To thy sacred text be true.
Subtext: accepting that being true to it
involves on occasion denying aspects of it.*

— Tony Campbell —

Contents

Part Two
THE BOOK OF JOSHUA AND ENIGMA

Part Three
THE BOOKS OF SAMUEL AND REALITY

Abbreviations

AB	Anchor Bible
An Bib	Analecta biblica
ANET	*Ancient Near Eastern Texts*
ATD	Das Alte Testament Deutsch
BETL	Bibliotheca ephemeridum theologicarum lovaniensium
BKAT	Biblischer Kommentar, Altes Testament
CBQMS	Catholic Biblical Quarterly Monograph Series
FOTL	Forms of the Old Testament Literature
HSM	Harvard Semitic monographs
ICC	International Critical Commentary
IEJ	*Israel Exploration Journal*
JB	The Jerusalem Bible
JPS	Jewish Publication Society, The Holy Scriptures, 1955
JSOTSup	Journal for the Study of the Old Testament: Supplement Series
KAT	Kommentar zum Alten Testament
LXX	The Septuagint
NAB	The New American Bible
NCB	New Century Bible
NRSV	New Revised Standard Version, The Holy Bible, 1989
OBT	Overtures to Biblical Theology
OTL	Old Testament Library
WBC	Word Biblical Commentary

Introduction

As I have said elsewhere,
the time for debunking is past.
It is time to build for the future.
"To build and to plant." (Jeremiah 1:10)

The aim of this book is to look closely at what is happening in the study of biblical text (Older Testament) at the present time and to build on that in order to extract the maximum value from what otherwise might be seen as disturbing. In simple terms, what is the meaning of much of the Older Testament in the light of modern study? How do we make meaning from its texts?

Where the Pentateuch is concerned, the last couple of centuries have seen the elimination of Moses from the originating stages of the pentateuchal text — Moses removed from the origins of the Pentateuch. The moves are now in place, and have been for some time, that make it likely that the next century or so will see the elimination of the Pentateuch itself from the originating stages of the text of Israel's story — the Pentateuch removed from the origins of Israel. The composition of its text has long been accepted as exilic or later; its constituent traditions are another question, but are usually out of our reach. Rather than being at the beginning of it all, the formation of these traditions as well as their shaping into the present biblical text will more likely be seen as having emerged around the end.

A strong pointer in this direction is the publication in the United States of *A Farewell to the Yahwist?* providing papers read at a symposium of the Society of Biblical Literature (see under Dozeman in the bibliography). It brings to the fore, for consideration in American and English-language circles, issues that have been under discussion for some time in Germany. The debate is likely to be ignited more broadly than hitherto. The publication by Mark O'Brien and myself

1

OLDER AND NEWER: An Aside

The terms "Older" and "Newer" Testament are used here in place of the traditional "Old" and "New." The primary purpose is simple: not to detract from the unity of the Bible from a Christian point of view. "Old" is understood by some to mean "outmoded" or "bypassed," a view that should not be encouraged. The old split between "God of wrath" and "God of love" has long been recognized as nonsense and has gone by the board. "Old" and "New" may need to go the same way. "First" and "Second" Testament to my mind will not be accepted; "First" and "New" is worse, positively inviting replacement thinking. The current "Hebrew Scriptures" is a tad on the narrow side as well as misleading. For the early part of the Bible, the Protestant canon is the same as that of the Hebrew Bible as far as the actual books included are concerned; the sequence of the books, however, is quite different and significantly so — at least potentially (prophets last, pointing to Jesus; or "writings" last, pointing to the Temple). Not encompassing the deuterocanonical books, "Hebrew Scriptures," of course, ignores those of Roman Catholic, Orthodox, and other faiths. No terminology is fully satisfactory; "Older" and "Newer" is more ecumenical than most.

---

of *Rethinking the Pentateuch* opens the way to possibilities for a quite different view of the Pentateuch from the one that has prevailed in the West over the last two or three centuries.

Where the book of Joshua is concerned, it has been authoritatively claimed that:

> We must confront the fact that the external material evidence supports almost *nothing* of the biblical account of a large-scale, concerted Israelite military invasion of Canaan. . . . (Dever, *Early Israelites*, 71)

No informed scholar would disagree. Given this, how then do we understand the book of Joshua?

Alternatively, summarizing the papers from a 1992 conference at Brown University by half a dozen specialists, William Ward writes:

> If one were to characterize briefly the general thrust of this conference, it is that the empirical evidence of archaeology and language does not remotely resemble the biblical narrative of the Exodus and Conquest. (in Frerichs and Lesko, *Exodus,* 111)

Where the unified kingdom of David and Solomon is concerned, grave doubts have been expressed about the achievements of both and the timing of Davidic texts. One view can stand for many:

> Do the descriptions of David's wars and building projects mesh with the archaeological reality of that era? Are the dynastic intrigues that play such a major role in the "Court History" conceivable in David's time? ... The answer is certainly negative. ... The evidence clearly suggests that tenth-century Jerusalem was a small highland village that controlled a sparsely settled hinterland. (Finkelstein and Silberman, *David and Solomon,* 94–95)

My concern, as is well known, is less with the historical value of such texts but with their reflection on human experience and their theological value for assessing life before God. Nevertheless, the issues of such texts have to be taken into account. Truth should not be based on unconscious falsehood, legendary or not. An exploration of the Davidic texts from this point of view is highly desirable. The Solomonic texts (1 Kgs 3–11) are, in my judgment, an oddly assorted lot with an unusually high percentage of the legendary (unless one makes allowances for the standard political exaggeration found in similar Egyptian, Mesopotamian, and Neo-Hittite texts); the Davidic texts, on the other hand, bear close examination. They are surprisingly down-to-earth. The archaeological findings may be meager; the claims in the text are not grandiose.

For many people of devout faith the Bible has been the word of God that tells it as God sees it; maybe not everything is there in modern scientific detail but everything we need is there for seeing our modern world with the eyes of religious faith. Fortunately or unfortunately, a simple careful reading of the biblical text tends to contradict this.

If God were giving the definitive account of creation in Genesis One (shorthand for Genesis 1:1–2:4a), why does the Bible present half a dozen other images of creation that are quite different? Psalm 104, for example, begins with the oceans, touches on the springs and streams, moves to plant and animal life, and how all of this, magnificent in its multiplicity, depends on the goodness of God and is constantly renewed by God's spirit. Proverbs 8 takes a different tack, starting with wisdom ("me"), before the oceans, before the springs, before the mountains. As God worked on the heavens, on the deep, on the skies, on the limits to the sea and the foundations of the earth, wisdom ("I") was there beside him, rejoicing and delighting in the inhabited world (Prov 8:22–31).

The book of Job has several images of creation. There is the earth that God hangs out over nothing, with the waters bound up in the thick clouds (26:7–11). Right alongside this is the God of irresistible power, overwhelming the monsters of the deep, stilling the sea and targeting the fleeing serpent (26:8–13). "The thunder of his power who can understand?" When the text has God question Job, first come the foundations of the earth, then the limits set for the sea, clothed by God in clouds and darkness, mysterious but fixed in its place and no threat (38:4–11).

If Israel had the wealth of these images, and many more, at its disposition, we may have to reflect a little more over what is the meaning to be found in the magnificent text of Genesis One? We did not need to wait for modern science to tell us that Genesis One was not giving some sort of a portrayal of the way creation actually happened. The Bible knew better than that.

Israel's time in the wilderness is described in the books of Exodus and Numbers as a period of unmitigated rebellion. Toward the end of it, God is portrayed saying to Moses: the people who have seen my glory and my signs, in Egypt and the desert, nevertheless "have tested me these ten times and have not obeyed my voice" (Num 14:22). But for the prophets Hosea and Jeremiah, the time in the wilderness was one of honeymoon fidelity (see Hos 2:14–15 or Jer 2:1–2). There is a tension here that does not sit comfortably with an insight into historical reality "as God sees it."

Later in Israel's story, the monarchy emerges as the form of central government. In one account, the monarchy comes at Israel's request, on grounds of internal justice. "You [Samuel] are old and your sons do not follow in your ways; appoint for us, then, a king to govern us" (1 Sam 8:5). A second account has God give monarchy to Israel, on grounds of external defense. "He [Saul, shortly to be king] shall save my people from the hand of the Philistines; for I have seen the suffering of my people, because their outcry has come to me" (1 Sam 9:16). According to a third tradition, the move to monarchy is sheerest defiance of God, the sort of unfaithful apostasy that had dogged the people of Israel from the time they came out of Egypt (see 1 Sam 8:7–18; 10; 17–19). The intricacies of these passages keep biblical scholars in full puzzlement. But if we want to know what actually happened back then, the biblical response has to be along the lines of: "Go think!"

We could line up many more examples from Older and Newer Testaments. This may not be what some of us learned in kindergarten, CCD, or Sunday school. But it is there in the biblical text; it doesn't need any fast talking or sales patter from me. In broad Australian, Blind Freddie would have no trouble seeing it. Yet this is the Bible, the sacred scripture of the Jewish and Christian faiths. Rightly, it has been revered over centuries. Over centuries, alas, people have simplified matters, smoothed out tensions, turned a blind eye to contradictions. Part of the fascination of this ancient and sacred text is the question it is constantly putting before its readers: What is the nature of this text? How does it function?

Another issue concerns our interpretation of an ancient text. Once upon a time, the goal of critical scholarship was thought to be discovering the intention of the author of a text. Later reflection in literary circles revealed the weaknesses in this formulation. As Paul Ricoeur remarked, the author was always a "function" of the text; that is, we can reach the author only through the text. The author does not interpret the text; the text reveals its author. It is more accurate to speak of discovering the meaning of the text. This opens up interesting avenues. A text has meaning in its past and in our present. The

interpreter contributes a subjective element to the discovery of meaning in both times. To spell that out: (1) the interpreter discovers in the
text a meaning that is judged appropriate to the text's past; (2) the
interpreter discovers in the text a meaning that is judged appropriate to the interpreter's present. In both cases, the interpreter has a
subjective role to play in identifying a meaning derived from the text
(i.e., "that is judged appropriate" by the interpreter). In both cases,
the text has a role to play in exercising control over the subjective
activities of the interpreter. Important to both cases is the concern for
what is appropriate to the distant past of the ancient text, as best that
past is known to us, and the concern for what is appropriate to the
present of the interpreter, subject to the control exercised by the text.

The value of this understanding is to realize that we have the right
to an interpretation of an ancient text that is appropriate to our own
present context. Of course, this has to be balanced by the right of the
text to an interpretation that is appropriate to the text's own ancient
context. Both interpretations can be valid. Both are available to us.

One further issue needs to be raised. A saying that I have not heard
contested or queried over the years sharpens our thinking. By the way,
the saying is a matter of observation, observing what people say and
do; it is not claimed to be a self-evident axiom.

> We do not believe something because we can quote it from the
>   Bible;
> we quote something from the Bible because we believe it.

This confronts us with two questions:

1. By what process and for what reasons do we come to believe
   something of relevance to our faith, if it is not on the authority
   of the Bible?

2. Why then do we quote from the Bible in support of what we
   believe? What need is operative in us?

It would be folly to attempt answers without first exploring the
biblical text and exploring its impact on religious faith. Only in the
course of this exploration can we hope to encounter the biblical text
closely enough to begin to understand its nature.

AVOWAL

The introductions to many of my books seem to contain or conclude with an Avowal. None is more appropriate than here.

The wisdom that comes with age has brought me to be fully aware "that I have always wanted my Christian faith to be justifiable as a respectable choice — probably better, an intelligent and reasonable choice" (Campbell, *Whisper of Spirit,* xi). All my life as a biblical scholar I have experienced the Bible as a respectable work, witness to the best of thought and insight. I have not wanted a reliable historical record when the Bible is not a history book. I have wanted and found a serious and responsibly reflective book that ponders the manifold experience of life and God.

Among my primary passions is a passion for integrity. Where religious faith interacts with the Bible, that passion for integrity means the exercise of great care to be sure that faith claims relating to the Bible are expressed in such a way that they accurately reflect a full understanding of the relevant biblical tradition. All too often, they do not; all too often, tradition is supported by a selective reading of the Bible, at best. Far too often, people who should know better quote the biblical passages that they agree with and do not even acknowledge, much less deal with, the biblical passages that they do not agree with — that do not agree with them. The Bible often invites us to reflect, to "go think." It frequently retains contrasting views; it seldom adjudicates between them.

It pains me when, after an outdated science has been wrongly imposed on the interpretation of biblical text, updated science is presented as discovering the Bible as wrong — rather than the outdated science as out of date. In a fuller understanding of the biblical tradition what updated science has now asserted had always been allowed for by the Bible. Creation is a good example of this. Cosmological science moved toward a 4.5-billion-year-old earth and a universe some 13.7 billion years old, at least. Focused on the six days of Genesis One, the biblical tradition was dismissed. Evolution triumphed; the Bible cringed. A fuller understanding of the biblical tradition always allowed for such cosmological science. The biblical tradition was clear: it believed that God had created the world. A fuller grasp of the tradition was equally clear: given multiple portrayals of creation, it was clear beyond doubt that the biblical tradition bestowed no favor on any one way in which creation might be portrayed (see not only Genesis One and Genesis Two, but also Ps 104; Prov 8:22–31; Job 26 or 38; and more).

Much the same pain is present for me when archaeological discoveries are opposed to biblical text. It is not the case that incontrovertible material discoveries of archaeology are opposed to faith-filled fictions of biblical text. It is a particular interpretation of archaeological discovery that is opposed to a particular interpretation of biblical text. As biblical scholars should be well aware, once upon a time archaeology was claimed to prove the Bible right. Inaccurate, of course, but the claim was made. Now, in some circles, the claim can be heard that archaeology proves the Bible wrong. Inaccurate, of course, but the claim is made. What is at stake, in both cases, is interpretation, interpretation of biblical text and interpretation of archaeological discovery. A particular view of biblical text, often far too narrow and selective, saw itself confirmed in a particular and often narrow view of certain archaeological discoveries. Conversely, new archaeological discoveries are sometimes seen to oppose the Bible. In reality, such discoveries, like many others, open the way to a wider interpretation of the biblical text, an interpretation that has always been possible but too often ignored.

Many factors contribute to loosening the shackles that hold us bound, to removing the shades that impede our vision. The passion for integrity and the making of meaning fuels much of my faith and biblical interpretation.

Part One

The Pentateuch
and Revelation

The Pentateuch may turn out to be substantially late in the story of Israel. As substantially late, the Pentateuch makes a significant contribution to modern Christian faith and the revealing of God. Three questions:

> *Who are we?*
> *Who is Israel?*
> *Where is God?*

Chapter 1

Israel's Traditions about Humanity

INTRODUCTION

It is generally a good idea to have a look at something in its context before reaching for the magnifying glass or microscope. The collection of the Garden of Eden story, the material on Cain and family, the flood story, and the tower of Babel story makes a context that is well worth looking at.

There are good reasons for not seeing this collection as a report of human beginnings; we'll touch on some of these reasons later. Rather than a report of human beginnings, it is a remarkable reflection on human nature and human living. According to these texts, we are a wayward lot and nevertheless our relationship with God is secure. So much religious language has God punish evildoers; of course, most religious folk hope to be reckoned among the saints. But there is a persistent strand in the Bible, Older and Newer Testament, that has God on the side of the sinner. Perhaps the most outrageous and clearest Older Testament example of this is in the book of Hosea, where the biblical text has God order Hosea: "Go love a woman who has a lover and is an adulteress, like the love of God [*yhwh*] for the people of Israel even though they turn to other gods" (Hos 3:1) — a symbol of how I [God] love the people of Israel, even though they do not love me. To my mind, that is absolutely extraordinary, quite something — to put it very mildly.

What is captivating about Genesis 2–11? For an ancient text, it is surprisingly part of our world. There is nothing idyllic or dream-like about the first story, the Garden of Eden. Given half a chance, the human race faced with a single boundary within which to live

11

harmoniously will breach the boundary and destroy the harmony. Innocence we do not have. Consequences are spelled out in various ways, but the upshot is clear enough: what we are is what we always were.

There is nothing idyllic about the final story either, the tower of Babel. Gifted with a sense of their ability to achieve, the people bake bricks for a city and a tower; they are going to make a name for themselves (11:4). Their destiny is in their hands, and they will make it happen; nothing is impossible for them. We may find ourselves much the same. Faced with global warming and a crumbling world, most moderns are confident technology will find a way through and all will be well. True, perhaps, but only if human ambition is restrained and is responsive to nature's needs. For Babel, symbolic of human experience, human ambition led humans astray.

The big story in the middle of the collection is the flood. Two surprises are too surprising for many readers. First, the human race will not get any better. Second, God will never wipe it out again. The key verse is Genesis 8:21.

> I will never again curse the ground because of humankind, *for the inclination of the human heart is evil from youth;* nor will I ever again destroy every living creature as I have done.

This is in flat contradiction with Genesis 6:5, of course. In such cases, the biblical advice to us can only be: "Go think!" While 8:21 may be in flat contradiction with 6:5, it is not alone in the understanding of the flood story and it is fully supported by the exilic prophet in the book of Isaiah:

> This is like the days of Noah to me:
> Just as I swore that the waters of Noah would never again go over the earth,
> So I have sworn that I will not be angry with you and will not rebuke you. (Isa 54:9)

Conclusion: we are a wayward lot and nevertheless our relationship with God is secure. When we "go think," we may reflect that God's decision never again to destroy, with no conditions attached, is theologically akin to a second creation. In which case, is there any need for some initial catastrophe, some doctrine of original sin?

In our modern world, many people do not care all that much about God; frankly, what does their relationship with God matter to them. We are here, and that's for sure. God may be there, but that's not so sure. And anyway, for those who do not care all that much about God, it hardly matters. For those for whom God does matter, we may not be impressed by the theology articulated in the biblical flood myths and we may be puzzled by oppositions such as Genesis 6:5 and 8:21. On the other hand, we may be encouraged to find that at the heart of the paradox is faith that the God we believe in is somehow well disposed toward the human race, messy though it is.

Let's reach for the magnifying glass and the microscope and look at these stories a little more closely.

CREATION

In today's modern world, we have little doubt about the 15 billion years or so (13.7 billion to be precise at the moment) needed for our universe to emerge and the billions of years needed for our planet to emerge as part of it. Only a few of the benighted blind believe Genesis One related to such a process. Nobody in the Bible's ancient world knew about these billions of years. Nobody in the Bible's ancient world believed that Genesis One offered an exclusive portrayal of the way in which God was responsible for our world's coming into being. A powerful and magnificent portrayal, yes; an exclusive or factual portrayal, certainly not. Why would this have been so blindingly evident to the ancient biblical world so far before the advent of modern science? Simply because the Bible imaged God's activity in creation in a wide variety of ways. Some were in Psalms and Proverbs, others were in Job and Isaiah (chapter and verse details for some are given earlier). Some were stately with emphasis on the effortless authority of God; others hymned the triumphant victory of God in combat with the forces of chaos (e.g., Rahab, Tannin, Yamm). Intriguingly, the most sophisticated literature (Psalms, Isaiah, Job) has the references to the purportedly "primitive" combat mythology; something is going on here that escapes us.

It is the height of arrogance for moderns to assume that the poor primitives did not know any better. To the contrary, in some areas they knew better than we do. That may not be a great compliment, but it is a compliment we are obliged to pay.

Genesis One is beyond any shadow of doubt a magnificent piece of literature; no other creation passage is so measured, so thorough, and so structured. In stately fashion, it moves from chaos to order, from darkness to light, from emptiness to a world full of life, capped by man and woman. All of this occurs in six days of meticulously structured movement; the seventh day is left clear, hallowed, and free for rest. Once upon a time, we were clear about what this text meant; it was the start of a narrative that ended in sight of Canaan. Developments in biblical scholarship have brought us to the point where we have differing views of what the text's function might have been; certainty, alas, we do not have.

Once upon a time, Genesis One was almost universally regarded as the account of creation with which the pentateuchal Priestly source (P) began. While this view is still possible, developments in biblical scholarship have made it much less sure. The definitive account of creation it cannot be; there are too many others. One can hazard the possibility that it depicts our world as it came from the hand of God, declared to be "very good"; in which case, all that follows Genesis One depicts our world as it has come from our human hands. Biblical sources on a pentateuchal scale (i.e., from Creation to Canaan) have been losing favor for some time now in pentateuchal studies. This development will need discussion shortly.

If Genesis One was the opening chapter of a priestly source (P), then the question of its purpose is answered: it depicts the world from which Israel came, a world that was "very good." It is an ordered world, abstracted from all the irregularities of reality, a secure and stable world, a world in which sabbath has a crowning role to play. Above all, it is a world where God is supremely sovereign. In my judgment, two factors militate against Genesis One having this "opening chapter" role. First, close study of the vocabulary of Genesis One shows that "it is certainly possible that P composed Genesis One; it is certainly not necessary that P composed Genesis One." Second, close comparison of Genesis One and the priestly flood text reveals that commonality of authorship is not impossible, but "given the extent of the difference between them, such unity of authorship must be considered highly unlikely" (see Campbell and O'Brien, *Rethinking the Pentateuch*, 107–15; indignant squeals of outraged prejudice are understandable but hardly appropriate. The evidence, principally a careful assessment of the use of language and of category modeling, has to be evaluated).

Three other understandings can be envisaged. They do not exclude each other; combinations are possible.

1. With some sort of priestly text being put together from already existing multiple priestly writings, a creation passage (Genesis One) was composed to function as its beginning. This would satisfactorily account for the differences from other priestly texts; but it seems impossibly difficult to demonstrate such a case.

2. A further possibility would be that Genesis One was composed to highlight the significance of sabbath. In such a hypothesis, the world would be seen as not precisely made for sabbath, but close to it; the culmination of the creation process was God's rest on the seventh day. Appeal to a pentateuchal source would be unnecessary.

3. Another possibility to be entertained is that the peaceful, orderly, and alive image of the world, presented in Genesis One, should be seen as the image of the world that could be brought about if God's law (most likely, the deuteronomic law) was properly observed. There is deuteronomic vocabulary in Genesis One; there is priestly terminology in Deuteronomy (e.g., the classification of clean and unclean in Deut 14:1–20). Above all, the deuteronomic insistence on the centralization of sacrificial worship in the Jerusalem temple would be of enormous interest for a major section of the Jerusalem priesthood.

The notion of pentateuchal sources ("pentateuchal": extending from Creation to Canaan) has been losing favor for some time now.

The idea of sources for the Pentateuch took root back in 1753, with Jean Astruc's anonymous publication identifying two principal documents (*les mémoires originaux*) used by Moses, Astruc argued, to compose the book of Genesis. Division was by divine name, *elohim* or *yhwh*. With subsequent study, the *elohim* material was distributed across two sources, the earlier Elohist and the later Priestly Writing. Difficulties were there from the start. Further smaller collections were needed to account for the material that did not have a place in Astruc's two principal documents. Starting with legal materials, the combination of various collections was another possibility put forward (the fragmentary hypothesis). Supplementary editing of one original base source was suggested in place of several sources (the supplementary hypothesis). Toward the end of the nineteenth century, something of a consensus settled on four sources, in the well-known sequence, J, E, D, P. Around the middle of the twentieth century, this consensus began tranquilly to collapse. It was not replaced; but it was not trusted. A presentation of this classical consensus is available in Campbell and O'Brien, *Sources of the Pentateuch* (where, from the outset, both authors express their disagreement with this source-critical model, ix–x).

The Elohist (E) was the first to fall from grace and in due course lapse into oblivion. The passages of text and their characteristic features remain, of course; they are accounted for in various ways, but not by appeal to the figure of an Elohist and an E source (see *Sources of the Pentateuch*, 161–66). The Yahwist (J) too has fallen from grace over the years; a similar lapse into oblivion, for the figure of the Yahwist and a J source, has begun. In my judgment, the Priestly Writing (P, whether source or redaction) will follow soon enough. The writing is already on the wall; it will probably take a generation or two for it to be more widely accepted. As a source, for example, there was once a consensus that P ended with Deuteronomy 34:7–9 (e.g., Noth, Elliger). Now that ending has been pushed back to perhaps Leviticus 16 (Christophe Nihan) or Exodus 40 (Reinhard Kratz). Both are good places for something to have ended; it is doubtful that the "something" will turn out to have been a P source that began at creation. Even the relatively advanced 2006 book *A Farewell to the Yahwist?* refers to pre-Priestly, post-Priestly, non-Priestly, etc., using an upper case P to designate the Priestly code, Priestly editing, or Priestly Writing. In due course, aware of the difficulty of establishing the unity of a P source (beyond issues of language and culture that can be common over generations), I suspect the lowercase "priestly" will be preferred, allowing for terms like "early material" or "late material," "priestly" and "non-priestly," etc. It is happening for J; I believe it should and will happen for P. For example, Rolf Knierim has recently written: "The expression 'Priestly writings' refers much more to a history of ongoing priestly traditions rather than to a uni-level source" (*Numbers,* 7). We will see evidence for this along the way, as we discuss some of the texts that lie ahead.

As we have seen, the issue of Genesis One as the opening chapter of a priestly source is dependent on the recognition of that P source. To repeat: the presence of priestly writings in the Pentateuch is not in dispute; the presence of a P source will be. Once the independence of priestly writings is recognized, the acceptance of a P source demands that some sense of unity be demonstrated across the relevant priestly writings associated with the P source. Issues of style, theme, and theology, alleged as indications of unity by some, are difficult to pin down in terms of such unity. Those writings, considered to belong to the P source, need to be distinguished from other priestly writings that are not to be associated with the presumed source.

What fascinates me in all this is to watch the interaction between past tradition, modern science, and modern biblical interpretation — and finally then the incorporation of this into an enriched faith in God. In many respects, past tradition has seen Genesis One as *the definitive* biblical account of creation. While evidence that this is not the case was present in multiple biblical texts, it was ignored. When modern science asserts the contrary of past tradition, the valid conclusions of science must be accepted. In the case of creation, the acceptance was often grudging, probably because science was assumed to be inimical to religious faith. In due course, biblical interpretation itself gave greater emphasis to the Bible's own contradiction of past tradition. Finally, a greater freedom to look at the biblical text without preconceptions allows a deeper understanding of faith in God to emerge.

In the present case — as will be developed later in this book, but can be adumbrated now — the encounter with God in today's experience leads to a selectivity in the passages of scripture that are read. In Israel's past, the encounter with God in Israel's experience often led to a selectivity in the passages of scripture that were written. As a result, the revelation of God is not shrouded in the mists of a distant past; the revelation of God is found in the clarity of an immediate present.

~MODERN FAITH~

Genesis One, with its six days of creation, seems tame and desperately out of date when confronted with modern science's awareness of our 13.7-billion-year-old universe, the untold billions of stars in our galaxy, the equally untold billions of galaxies in our universe — and so much more.

The presence of other and different portrayals of creation or references to creation in the Older Testament should stir our thinking and protect us from jumping to rash conclusions. The absence of any other sequence of six days anywhere else in the Bible should also stir our thinking and protect us from jumping to rash conclusions. In ancient Israel, with awareness of the breadth of Israel's traditions — no easy task in the absence of books, concordances, and libraries — few would have indulged the idea that Genesis One gave a picture of how God had created the world. Given the "other and different portrayals of creation or references to creation" in the biblical texts (such as Prov 8, Ps 104, Job 26 or 38, Gen 2, and more), we can conclude that Israel believed God created the world and Israel's theologians were aware that they had no idea as to *how* it might have been done.

Then as now, the six-day structure of the chapter highlighted the place of sabbath in the world of Israel. Then as now, the chapter portrayed a sovereign God. Then as now, the chapter portrayed an ordered world. These are positions of faith. They could have spoken to Israel in its past. They can speak to us in our present.

On whether chaos pre-existed creation, Genesis One is unmistakably ambiguous (either the chaos was there or God created it);

modern cosmological science today is still undecided. "Let there be light" is a grand opening line. Light separated from darkness, waters above separated from waters below, earth separated from sea — it all constitutes a hard act to follow. Vegetation on the land, fish in the sea, birds in the air, wild animals and all — eminently sensible. Finally, humans in God's "image and likeness." A bit of a mystery that; it sounds good, but what does it mean? What the text portrays God doing over the six days we humans certainly cannot do. But "image and likeness" ties humans into God in a way that is not done for anything else. We humans exercise our creative power in other spheres. Exalted we may be, but the text nevertheless makes us aware of a power and sovereignty we do not have. It is a grand portrayal of a sovereign God.

Genesis One is also a grand portrayal of an ordered world. Chaos has been banished; everything is in its place. All is good. This is hardly irrepressible optimism of the Pollyanna variety. It is not the world we live in and the world we experience that is described this way; it is the world coming, in the text, from God's creative hand. Experience can encounter a chaotic and messy world. Israel's experience certainly did. In all the chaos and mess, some in ancient Israel expressed a longing for order and stability. They portrayed it with the images of a world coming from the creative hand of God. Each week, they celebrated it on the seventh day. Christians today can rise to the imaginative challenge of finding longed-for order and stability in the image of a crucified God.

Language such as "from God's creative hand" can sometimes create a problem. Speaking of creation in terms of the universe, the image of an anthropomorphic God — the little old man with a long white beard — is out of the question. Where "creation" language may risk being associated with a hands-on God, too closely involved in the detail, language of God's "envisaging" created beings "emerging" within the universe God had made may be found preferable. Joseph Ratzinger rightly pillories the outdated image of a creator God today as "the expression of a naïve anthropomorphism, of a primitive mode of thought comprehensible in a situation in which man [*sic*] still lived in a small world, in which the earth was the centre of all things and God had nothing else to do but look down on it" (*Introduction to*

Christianity, 101). Language of God's envisaging what in due course will emerge may be less open to misunderstanding, provided the basic concept of creation remains.

THE GARDEN

The Garden of Eden text is undoubtedly a good story. Like many a good story, it involves two strong human passions. Both lurk deep within us, at different depths but deep enough that, for many, a level of rare reflectiveness is needed to reach them. The first is the human yearning to reach beyond the present to a past that was perfect and its correlative, our turning from a present that is not. The second is a yearning to reach beyond the human. Alas, in much dealing with the Garden story, the first has long obscured the second. In recent years, the text has been freed of the tag of paradise lost; the tag of innocence lost is yet to be firmly attached. The knowledge gained is another story.

It is important to realize that it was not paradise the couple lost, through a sin of disobedience with corresponding punishment; there was no paradise to lose. It was innocence they chose to lose, through an act of folly with corresponding consequences. Is there a significant difference? I believe the difference is immensely significant. Summed up almost too simply, it is: God didn't do it; we did. Summed up only a little less simply, it is: God was not involved in it all (crime and punishment); we were involved in it all (act and consequence). Very basically, it was not a legal rescript that said we were not divine; it was a matter of human nature. Just as basically, it was not a sin against God that is portrayed; it is a sin against ourselves. As to less basic matters, first, our world has not changed from a paradise to the way it is now. Allowing for change, how it is now is how it always was. Second, our human nature and our human lot have not changed significantly. Allowing for the passage of the centuries, how we are now is how we always were. One can dream of a mythic moment in which humans might have been innocent; it is no more than a mythic moment. What is depicted as the first human act revealed that mythic moments have no duration.

The text does not portray divine punishment bringing us to where we are; the text portrays human folly with its consequences — our longing for an autonomy that is not ours. What the text portrays is the folly innate in any human being of wanting to be more than we are, along with the consequences that automatically flow from that folly. The significance lies in the observation that the text does not portray a sin against God bringing deserved punishment. Instead, the text portrays an act of folly, against God's warning, bringing natural consequences in its train. In the context, the order not to eat of the tree of the knowledge of good and evil can be understood as more of a warning than a prohibition (no reasons are given); it is folly to want to be like God (even if invited by the snake). The story says we attempted it from the outset; the consequences may be seen as with us now. They are not the result of punishment because of sin; they are the consequences of what humans do. They are not divine punishment; they are the effects of human causes.

The Garden of Eden stands as a synonym for paradise. When we read of "edenic" qualities, we know what is meant, even if we have never seen the word before. It refers to qualities of perfection. When an author writes of childhood as an "edenic prelude before the blood, sweat, and tears of adult life," we know what is meant, even when we know that many childhoods are not edenic at all. There is a hankering in us for a golden age, the "good old days" that we know as probably not all that old and certainly not all that good. Correlative with that hankering for the past is pain with the present. The underlying logic is simple, even if unavowed: what comes from the hand of God is good; much of our present is not good; our present as it is cannot have come from the hand of God. The Garden of Eden is somehow the supreme symbol of that hankering for a Golden Age.

The human yearning to reach beyond the merely human, a yearning for something in life that is not limited by human realities, is less easy to pin down, less explicit in literature. Yet it is constantly there. Perhaps the word that leads us most easily to the idea is "ecstasy," the experience of being taken outside oneself. The term has an exalted pedigree in religious language and religious experience, where it is akin to rapture. The pedigree is less exalted where drugs are concerned; the experience, however, can at times be much the same, a departure from the ordinariness of the day-to-day. Where motion is concerned, skiers and surfers know the sensation well, as do skydivers and glider pilots. The experience can happen to us on mountain peaks or in hermits' huts; it can happen to us in massed crowds or massed choirs, in concert halls or sports stadiums. To be human can be grand; to be more than human can be grander still.

According to the biblical text, however, the Garden of Eden is no golden age, no paradise, although popular tradition has often made it so. It is quite possible that an early story told of the achievement of completeness through the creation of woman as the counterpart of man. To use that story as an introduction to Genesis 3, only a few verses would have needed to be added. They would include:

1. Genesis 2:9b, "the tree of life in the midst of the garden and the tree of the knowledge of good and evil." There is not much point in the prohibition without the relevant tree.

2. Genesis 2:16–17, the prohibition against eating of the tree of the knowledge of good and evil. The issue is serious enough to be sanctioned with the formal death penalty.

3. Genesis 2:25, "the man and his wife were both naked, and were not ashamed."

The structure of the two chapters (Gen 2–3) is clear. There is lead-up to a core story (Gen 2:4b–24); there is the core story (Gen 2:25–3:7); there is follow-up to the core story (Gen 3:8–24). It is helpful to recognize the role of all three parts and to be aware of what may once have been behind lead-up and follow-up.

The story is about human completeness; it has nothing to do with a paradise. Humans were expected to work: "there was no one to till the ground" (Gen 2:5); the man was put in the garden "to till it and keep it" (Gen 2:15). To keep it means to protect; work and protect: any fruit-grower knows the work involved in caring for an orchard of fruit trees. The trees were "good for food" (Gen 2:9a), and their fruit was available to be eaten. They did not, however, bend down to the hungry; that only happened in apocryphal gospels and this is not an apocryphal story. It is set in totally primal times; there are no cultivated grains, no domesticated animals. Its focus is on a man and a woman, their complementarity, and the nakedness of which they were unashamed. Unashamed nakedness is universally a symbol of innocence.

The yearning for a golden age has as its correlative a pain that the world we know is not what it could be. Because it is thought the world could not have come from God in this state, humans yearn for an explanation of its sad and sorry state. The latter part of Genesis 3 has all too often been loosely interpreted to provide this explanation. The result is that, thanks to this yearning, the Garden story is misinterpreted and misunderstood. Technically, the latter part of Genesis 3 is concerned with the man and the woman — and the man and the woman only. It may well be that the verses (esp. 3:16–19) do allow for an explanation of the world's sad and sorry state. As we will see below, according to the letter of the text, these verses do not provide such an explanation; with some modifications, they might do so. Focus on this explanatory function may blind users to the core of the story: the loss of innocence. In the core of the story, the action occurs within the act and consequence of the natural order; no intervention from God is needed. It is a sequence of act and consequence, not of crime and punishment. The appeal to God's subsequent intervention is fully legitimate, but it is to be recognized as subsequent intervention. At a significant level, it detracts from the story's central message: the longing to be like God can cost us our innocence. The ultimate boundary within which we humans have to live is recognition of and resignation to the fact that we are not God. It can, indeed, be very fulfilling to be fully human. It is not, however, the state of being God.

Pushing beyond boundaries is part of being fully human. The issue is which boundaries to push beyond; it is never simple. If we did not push beyond boundaries in so many areas — communications, medicine, technology, travel, to name a few — we would still be stuck in a static and limited world. The Garden story is about a boundary, an appropriate limit, not an arbitrary prohibition. It is a limit with the death penalty attached, so it is to be understood as deadly serious, a matter of ultimate seriousness. (The language is that of the death penalty; the language of immortality is different, see Gen 3:22.) The action is not portrayed principally as a human transgression of a divine prohibition; rather it is about accepting to be human, about not seeking to be divine. The temptation is to be "like God," knowing what God knows (Gen 3:5). The story is about more than disobedience to God. The temptation is the desire to be as God is. There is no shame in being human; there is folly and illusion in thinking one can be divine.

The use of language is extremely skillful, as might be expected in what is probably best described as a wisdom vignette. The key wordplay is based on the meanings of three associated Hebrew words, *arom, arum,* and *eyrom,* meaning respectively "naked," "clever" or "crafty," and "naked" again. The Hebrew consonants in all three are the same: ayin, resh, and mem. In 2:25, the couple, "both of them," were naked (*arumim*); in the next verse, 3:1, the snake is crafty (*arum*); finally, in 3:7, the eyes of the couple, "both of them," were opened and they knew they were naked (*eyrumim*). Innocence has been lost; knowledge has been gained, at a cost. The absence of shame is explicit in 2:25; shame's presence is not explicit in 3:7, but the couple reach immediately for fig leaves.

Note: the "knowledge of good and evil," promised by the snake in 3:5b, is a distraction in relation to the core. It is not mentioned again until 3:22a, where it may belong in the context of an alternative version of the story (of which there were clearly several; see Westermann). An appropriate meaning for the phrase can be constructed (see the extensive discussion ["the many possible meanings"] in Westermann, *Genesis 1–11,* 242–48); most simply but also most abstractly, it is knowing something that God knows. The phrase does not of itself contribute the specifics of a meaning that is helpful in the context.

The play of language in the core of the story is skillful and subtle. Beyond the core of the story, the equally skillful thematic movement needs observation. First and foremost is the recognition that the action of the core story is a matter of *act and consequence,* of *cause and effect.* God's intervention is not needed. The couple eat, their eyes are opened, they see. God's intervention in what follows, beyond the core of the story, is presented as *crime and punishment.*

God's address to the snake begins, "Because you have done this"; similarly for the man, "Because..." There is nothing equivalent for the woman. The accusation of the crime presents the further impositions as divine punishment rather than as natural consequences.

One aspect of the punishment needs to be noticed: the snake is cursed; the woman and man are not. Curse is not mentioned in association with the woman. In association with the man, it is the ground that is cursed, not the human. A second element binds the whole story together. In their excuses (3:12–13), the man blamed the woman God had given him; the woman blamed the snake (the focus in the story returns to the illusory promise). In his address to the man, God evokes first the core story and then the narrative's beginnings back in the Garden. To the man God says: "You listened to the voice of your wife"; that is from the core story. God goes on: "You did not listen to me; you ate of the tree I told you not to"; "I told you not to" is from the story's beginning in the Garden.

The core story is simply told.

BEFORE (2:25): the two were naked and unaware (no shame)

3:4 The promise: "Your eyes will be opened, and you will be like God," knowing what God knows.

3:6 The reflection: it is attractive — valuable for nutrition, aesthetics, wisdom.

3:7a The reality: "The eyes of both were opened, and they knew that they were naked."

AFTER (3:7b): the two were naked and aware (shame: fig leaves)

The promise was: "Your eyes will be opened, and you will be like God."

The experience was: Their eyes were opened, and they were not like God.

The point of the story: When we humans ambition to be like God, we deceive ourselves.

The movement is clear:

The seed is sown — when you eat, your eyes will be opened and you will be like God.

The seed is cultivated — the fruit is attractive: good for food, delight to the eyes, desirable for wisdom.

The seed sprouts — they eat, their eyes are opened, they see they are naked so they reach for fig leaves.

This only takes us seven verses into a twenty-four-verse chapter. But the story is complete: its beginning is with innocence; its middle is the movement from promise/temptation to reflection and finally to action; its end is the discovery that innocence has been lost. No more is needed. The story, begun in Genesis 2:4b, has reached a culmination with Genesis 3:7. The Garden has been planted and populated, the prohibition has been promulgated and repudiated, human life has not been enhanced but diminished. Innocence has been lost. In a culminating episode, the snake has articulated the illusory, the promise that is temptation. The woman does not devote attention to the temptation; her attention has been attracted to the fruit and her evaluation of it is wise and insightful and, alas, a distraction. Finally, the two move to action and both eat — and discover that their innocence is lost. To excerpt from Claus Westermann: "Something has been lost . . . the state of unaffected innocence" (*Genesis 1–11*, 251).

In fact, this core story can be expanded in seven clear stages. Read in this way, attending to its core and then to these potential stages in its unfolding, the story can be read more satisfactorily and understood more fully. Two factors need to be insisted on here. First, this process is not arguing for or tracing the development of the text from an identifiable original to the present text we have now. This is not the case; it is not the point of the present discussion; it is not even faintly suggested here. What is suggested is that it may be helpful for readers or users to recognize the core story as such and to recognize what each potential stage of the unfolding of the text adds to the development of that core story. To my knowledge, the evidence does not exist to claim any of these stages as editorial additions. There may be occasional hints; there is nothing that can be termed adequate evidence. What is proposed, then, is one way of reading the present text that may be found to be insight-generating and helpful.

Second, there is nothing in any of the seven stages to claim God's action as bringing about the present human condition. Loss of innocence, yes; God's punishment of the pair, as individuals, yes; God's action resulting in the present human condition, no — absolutely not! Given the massive weight of Christian tradition wrongly favoring this misinterpretation, it needs the careful attention of each one of us. This issue of misinterpretation can be generalized: "No text in Genesis (or likely in the entire Bible) has been more used, interpreted, and misunderstood than this text. This applies to careless, popular theology as well as to the doctrine of the church" (Brueggemann, *Genesis*, 41).

Stage One: Estrangement (3:8)

There is probably no greater separator from God than shame. The couple were ashamed; they knew themselves to be naked and promptly fixed fig leaves to cover that nakedness.

The man and his wife hid from the presence of God. It is a lovely image, prior to the loss of innocence, of the LORD God walking with the naked couple at the time of the evening breeze, among the trees of the Garden of Eden. Anthropomorphic? Of course. Sentimental nonsense? Well, yes, perhaps. But symbolically lovely. The symbolism: between Creator and creature there is a bond that was felt to be there and judged to be real. With the loss of innocence, the felt bond was weakened. Not gone, as the "garments of skins" (v. 21) bear eloquent witness, but weakened.

At this point, reading the story can pause at 3:8. No more is needed.

Stage Two: Blame (3:9–13)

Once the "I was naked" was out in the open, the follow-up is illuminating: How do you know? What happened?

The man, whose own role as portrayed in the story has been mute and inglorious, blames God. "The woman whom you gave to be with me," she gave it to me; you gave her to be with me, so it is fundamentally your fault, O God. The woman simply calls it as she saw it. "The serpent tricked me." And God is left with the sorrowful "What is this that you have done?"

With this stage of expansion, reading the story can pause at 3:13. No more is needed. Those who want longer endings for Mark's Gospel (to take this as an example of our natural dispositions) will want further expansion here. Those content with a short ending to Mark will recognize that the story could stop right here — as it could have stopped at 3:7 or 3:8.

Stage Three: Future generations (3:14–15)

Those who lived with snakes around could hardly have left a bit of etiological vengeance out of the story. The innate human fear of the poisonous reptiles had to be given its due.

What is worthy of particular note about this stage is that, apart from a quite different reference in 3:20, it is the only point in the entire chapter where future generations are referred to, "your offspring and hers" (3:15). Nowhere else do future generations merit a mention.

At this stage of expansion, reading the story can pause at 3:15. No more is needed.

Stage Four: Present couple (3:16–19)

With God having been brought into the narrative at stage three, the idea of having God address both man and woman would be irresistible. What most moderns do not pay attention to, naturally enough since they are not reading Hebrew, is that the second-person singular is used, so that only the individual present is being addressed. What most moderns should pay attention to, whether reading Hebrew or not, is that future generations are not referred to. Unlike the case of the snake, offspring are not mentioned.

Given Christian tradition's massive weight favoring misinterpretation here, it needs to be clearly seen that the singular only is used, that subsequent generations are not mentioned (even though it would have been easy to mention them), and that punishment is assessed for the two, not the human condition changed for us all. Whatever may be implied or inferred about the human condition, it is important for the sake of truth and honesty to be fully aware of what is not said —

but so easily could have been — before moving to what may, perhaps, be inferred or considered to have been implied. The reflective will realize that later generations may not have had the same text we have; it is highly unlikely that they had the wherewithal to consult texts as we do. For further details, see below.

In these two utterances, one to the woman (v. 16) and one to the man (vv. 17–19), very minor but subtle quirks appear that raise the possibility that an author's attention has strayed from close focus on the story text.

Two things are said to the woman: first, I will greatly increase your pains in childbirth; second, your desire shall be for your husband. The first is not "I will cause pain in childbirth for you and your daughters after you" but "I will greatly increase your pangs in childbearing." There have been no children born so far in the story; pain in childbirth is not mentioned in what is to come. Technically, therefore, there is everything to cause and nothing to increase. As a quirk, it is a minor technicality. The second is "your desire shall be for your husband," but in all history, whether biblical history or human history, the dominant image is of men's desire being for women, not the reverse. The term used here for "desire" is rare (Hebrew: *teshuqah*); it occurs in two other places in the Hebrew scriptures. In Genesis 4:7, it is the attitude of sin to Cain, crouching at his door, where it is quite different from 3:16. In Song of Songs 7:11, *his* desire is for *her*, in a context of love and belonging — not domination. One suspects the possibility of a depth of reflection around desire that is not made explicit for us.

What is said to the man is not "Cursed are the trees because of you; they shall no longer bear fruit for you." Instead, the ground is cursed, in toil will the man eat of it, thorns and thistles will be its produce, plants of the field will be his food (exact meaning has to come from the context; field growth can be feed for livestock, e.g., Deut 11:15; the context expects something more sophisticated) — "all the days of your [singular] life" (Gen 3:17–18). The man was to "work" the Garden (2:5, 15). Nevertheless, in the story the image of the Garden with its fruit-bearing trees is of an area where cultivated plants and domesticated animals are not taken into account. The language of a curse on the ground does not reflect the earlier story; it suggests the verses reflect something of the conditions of later life. The quirk, if it is one, is minor but noticeable.

At this stage of expansion, reading the story can pause at 3:19. Enough has been said.

However, whether passages are original or additional, the text as it is now constituted is entitled to interpretation. If we go back to 3:14, there is a minor oddity in that, while two actors are involved ("enmity between"), the *blame* is laid on only one of the two parties (the snake), but the *burden* is laid on the two, on both parties (the snake and the woman). The text appears to resemble more closely accounting for a current state of affairs than assessing a burden for the future.

Where the sayings regarding the woman and the man are concerned (3:16–19), whatever the quirks, a couple of factors are beyond doubt: first, the address in each case is singular; second, there is no reference to children, descendants, or subsequent generations. Given the factuality of these observations, they cannot be ignored.

A narrator, working at any time, who pitches a story "at the beginning" and who assumes the stance of a narrator at that "beginning" time can look only to the future from that beginning. Narrators, working at some later time (e.g., exilic or post-exilic), who pitch a story "at the beginning" but who, without specifying it, assume something of the stance of their own later time naturally experience as past what would have been viewed as future "at the beginning." The future of such a "beginning" was, by the time of exile or later, well and truly past. Unless a storyteller with full awareness took up the stance of a narrator back at the beginning, the future unfolding from that past time did not need to be mentioned or foretold; it was already past experience.

In this light, a narrator located in the present, looking back to the past, would not have needed to refer to children, descendants, or subsequent generations. They were taken for granted as part of the past, as part of what had already been experienced. What such a narrative stance might be understood as saying is that what is now experienced in the present, and what has been its past, is what was once the situation in the beginning. From the very beginnings of human life, humankind chose to lose its innocence. According to the text, they were forbidden this tree and were warned of the seriousness of the consequences (death penalty). They knew. They ate; and in that act, they lost their innocence. Their eyes were opened; they were not God. Forbidden and warned, knowing something of what was involved, the couple walked into it; we have been walking into it ever since. A late setting would make particularly good sense if subsequent texts — e.g., the flood, the ancestors, aspects of exodus and Sinai — are best understood as belonging in the later period, which is possible.

In the narrative, is the situation in the beginning portrayed as the result of God's action or of human action? With God involved in human living, the question is not easily answered. Our present Genesis text is not of great help. To the snake, it has God say: "I will put enmity between you and the woman"; to the woman, it has God say: "I will greatly increase your pangs in childbearing." But after that the divine "I" disappears. "In pain you shall bring forth children" does not involve the divine "I." "Cursed is the ground because of you" does not involve God's "I."

There should be no doubt that, in eating the forbidden fruit, the couple lost their innocence — and that was their doing (Gen 3:6–7). The text is clear; the human condition results from human action. Action is not needed from God. The results of that loss of innocence are unfolded in the rest of the chapter. Whether these results are portrayed as a punishment proclaimed by God or as the consequences of human folly declared by God is open to interpretation. The absence of reference to children, descendants, or subsequent generations leaves the future unaddressed. Viewed from a much later time, the time of the narrator's present, children, descendants, or subsequent generations would not need to be addressed. They are not the future; they are the past that has been experienced since the beginning.

In all of this, one thing is certain: uncertainties in this text are unavoidable. Among them: an appropriate understanding of the death penalty (2:17); the meaning of "knowing good and evil"; the role of the trees; the context of the last three verses (3:22–24); the primary focus of the narrative (disobedience, loss of innocence). When working to fathom this text — what to highlight, what to leave in obscurity — a great deal of discretion must be left with the interpreter.

Stage Five: Mother of all the living (3:20)

Fittingly, the woman's name is given as Eve. In this, there is a tie to universality (Eve: a name that evokes the Hebrew for life); she is the mother of all the living. What is found in her may be present in all. The verse does not affirm that what was said of her in 3:16 is to be said of all the living. Some may wish to infer it or claim that it is implied; it is certainly not explicit.

At this stage of expansion, reading the story can pause at 3:20. No more is needed.

Stage Six: Relationship with God (3:21)

The "garments of skins" is a lovely narrative touch. The couple had lost their innocence; they had not lost their God. The relationship with God is not broken. It may be stretched; it is not broken. The same faith is expressed at the end of the flood in Genesis 8:21–22 and Genesis 9, where an unconditional covenant is claimed between God and a world with fear and dread, with murder and capital punishment (see 9:2, 6).

The garments of skin would have been beautifully in place after the fig leaves of 3:7. Look what they did; look what God did. What God made was so much better. Skins sure beat fig leaves. More important: they have lost their innocence; they have not lost their God. However, beautiful as it may be, it is not advisable for us to rewrite biblical text without good cause. It is important, however, to realize that the God who might well have been portrayed abandoning the human race is instead portrayed as committed to it.

At this stage of expansion, reading the story can pause at 3:21. No more is needed.

Stage Seven: Banishment (3:22–24)

This stage unquestionably belongs with the story in its present form. There are two trees; one has been eaten from. This is the story we have been hearing.

Nevertheless, the differences are marked. The focus of the story in these three verses is not on the couple, man and wife, both of them, as it has been up till now in the text. The focus is on the man alone: "the *man* has become like one of us…*he* might reach out

his hand . . . the LORD God sent *him* forth, . . . He drove out the *man*"
(3:22–24). In these last three verses of the chapter (3:22–24), Phyllis
Trible understands HA-ADAM ("the man") to become generic (i.e.,
including both man and woman) and thus allowing the verses to be
part of the total narrative (*Rhetoric,* 134–39). In my judgment, this
is unlikely. Apart from the general context of the story, the fact that
the tree of life and the language of eternal life recur here for the first
time militates against any such understanding.

Nakedness is no longer mentioned; "knowing good and evil" has
taken its place. After the opening of their eyes in 3:7, the text does
not say that they knew good and evil; instead, it says that they knew
they were naked. They had reached beyond their boundaries and lost
their innocence. The emphasis has shifted in 3:22. Earlier, it was
about boundaries; when they transgressed the boundary, "the eyes
of both were opened and they knew that they were naked" — they
were not like God (3:7). Now the concern is different, for — to the
contrary — the man has indeed become like God; "See, the man has
become like one of us, knowing good and evil" (3:22). The motif of
knowing good and evil (better: good and bad) occurs in the words
of the snake (3:5) and in the words of God (3:22). A grasp of its
meaning has eluded biblical scholars over the generations; we can
speculate, but we cannot know with accepted clarity. Note the half-
dozen pages consecrated by Westermann to the three-word Hebrew
phrase (*Genesis 1–11,* 242–48). W. G. Lambert is quoted by Westermann saying: "The expression describes that which is required to
gain something beyond what is human" (244). Westermann himself
concludes: "It is concerned with a divine and unbridled ability to
master one's existence" (248). With appropriate restrictions, "to be
like God" adequately catches the core of what is meant.

The tree of life receives a prominence in these verses that it did not
have in the story before. The threat of the death penalty has been
replaced by concern for eternal life (compare 2:17b with 3:22b).

The fragment has been blended into the story of the tree in the
middle of the Garden, which is now for us the tree of the knowledge of good and evil. Enough difference is preserved to suggest the
possibility that a different story might well have been told focused
instead on the tree of life in the middle of the Garden. Given the fact

of differences and the possibility of a different story, extreme caution is in order when it comes to using material from these three verses to interpret the main story. Westermann's comment sounds that note of caution: "The state of scholarship with regard to the three last verses of Gen 3 is very confused" (*Genesis 1–11,* 271).

As we move to examine these two chapters in greater detail, it is worth reiterating what this discussion has been about and what it has not. It has not been an attempt to reconstruct the growth and development of the text. There is inadequate evidence for any solid base to start from. What the discussion has been about is proposing a possible approach for readers today to recognize a potential self-contained core, ending with 3:7 and then unfolding the rest from there. The core story is found between temptation and reality. Temptation: if only you eat, your eyes will be opened and you will be like God, knowing good and evil. Reality: they ate, their eyes were opened and they were not like God; what they knew was that they were naked. Readers or hearers can recognize in that a story of the loss of innocence. The potential stages that follow are no more than insights that help complete the unfolding of that reality, that loss.

What has been done so far has been tracing a global overview of one approach to the reading of the text. What needs to follow now is attention to certain aspects of detail. The story bears looking at closely.

As we have seen, it is a story that is rich in insights and surprises. Right at the beginning, there is a significant insight; toward the end, readers are left with a surprise. At the beginning, work is taken for granted. It is not the result of some sin; work was assumed from the start. Why was the earth barren? Because there was no water to wet the world and there was no man to work the ground (Gen 2:5). Work is intrinsic to the human condition; productivity does not happen without it. Toward the end of the story, the offspring of the snake and the offspring of the woman are mentioned as at odds with each other (3:15). After that, there is no other reference to offspring, descendants, later generations, or anything like that (apart from the quite different 3:20). For interpreters who link this story to some notion of original sin, that is more than a surprise; it is a serious problem.

The narrative begins with the creation of the Garden and its occupants. So far so good; it is a fine garden, meeting all the needs of its
occupants. The story moves on to the one condition governing life in
the garden, related to the tree in its center. The motif of the sacred
tree is widespread in the imagery of the ancient Near East. Heraldic
animals are associated with the tree, perhaps as guardians, suggesting that it may be forbidden, protected, or otherwise inaccessible.
Most of the images are small, coming mainly from cylinder seals; a
large-size mural, substantially complete, adorned a wall in the palace
of King Zimrilim of Mari (from the period 2040–1870 BCE, now
in the Louvre). This mural, which stands 1.7 meters (c. 5ft. 7in.)
high, presents considerable detail. The sacred tree itself is as it were
bisected, represented on either side of an upper and lower central
panel, the whole flanked by two palm trees each with its attendant.
There are three winged sphinx-like beasts on either side, actually
standing in the tree, one above the other. In the upper central panel,
the king stands before the goddess Ishtar, with other deities present.
In the lower central panel are two goddesses each holding a jar from
which four rivers flow (with fish in them), reminiscent of the four
rivers flowing from the Garden (Gen 2:10–14). The mural dates to
early in the second millennium. The motif is thoroughly traditional,
however, and unlikely to be of use for even suggesting a date for the
composition of the biblical narrative.

The nature of the tree in the ancient images is mostly unknown;
it is clearly of sacral significance, but whether tree of life or tree of
knowledge it is often impossible to tell. How would a tree of life be
distinguished imagistically from a tree of knowledge? The Garden of
Eden story is a text, not an image. In monotheistic Israel, the gods
and goddesses are replaced by the one god of Israel. The protective
guardians are replaced by the divine prohibition. But — an alert for
the interpreter — there are two trees in the middle of the garden.

Despite poring over cylinder seals and the like, the symbolism and
the significance of this tree in the ancient Near East are two issues
that have been neglected or inadequately explored in my education.
What is the significance of a tree that is found widely spread across
the art, and especially the glyptic, of the ancient Near East? It is
often located in the heavens; kings and goddesses can be found in

association with it. The Zimrilim mural pictures the rivers that bring life-giving water to the world flowing from jars held by goddesses associated with the tree. Heraldic animals form its honor guard. The symbolic significance of the tree is clearly huge. It is not surprising that in the Genesis story the symbolic significance attached to the tree should be equally huge. There is an extensive exploration waiting to be made. Jungian analyst and storyteller Clarissa Pinkola Estés speaks of the names given such a tree in ancient myth and folktale as "the Tree of Life, Tree of Knowing, Tree of Life and Death, or Tree of Knowledge" (*Run with the Wolves*, 415). These stories probe the inner dynamic of human living.

According to the biblical text, both trees are in the garden: "the tree of life ... in the midst of the garden, and the tree of the knowledge of good and evil" (Gen 2:9; the NRSV includes an "also" that is not in the Hebrew). The woman refers to "the tree that is in the middle of the garden," which would be most confusing if there were two of them. The main story is about the tree of the knowledge of good and evil. An alternative story centered on the tree of life could, presumably, be easily crafted from the tradition. Pointers to a third story lurk at the end of chapter 3 (vv. 22–24). The main story has been told inclusively, of a couple. As noted earlier and highly significant, there is a marked change of tone in these last three verses with the woman absent from the narrative; the language is exclusive and only the man is mentioned. "See, the *man* has become like one of us ... *he* might reach out *his* hand ... God sent *him* forth ... he drove out the *man*" (Gen 3:22–24). The shift is striking; it may point to another way in which the story was also told. Mimicking the heraldic guardians of the tree, the cherubim guard the way to the tree of life (3:24).

In relation to the tree of life, Westermann speaks of "a second voice as it were together with the melody" (*Genesis 1–11*, 213). While this highlights the phenomenon, and much scholarship has addressed it (Westermann: "protracted and endless discussion"), the significance may be much more than simply "a second voice." It is possible — by no means certain, but possible — that the text of Genesis 2:4b–3:24 holds pointers to at least three stories. In such a case, the text we have is not so much the finished product but the base from which the telling would be launched (see Campbell and O'Brien, *Rethinking the Pentateuch,* 15–20). In the main story, two characters are active as principals, the man and the woman. To the contrary, in the story reflected in the last three verses (3:22–24), there is only one active principal, the man. The possibility of a story centered on the tree of life is allowed for in 2:9; either inclusive or exclusive versions are possible.

If we allow for its users, those who used the text of Genesis 2–3 or its equivalent as a launching pad for their storytelling or theologizing, the possibilities are clearly important and multiple. In line with the pointers preserved in the text, a story could be told around the issue of the tree of the knowledge of good and evil — so named now from the present context (see Gen 3:5, 22), but once probably the tree "in the middle of the garden" (Gen 3:3). The story could be told with a communal focus (the couple); it could be told with an individual focus (the man alone). A story could be told around the issue of the tree of life. How are humans best to experience the fullness of life and depth of life? Equally, the story could be told with communal or individual focus. Fundamentally, two issues are basic here: What is good for us? How do we live best? No single text, no single story can provide the answers to such questions. What a story may do, what one of the stories in Genesis 2–3 may do, is stimulate some thinking around the issue.

Two considerations come into play for a text of this profundity. First, is it more helpful to consider the texts we have as finished products or as user-bases to be selected from and expanded? In this case of the Garden, the presence of two trees and the issue of communal or individual context has considerable impact. The "finished product" view is not excluded; the text we have may be understood as a finished product. The "user-base" view is not mandated; it is obviously possible. It was possible then; it is possible now. Second, there is the possibility of ancient texts being given meanings according to our understanding of what was possible in their past time and the possibility of such texts being given meanings that specific interpreters find appropriate for our present time. When the biblical text has invited us to "Go think!" both these considerations may need to be taken into account.

The story moves on from the prohibition to the action of the couple. It is a text with possible stories of the first couple in the first garden; it is by no means certain that it is a story of human beginnings with consequences for the history of humankind. It could well be a late story about human proclivities, located at the beginning of human life, with the refrain "as it was in the beginning, is now, and ever shall be [world without end. Amen]."

There is much to be said, but two observations will have to be enough for us. The first concerns the woman's dominance in the text leading up to the transgression. The second concerns the closed nature of the story that does not claim to extend beyond its own boundaries.

The lead-up to the transgression is begun by the snake but is then taken over by the woman, who remains dominant until the transgression itself. The snake's opening gambit, as we know, is a loaded question: "You can't eat from any tree in the garden, eh?" The woman's reply embroiders the original slightly: "Yes we can, but not from the tree in the middle of the garden; we can't even touch that, lest we die." The snake rebuts this and disappears from the story (in any active role). First, "you will not die." In relation to this, we need to recognize that they ate and did not die, despite the associated death penalty. Mortality or immortality should not be the issue; that issue belongs with the tree of life, not the tree of knowledge (see Gen 3:22–24, which may be flagging a potentially different version of the story). Second, "your eyes will be opened, and you will be like God, knowing good and evil." In relation to this, we need to recognize that their eyes were opened — but they were not like God (3:7).

In the text, however, the woman disregards what the snake has said; instead, she turns to the forbidden fruit. She evaluates it under three significant aspects: nutrition, aesthetics, and wisdom. The first two — in reverse order and slightly different language — are already affirmed in Genesis 2:9. The third is her own observation: "to be desired to make one wise." This is the contribution given the woman: nutrition, aesthetics, and wisdom. After this reflection, she eats. She gives to her husband with her. The text does not give him a moment's thought. He eats. What sort of a text is this? She knows full well what she is doing; 3:3–4 assures readers of that. The text does not have the man contribute a word; in the circumstances, an extraordinarily strange silence. He is mute.

What kind of portrayal is this? The woman corrects a slanted view of things, reflects independently, and acts. The man who has received God's prohibition directly is portrayed as totally silent, although he is with her. Without the text giving him a moment's reflection, he defies God's prohibition; he eats. Today's feminists may be unsurprised, assured that women evaluate things reflectively and men act unthinkingly and instinctively. But this is an ancient text, and it has found a significant place in the biblical canon. What kind of portrayal is this? We know nothing of its author. We do not know how it came to be where it is. We do know that there is an accuracy in its portrayal; given a boundary, it is human nature to test it. In this case, the boundary proved to be between the human and the divine.

It will help to reflect on what has been said. The snake's opening question was a classic half-truth. Half-truths are a sure route to a distorted perception of affairs and seriously distorted perceptions often precede serious evil. In the story, the snake has done its job well. The woman's rebuttal establishes a protective hedge around the law ("nor shall you touch it"); it is a well-known rabbinic approach. In the story, she is portrayed acting wisely. However, the snake's half-truth has successfully drawn attention to this particular tree and highlighted the temptation: with opened eyes to be like God. Three attributes of the tree (and presumably its fruit) are noted: "good for food," "a delight to the eyes," and "to be desired to make one wise" (3:6). The first two, as we have noted, are already affirmed in 2:9 ("pleasant to the sight and good for food"); the third is new and lies on a more ambitious plane. Its verb has a range of meanings from "to have insight" to "to achieve success"; the emphasis is clearly positive.

After the full verse given to the woman's reflection, the text also attends to her action: "she took of its fruit." It is not said that she touched the tree; it may be implied but it has no part in the narrative. Having taken the fruit, the woman eats. After all this, the Hebrew text gives five words to the next action: "and she also gave some to her husband, who was with her, and he ate" (3:7). In the text, he is "with her" and he is silent.

Where does such a text come from? As is well known, attitudes to women vary widely in the Bible; some are appalling. Not so here. A few chapters further on, Sarah will see to it that we are children of Isaac, not of Ishmael (Gen 21). It may be that the closest parallel to Genesis 2–3 in the Hebrew Bible is Genesis 27, where Rebekah is given a dominant role in relation to an apparently feeble son, Jacob — potentially a more significant ancestor for Israel than Abraham. The initiative is Rebekah's: "Rebekah was listening when Isaac spoke to his son Esau" (Gen 27:5). The instructions are Rebekah's: "Now therefore, my son, obey my word as I command you" (27:8). The responsibility is Rebekah's: "Let your curse [the curse meant for you] be on me, my son; only obey my word, and go, get them for me" (27:13). Even the outcome devolves on Rebekah: "Now therefore, my son, obey my voice; flee at once to my brother Laban in Haran" (27:43).

Where do such texts come from? How did Genesis 2–3 get to be where it is? The answer is extremely simple: we do not know. But it is clearly the fruit of much reflection. That is why I find it captivating.

The naming of Jacob's sons, the sons who give their names to the tribes of Israel, is another puzzling text (Gen 29:31–30:24). It is not a parallel but it has a surprising affinity with what we have just looked at. Eleven sons (Benjamin comes later) are born to four women (Leah, Rachel, Bilhah, and Zilpah) from one man (Jacob). All eleven are named by only two of the women, Leah and Rachel. All eleven sons are given names relating directly to the inner emotional states of these two women, Leah and Rachel. Comparison with Genesis 49 only heightens the question: where on earth does such a text come from? There are aspects of intellectual life in ancient Israel that we know very little about.

Of course, reflections on a reflective text usually mirror their time or their context. So Hermann Gunkel (1910) says of the woman (concerning not touching the tree): probably an expansion bringing out the eager nature of the young woman/wife (*Weib*). Von Rad (nine printings, 1949–72) remarks that "the woman is quite ingenuous (*ganz unbefangen*)...goes a bit too far in her zeal." Westermann (1974) says simply: "The woman acts independently in transgressing the command and so is fully responsible. One could also say that the woman is led astray by her desire." There is not a word in the text about her desire ("delight to the eyes" [even if the Hebrew can mean "craving" in other contexts] refers to the tree, not to the inner state of the woman); there is not a word in Westermann about her reflection or the man's silence. Wenham (1987) has more than one hundred lines consecrated to the snake and less than ten lines to the woman in 3:6. His arguments for attributing "covetousness" to the woman are totally inadequate. The man's silence does not rate a mention, but the man is said to be associated with the woman in the eating; "Indeed, his eating is the last and decisive act of disobedience...." Finally, in 2004, from the United States (admittedly in the context of Sir 24:25 and 1 Tim 2:14): "One may reasonably infer from the text of Genesis that the serpent approached Eve first because she was weaker, but Adam still bears the primary responsibility in the story" (Collins, *Introduction*, 74). So it goes!

To conclude reflection on this first observation, it is worth noting the movement in the text. The man is alone for most of the first chapter (Gen 2:4b–20); the woman is dominant in the first part of the second chapter (Gen 3:1–7); God is given the role of pronouncing the fate of the snake and its offspring and of pronouncing the punishment of the woman and the man (Gen 3:14–19). The two chapters are open to a depth of reflection they seldom receive. At the same time, this "depth of reflection" has to be put in its proper place. It belongs to a story reflecting on the human condition, the state of human nature, and therefore located in the Bible among stories of its kind. It is not a story explaining how the human condition came to be the way it is. Downplaying its weight appropriately, Walter Brueggemann remarks: "It has been assumed that this is a decisive text for the Bible and that it states the premise for all that follows. In fact, this is an exceedingly marginal text" within the Hebrew Bible (*Genesis*, 41).

The second observation concerns the closed nature of the story that does not claim to extend beyond its own boundaries. Perhaps it will be best to preface discussion of this observation with a passage from Claus Westermann, one of Germany's great twentieth-century biblical scholars, protesting against the long-standing, traditional misinterpretation of the story as portraying a "fall" from a previous graced state akin to paradise.

This is illustrated by the description "the fall" which has become the title of the story in all Western languages. . . . It has rarely been contested up to the present, so deeply is it rooted in Western tradition. . . . Quite apart from any theological judgment one may pass on this line of tradition [of a "fall"] from late Judaism through Paul to Augustine, one can no longer say that it accords with the intention of Gen 2–3. . . . The narrative of Gen 2–3 does not speak of a fall. One should avoid therefore a description which differs so much from the text and is so inaccurate and deceptive. (Westermann, _Genesis 1–11,_ 275–76)

Brueggemann expresses the same conviction. "The text is commonly treated as the account of '_the fall._' Nothing could be more remote from the narrative itself" (_Genesis,_ 41).

If one's theology requires some initial catastrophe to explain the troubled state of our present world, there is nothing to prevent theologians from affirming such an initial catastrophe. The only thing that honesty demands of such theologians is that they do not claim to find the report of this catastrophe in our Genesis 2–3, beyond the human loss of innocence at the start of Genesis 3, before any follow-up by God (i.e., Gen 2:25–3:7). Among many things, discoveries at Qumran have heightened awareness that different versions of texts circulated at times in antiquity. However, instead of one initial catastrophe, it may well be that "the troubled state of our present world" has come about because of a multitude of decisions by a multitude of people. The transgression in Genesis 2–3 may be a supreme symbol of such decisions. There is no flaw in the garden God has made; it may be that there are flaws in the humans God has also made (or allowed to become).

Close attention to the biblical text is what underpins any understanding of the story as closed and self-contained. Half a dozen observations need to be noted, some already discussed briefly. As we have noted, two in particular obtrude, when allowed to. First, focusing on 3:8–21, we have recognized that only the singular is used, both for the participants and for the consequences. In a self-contained story, this is not surprising; in a story with more extensive ramifications, it would be. Second, in relation to the man and the woman, there is no reference to children; not to subsequent generations as there will be in the promises to the ancestors; not to future descendants as there will be in the guarantees of dynasties to kings. It is to be observed that such a reference, looking into the future, is present for the offspring of the snake and humans (v. 15); but it is also to be observed that there are no corresponding references to the future given for the woman or the man. The story has no further reference to the future for the human players to come. There is ample space for this in vv. 16 and 17; the space is not used. The story is self-contained. The possibility has been adumbrated that, in a relatively late story, humanity's future — children, descendants, and all that — can be taken for granted as already part of the storyteller's past.

Further details in the biblical text (our "quirks" earlier) may confirm this understanding. The woman's pain in childbirth is spoken of as greatly increased (v. 16); the assumption is that some pain was already there, but the text has no reference to any previous offspring. The births of Cain and Abel (4:1–2) are reported, without any allusion to 3:16 (also Seth and Enosh, 4:25–26). A curse is laid on the ground all the days of the man's life (v. 17); again, no reference is made to his offspring. The vocation of Cain to be "a tiller of the ground" (4:2) is noted, without any allusion to 3:17 (cf. 4:12, where a reference might be expected but is not present). Finally, vegetarianism appears to be stipulated, in speaking to the man (v. 18; cf. 1:29). Any such restriction ceases after the flood (9:2–3).

All things considered, the story appears to be a portrayal of the first example of natural sin, reflecting the innate human tendency to push beyond apparent boundaries, to ambition more than lies within the reach of human destiny. It may be significant that neither Adam nor Eve, Cain nor Abel, are mentioned in the Hebrew Bible after Genesis 5:5 (for Abel, after Gen 4:11; for Cain, after 4:24; and for Eve, after Gen 4:25). Adam, of course, heads the list in 1 Chronicles 1:1. Adam also rates a mention, though rather as an afterthought, in the deuterocanonical Ben Sirach (Ecclesiasticus): "above every other created living being was Adam" (Sir 49:16) — rather too laudatory to be said of the Adam of Genesis 3.

The name or designation used for God in Genesis 2:4b–3:24 is an unusual one, in Hebrew *yhwh elohim,* in English Lord God. While computers show it occurring some thirty-eight times across the range of Hebrew scriptures, this passage (Gen 2:4b–3:24) is the only example of sustained use (some twenty occurrences). The usage is not fully explained, but it may be a pointer to the self-contained and independent nature of this text.

~ MODERN FAITH ~

The Garden story may be much more than the sad story of a sinful couple, at the beginning of the race, who threw a monkey wrench into the works of God's well-ordered world. Maybe there is something in the story that is more deeply symbolic, more profoundly probing of the human nature that is ours. Beginning with the widespread presence of the sacred tree in the art of the ancient Near East, we have pointed to possibilities for the tree of knowledge and the tree of life as symbols giving access to understandings of human nature. We can point here; we cannot do more.

Allowing for the development of psychological perspectives in modern understanding, there are at least three ways in which the Garden story might be understood:

1. given one prohibition only, the couple *should not* have transgressed it;

2. given one prohibition only, the couple *couldn't not* have transgressed it;

3. given one prohibition only, the couple *oughtn't not* have transgressed it (i.e., one might say that the couple were morally obliged to transgress it; see below).

The first of these is the traditional understanding of the Garden story. God is understood as a force fostering life. Fullness of life is laid out before the couple in the Garden. From only one tree must they not eat. The eating of the fruit of that tree was in some way a transgressing of the boundaries of human existence. The transgression reflects an aspect of what is endemic in human nature, the desire to push beyond its boundaries. In my judgment, this traditional understanding is correct for the biblical tradition. The traditional understanding of this as involving a change of state (the Fall) and as a transgression with consequences for the human condition is, of course, not supported in the text of Genesis 2–3.

The second of these interpretations looks at the everyday experience of human life and recognizes that given one single prohibition, humans will inevitably transgress it. The emphasis is on transgression as a bad thing. Some might rightly object that this everyday experience is of human life *after* the so-called Fall. The biblical text, however, portrays the transgression as the couple's initial experience of human life, the initial experience of human life itself — not subsequent to any prior failure.

The third of these interpretations, which as far as I know can be envisaged only in our present world, views such transgression as a good and necessary thing. Without it, human life as we know it would be impossible. God is not understood as a force fostering life but, in this prohibition, as a force constricting life. The human couple, or one of them, must transgress the prohibition, must disobey, in order to find life. With everything laid on for them in the Garden, human life, in this understanding, would have been unavoidably docile, passive, quietist, without challenge. "We open the successive doors in Bluebeard's castle because 'they are there....' To leave one door closed would be not only cowardice but a betrayal — radical, self-mutilating — of the inquisitive, probing, forward-tensed stance of our species" (Steiner, *Bluebeard's Castle,* 136). Should that human couple have left one door closed?

In order to face the creative challenge and reality of human life, the prohibition had to be itself challenged and transgressed. Robert Fulghum puts this understanding nontechnically: "I am talking about the forbidden fruit of the Tree of Knowledge.... To eat of it is always trouble; not to eat is not to be fully human" (*On Fire,* 105). "To be fully human" is all very well but honesty probably requires us to put next to it these fearful lines from Wilfred Owen concerning Abraham and the sacrifice of Isaac, in the context of World War I:

Offer the Ram of Pride instead of him.
But the old man would not so,
    but slew his son, —
And half the seed of Europe, one by one.

We are forced to ponder the painful reality of the gamut ranging from "always trouble" to "fully human" to humanly divine. Where do we find ourselves? What might innocence mean? What has the loss of innocence meant? There is a further option from lines near the end of the film *The Edge of Heaven*. In the context of the Muslim version of the story of Ibrahim and Ismail, a Turkish academic recalls having asked his father: "Would you have done that to me?" His father's reply had been: "I would make an enemy of God in order to protect my son." We are left to ponder what might have been Israel's story and ours if the same decision had been given to Abraham in the Genesis narrative.

This third interpretation requires an understanding of God as restrictive of life. In some recent modern Western societies, many would claim that this experience has unquestionably been verified. I know of no biblical context where it would be claimed; to my knowledge, it is almost impossible to find a context in the biblical world in which such a view would be at home. This interpretation also envisages human life as challenging but benign. "Challenging but benign," it seems to me, is verified in many a biblical context. I think of Qohelet's "There is nothing better for mortals than to eat and drink, and find enjoyment in their toil" (more literally: eat, drink, and see the good in what they do [Qoh 2:24; also 3:13; 5:18; and 8:15]).

There is a grave problem with this third interpretation. The interpretation may be understood to imply that the prohibition is no more than an exercise of God's authority. It may be that in the text the prohibition is better understood as an exercise of God's wisdom. The snake is portrayed saying to the woman: "your eyes will be opened and you will be like God," knowing what God knows. From one point of view, humans are like God, made in God's image and likeness (Gen 1:26). From another point of view, humans are clearly not like God. The snake's offer to the woman is to go against the guidance given and for the couple to become like God. It is not the breaking of the law that is at stake; it is the core understanding of human nature. We are not God.

While this third interpretation can be attractive to a number of modern thinkers, the fact that, for all the obscurity of the narrative, the prohibition is not an arbitrary exercise of God's authority but a caution against the illusory temptation to "be like God" weakens the probability for any such interpretation. Human nature must often push against arbitrary boundaries. The innate longing to be "like God" is not an arbitrary issue; pondering it is pondering the quintessence of human nature.

In any interpretation, the relationship with God is portrayed as distanced, not broken; rather than walking with them in the Garden, God makes clothes of skin for the couple, enabling life as we know it. In the present text, the expulsion from the Garden follows (Gen 3:22–24). With its exclusive focus on the man, it may be a pointer to another telling of the story.

It is indicative of the self-contained nature of this story that such a plurality of interpretations can be mooted. On the potential for such interpretations, see John Sanford, *The Man Who Wrestled with God.*

The interplay of salvation and redemption in modern theology also impinges heavily on this Garden story and the understanding of its text. First and foremost must be the importance given to salvation. If the overarching understanding of salvation is to be found in the acceptance in faith of God's love for humankind, it is important that this Garden story does not get in the way of that faith. Some Christians have traditionally sung at Easter of the *felix culpa,* the "happy sin" that brought about the presence of Jesus Christ in human life. God's love is then shown in the price paid for human redemption. A traditional hymn displays such theology at its worst:

> That guiltless Son, who bought your peace,
> and made his Father's anger cease.

Salvation, on the other hand, affirms God's love without the need for a price to be paid. The cross of Christ is indisputable evidence of God's love for us. "No one has greater love than this, to lay down one's life for one's friends" (John 15:13). Greater evidence than this one cannot have. It has long been recognized that the idea that the

God of all our universe should love us is unbelievable — but true (e.g., Ps 8). Christ's cross is irrefutable evidence for believing it.

Some worry that without an initial catastrophe to disqualify us all, the redemptive value of the cross of Christ is undermined. In such a view, if Genesis 2–3 is a closed text, reflecting the absence of innocence within humanity and without emphasis on hereditary consequences, it does not generate the need for redemption from some single hereditary sin alienating us from God, offending God so that somehow God needs placating. In such a view, without "some single hereditary sin," is the redemptive value of the cross of Christ nullified. Not so at all. The theological potential of the cross of Christ becomes enormous. For human life to be liberated from meaninglessness and fear, on the one hand, and from the situation brought about by a multitude of sinful decisions, on the other, is redemption indeed; not a debt paid to God but a gain won for us. The life, death, and resurrection of Christ (symbolized above all in the cross) express as nothing else can the almost unbelievable commitment of God to humankind, the value God sets on humankind, the love God has for humankind.

"The incarnation is not a means of divine redemption but an expression of divine love" (Campbell, *God First Loved Us*, 53). Salvation, understood primarily as our becoming aware of God's love for us, is a less ambiguous and clearly preferable term. There can be no greater proof of love than to give one's life for another. As we have just noted from John's Gospel, that is precisely what Jesus did for us: "No one has greater love than this, to lay down one's life for one's friends" (John 15:13). Words are wonderful, but deeds are hard to better. That the God of all our universe should love each of us in the ordinariness of our human lives is in ordinary terms unbelievable — but apparently we had better believe it. According to St. Paul, reflecting on the message of the cross, the proclamation of Christ crucified is a "stumbling block" and "foolishness" to those who do not believe, but to believers it is the "power" and "wisdom" of the God whose foolishness and weakness are greater than human wisdom and human strength (1 Cor 1:23–25). Jesus' life among us and Jesus' deeds — "the blind receive their sight, the lame walk, the lepers are cleansed, the deaf hear, the dead are raised, and the poor have the good news brought to them" (Matt 11:5) — speak of God's esteem for human life in all of its ordinariness. Through his life, death, and resurrection, Jesus speaks of God's love for us. What greater salvation can there be than this?

The shift of emphasis from a punishment decreed by God (Gen 3:16–19, which it is not) to a loss of innocence resulting from human action (Gen 3:1–7, which it is) reveals the Garden story clearly as a reflection on what it is to be human. There is in human beings a yearning to reach beyond the boundaries of what is human; yielding to that yearning brings distortion into human reality. What the biblical story makes clear is that the human yearning for eyes to be open and to be like God has been met since the beginning by the human reality of eyes that are open and a being that is not like God. What is portrayed in this text is not a human sin that is punished by God with the pains and suffering that are part of so much human life. What is portrayed in the Garden story is a matter of natural consequence, independent of God. God may have warned against it; the warning is ignored. The act is performed (the fruit eaten); the consequence follows (their eyes are opened). God is not involved at all, unless the story is unfolded further and it is time for the evening walk in the Garden. Did Israel envisage a human nature that came from the creative hand of God much as we experience it now? Apparently so, in this text at least. In Genesis 2:25, the couple were innocent ("not ashamed"); in Genesis 3:7, that innocence was lost (they needed fig leaves). God is portrayed as having warned them (the prohibition). The consequences of the act flow from the act itself, not from God.

Modern theology has moved in this direction, leaving aside the misinterpretation of the Garden story. The story portrays the capacity for wrong choice as an element of being human. It does not portray the implementing of that capacity, the making of wrong choices, as for the first time becoming part of human nature in the Garden, subsequent to creation. It is portrayed as being there with human existence. Nothing is said of any impact on future generations. Future generations share that same human existence which has been there from the beginning.

As a theologian, Monika Hellwig writes: "The doctrine of original sin is rooted, as are all Christian doctrines, in biblical narrative, basically in the third chapter of the book of Genesis." A little later, she goes on: "The position was suggested and in the course of time almost universally accepted among theologians and theologically knowledgeable people that what is meant by original sin is grounded in the common observation that each of us is greatly diminished by what has happened prior to our own decisions and actions.... We are concerned with the cumulative effect of choices and actions which were less than worthy of human freedom and community" (Hellwig, in Domning, *Original Selfishness,* 11, 15). Fortunately, close attention to the relevant biblical text to a large extent coincided with theology's focus of its attention where it properly belongs in this matter.

Where the reflection on human sinfulness is concerned, theology's focus has shifted from a biblical past to an experiential present. Where biblical exegesis is concerned, close attention to the Genesis text reveals that human sinfulness is portrayed as inherent from the beginning; it is not portrayed as inherited subsequent to that beginning.

CAIN

The Cain stories are clearly in a separate context and in a style that is different from what precedes them. As far as context is concerned, Cain says to God: "Anyone who meets me may kill me" (4:14). But with Abel gone, in the hypothesis of continuity there are only his parents. Second, he marries a wife when none has been accounted for. As far as style is concerned, the narrative leaves extensive gaps for its users to fill: What others are around who might meet Cain? Where does Cain's wife come from? Why should a wife and child be a base on which to build a city? Is there a link between advancing technology and increasing violence? The gaps are there; they are left unfilled.

The tendency to read this material as a single continuous reporting of what was believed to be the beginnings of humanity is unfortunate, a temptation to be resisted. The little cluster is best viewed as a unit (Gen 4:3–24); two passages are central, one on Cain and one on his family line. The first centers on the enigmatic saying: "If you do well, will you not be accepted? And if you do not do well, sin is lurking at the door; its desire is for you, but you must master it" (4:7). The second culminates in Lamech's fearful song: "I have killed a man for wounding me, a young man for striking me. If Cain is avenged sevenfold, truly Lamech seventy-sevenfold" (4:23–24).

At the end of the second passage, Cain disappears from the text altogether. Abel is replaced by Seth, and Cain's boy Enoch by Seth's boy Enosh; the names are similar in English, but notably different in Hebrew, with the "n" the only consonant common to both (Gen 4:25–26). Genesis 4:1–24 ponders the "Cain" interior to all humanity. Genesis 5–10 will ponder a different aspect of humanity, its relationship to God. Bridging verses (4:25–26) enable the two texts to be brought into association.

In the first passage, the motif is the ever-present fact of inequality, expressed in the story as God's having regard or disregard for the two sacrifices. Inequality is a painful reality of human life, often culpable but also often clearly inculpable. Many want God's regard and disregard explained. Wenham lists "at least five different types of explanation" that have been offered and ends with a wistful touch of frustration: "we might well expect an allusion" to elucidate this inequality (*Genesis 1–15*, 104); no elucidation is given. The last word can be left with Westermann: "The narrator wants to say that in the last analysis there is something inexplicable in the origin of this inequality.... When such inequality between equals arises, it rests on a decision that is beyond human manipulation" (*Genesis 1–11*, 297). In a different context, novelist John Fowles describes the unequal distribution of energy, talent, and good luck as the great genetic injustice of life. The biblical narrator has God comment to Cain: "you must master it" (Gen 4:7). So must we.

The Hebrew word used for "desire" here (4:7) occurs only three times in the Hebrew scriptures. The first is in the preceding chapter, for the woman's desire for the man (3:16). In the context of a distorted relationship, desire leads to dominance ("he shall rule over you"). The third occurrence is in Song of Songs, "I am my beloved's, and his desire is for me" (Song 7:11 [NRSV, 7:10]). In the context of a loving relationship, desire leads to belonging. Here, in the context of Cain, "desire" is possibly the symbol for that human imbalance that, exploited, is a cause of sin. Imbalance in society threatens the justice of human existence; humans must right the imbalance without sin. Cain is the prototype of our failure to do so.

The second passage begins not with Cain's taking a wife but with their intercourse and the birth of their son, Enoch. A city is then built and named after the son. So early in the piece, a city is puzzling. It is part of the style of this Cain material to explain nothing. There is no hint that the city is anti-God, as may be the case in the tower of Babel story. Somehow, all the same, its needless presence is ominous — needless because the text gives us only three persons. The text will hint at developing technology: stockbreeding, music, metalwork. The text arrives at the unquestioned increase of violence: sevenfold for Cain, seventy-sevenfold for Lamech. At the beginning of all this is the city; it is ominous. Does it reflect exiled Israel's experience of the Mesopotamian city? Does it reflect Israel's own experience of its less imposing urban culture? We do not know and the text leaves us free to imagine. What is beyond doubt, however, is that with Lamech in the seventh generation — Adam, Cain, Enoch, Irad, Mehujael, Methushael, Lamech — violence in human society has increased more than tenfold. "If Cain is avenged sevenfold, truly Lamech seventy-sevenfold." Alas, it is not an alien picture; nor is it a peaceful picture. The emphasis on technology comes with Lamech's sons; the mention almost in the same breath is hardly devoid of significance. It casts a darkening shadow on our human race, an inner light on aspects of the being of our human nature.

~ MODERN FAITH ~

The unequal distribution of energy, talent, and good luck may be a genetic injustice. Human activity in so many forms — whether the pursuit of power, the exercise of violence and war, the amassing of wealth, and so much more — has hugely exacerbated this unequal distribution.

The story of Cain's murder of Abel is symbolic for us of the failure to cope with that genetic inequality. The account of technological progress confronts us with the means for exacerbating inequality. Does the mention of stockbreeding hint at the wealth that comes from agricultural and pastoral advances and allows for heightened inequality? Are music and metallurgy symbolic of that wealth?

The biblical text opens with the affirmation that the world is good (Genesis One). The stories of the Garden and the Cain family remind us of how far the real is distanced from the ideal. How does modern faith find something of the ideal in the all-too-painful presence of the real?

THE FLOOD

The flood text is one of the most extraordinary theological documents in the whole Bible. Emphatically and explicitly, it expresses faith in two diametrically opposed convictions:

1. faith that God is committed to eradicate evil;

2. faith that God is committed to tolerate evil.

The outcome: faith that God has accepted a creation, God's creation, that is not only capable of evil but has, in fact, actualized its potential for evil.

The basis for this can be reduced to three elements:

1. The conviction in faith that God existed;

2. The experience in themselves that Israel existed;

3. The certainty that the world was not as it could be.

Most Bible readers accept the biblical flood narrative as the expression of God's opposition to evil: God destroyed the wicked world. Even now, many Bible readers give evidence of a visceral refusal to see the faith statement of God's commitment to the continued existence of a wicked world. The language is still heard among us of a new Adam and a new creation following the flood; these readers do not allow themselves to see that the two texts combined in the flood narrative both end with God's unconditional commitment to the continuance of the world that, in the time-frame of the narrative, was not as it should have been and in the future will not be as it could be.

The paradox takes a while to sink in; after all, this is biblical text. This biblical text begins by saying that the world was wicked. So God destroyed it, sparing only an ark-load. We agree; in the context, it appears perfectly fair. This same biblical text ends by saying that, after the flood, the world was still wicked. Because no time has passed, we are entitled to be surprised. But then God unconditionally commits to never destroying this wicked world again. If we are not profoundly puzzled, we are not paying attention to the text.

In a polytheistic context, with a multitude of gods, it is not so puzzling. One god or group of gods wants a destructive flood to wipe out humankind; another god or goddess or group of gods does not want such a flood. In a monotheistic context, with only one god to reckon with, it is a paradox indeed. According to the beginning of the biblical text, God was "sorry that he had made humankind" (6:6) because of the evil inclination of their hearts; at the end of the biblical text, this one and the same God, recognizing that "the inclination of the human heart is evil" (8:21), solemnly decides never to destroy life again. Monotheism leaves us with the paradox. Faith leaves us with the wonder of a God who is committed to us as we are. One single God, implacably committed against evil, unconditionally committed to life, to the life of one single human race. That life is our lives, our lives evil though they can be. It is not to be a fresh new world, not a second try with fresh bloodstock. It is our world, the world of Genesis 6:5 and 8:21. Noah's righteousness may have been given a role at the start of the story; it plays no role at the end. One single human race, wiped out once; the same tainted human race never to be wiped out again. The mystery of myth. Perhaps other peopled worlds exist elsewhere, but that should not distract us from concern with our own.

As we will see, in due course, there are two accounts of the flood within the core of the narrative, Genesis 6:5–9:17. Both of them have

MEANINGS OF MYTH: An Aside

Myth is a complex concept, used in scholarly writing in a variety of ways. It has been defined by one authority as "a large, controlling image that gives philosophic meaning to the facts of ordinary life.... All real convictions involve a mythology." At this very broad level, it is "any idea, true or false, to which people subscribe." Alternatively, myth has sometimes been defined more narrowly as "a narrative... of the origins of life or of the deeds... of supramortal creatures, often explaining the whys and wherefores of natural phenomena" (see Barnet et al., *Literary Terms*, 94–96). A recent understanding would see myth as a narrative seeking to combine the apparently uncombinable, reconcile the apparently unreconcilable (Lévi-Strauss). Myth certainly can on occasion be a vehicle for going to the core of an issue and plumbing the potentially unplumbable. The meaning given to the concept here focuses on that aspect of myth understood as "stories in which supernatural beings are the main actors; such stories generally explain why the world, or some aspect of it, is the way it is" (Powell, *Classical Myth*, 4; nuances can be left aside). My use of the word "myth" does not attempt to embrace all myth; it focuses on one particular aspect of it. Valuable considerations are available in Kirk, *Myth: Its Meaning*.

this same remarkable stance, the move from intolerance of human wickedness to tolerance of it. They express it differently; nevertheless the move is there in both. The old adage, "love the sinner and hate the sin," is not applicable here; in the flood, we are all sinners (except Noah and possibly those with him), and the sinners are all drowned, drowned dead. Difficult of access these texts certainly are. At the same time, the faith that produced them is truly astounding. These texts may be cast as reports of the past; they are in fact ponderings of the present.

An approach to the puzzle is the recognition that one of the great tributes we can pay to other human beings — parents, partners, and the like — is to speak of their unconditional love. Yes, they recognize flaws and failings in those they love; but they love them all the same. Genesis One affirms that we are made in the image and likeness of God. If at our best we can love unconditionally, surely God can; alternatively, because we believe God does, so surely we should try. Nevertheless, it may take a flood story or two to explore this.

It is time to turn to the text. Contrary to much current opinion, in my judgment the flood story unit is probably best understood to begin with Genesis 5:1 and end with Genesis 10:32.

As far as the beginning goes, Genesis 5:1–2 covers comfortably enough the core content of Genesis One. The human race is created, in the likeness of God, male and female, blessed and named. The two verses are suitable for a new beginning; they differ slightly from Genesis One and need not be a mere recap. As a beginning, 5:1–2 has the potential to be wholly independent.

After the introduction, a ten-generation genealogy takes us from Adam to Noah. At the other end of the unit, Noah's sons spread over the known world. Genesis 10:32 wraps it up: "These are the families of Noah's sons, according to their genealogies, in their nations; and from these the nations spread abroad on the earth after the flood." The tower of Babel story (11:1–9) occupies a different context, where "the whole earth had one language and the same words."

Seeing this unit (5:1–10:32) as consecrated to the flood story leaves two small units unaccounted for. First, there are four verses on what might be called "mixed marriages" (6:1–4); second, there is the account of Noah's drunkenness (9:20–26). The association of this latter with the story of Noah and the flood is natural enough. The former is a puzzle. It is hardly preparation for the flood, as an example of human wickedness; as Skinner noted correctly, back in 1910, "the guilt is wholly on the side of the angels" (*Genesis*, 143). The little fragment would be pretty much out of place anywhere.

Leaving these out of the way, we can come to the text of the flood. It is important to realize that we are dealing with a text, not an event. It is even more important to realize that we are dealing with one of the more complex texts in the entire Bible. Two reasons point to complexity and confusion.

1. *Because of time.* The flood account is located in the mythic past, which is where it has to be, but the evidence for key affirmations at the beginning and the end of the text rests solidly on experience from historic time. That is confusing.

2. *Because of topic.* The flood account deals with how we human beings stand before God; few if any issues are more complex. On such a sensitive subject, it places a flat self-contradiction firmly in the heart of God. That is confusing.

First, stories of a global flood can be located only in the mythic past. They are allowed there; they can even be credible there. A global flood, in historical time, in areas like the Fertile Crescent and the Mediterranean littoral, would bring any storyteller or storytelling tradition into disrepute. Memory of some sort — race memory, folk memory, body memory — would almost certainly disqualify any such idea.

Set in mythic time, the biblical text does not tell enough about human living in that time to legitimate its key assertions about humans. "Every inclination of the thoughts of their hearts was only evil continually" (Gen 6:5); "the inclination of the human heart is evil from youth" (Gen 8:21). Minor differences apart (to be discussed below), these two assertions are identical. Their importance is that the consequences drawn from them are diametrically opposed. "I will blot out from the earth the human beings I have created — people together with animals, and creeping things and birds of the air" (Gen 6:7); "I will never again...destroy every living creature as I have done" (Gen 8:21).

Essential here is to note that the evil of the human heart is *affirmed* at the start of the story. It is not *narrated* in the text which precedes. Even if one wanted to claim that the transgression in the Garden, the murder of Abel, and the violence of Lamech are to be included — as dubious a claim as this might be — these three crimes hardly legitimate the assertion that every inclination of the thoughts of human hearts was only evil continually. Frankly, this does not matter much. Storytellers can be left to expand texts where they believe it necessary. Storytelling texts can be allowed to assert without our insisting that they narrate what they assert. What matters a very great deal in this particular case, however, is that at the end of the story no time is allowed for behavior that might legitimate the repeated assertion of human evil. Some evidence of human evil is required and the timeframe of the story does not allow for it.

Without human behavior to legitimate the assertion, within the story text the narrator must base God's decision on something like the equivalent of divine insight into human nature, but not on repeated human failure. Within this narrative, God's decision promises a continuation of human existence, despite God's recognition that "the inclination of the human heart is evil from youth" (Gen 8:21). Remarkable!

Noah and his family disembarked from the ark (Gen 8:18). Noah built an altar to the LORD, offered burnt offerings, and "when the LORD smelled the pleasing odor, the LORD said in his heart,...the inclination of the human heart is evil from youth" (8:21). And this is the Noah to whom the LORD had earlier said, "for I have seen that you alone are righteous before me in this generation" (7:1). Human evil is affirmed, not narrated. But there is no way in which the affirmation can be based on post-flood evidence. In the text, Noah has not had a free moment to be aware of his inclinations, much less to act on them. Apart from divine intuition (which is probably not to be invoked), the only possible basis for this affirmation, made in mythic time, is what has been experienced in historic time. It is portrayed as divine knowledge that commits to the continuation of less-than-perfect human living.

Naturally, one may expect that texts are written in historic time and are, nevertheless, set in the mythic past. It is the fate of all myths. The implication for this flood myth, however, is that the causes that drive the story forward are grounded outside the story.

If the repeated description of humankind — "the inclination of the human heart is evil from youth" (8:21) — was disregarded, being claimed as a later addition (for whatever reasons), nothing essential in the text would change. Without some conditional clause to cover the possibility of future human evil (for example: provided humans do not lapse into evil again), the affirmation "never again" leaves God committed to humankind, no matter what. It is an incredible faith statement. That is precisely where the present text puts God.

That is precisely where the priestly text (in the next chapter, Gen 9) puts God when an unconditional commitment is given to a world where murder and capital punishment are envisaged (9:1–17). The meaning of 8:21, in Westermann's words: "God decides to put up with this state of evil" (*Genesis 1–11*, 456).

Is this any different from the Newer Testament's God who has the sun rise on the evil and good alike, who sends rain on the just and unjust (Matt 5:45)? Does it make a difference that God's "never again" occurs in the same story that began portraying God's regret over creation and God's decision to reverse it: "I will blot out from the earth the human beings I have created" (Gen 6:6–7)? Here the existence of just and unjust is not solely attributable to human behavior, introducing evil into the goodness of God's creation. Here, the text attributes the existence of just and unjust to God's decision never again to destroy and affirms God's commitment to the continuation of human existence into the future despite the text's portrayal of God's conviction of human sinfulness — i.e., that "the inclination of the human heart is evil from youth" (Gen 8:21). The flood text stands strongly against sentiments such as "Let sinners be consumed from the earth, and let the wicked be no more" (Ps 104:35). The decision never again to destroy is the negative equivalent of the positive decision to create.

The Newer Testament has the parable of the weeds among the wheat (Matt 13:24–30 [36–43]). The "harvest time" in the parable (vs. 24–30) may be thisworldly; in the allegory (vs. 36–43) it is otherworldly. It is clear that the parable is told in the context of belief in life after death. It needs to be equally clear that the biblical flood story is told in a context where there is no belief in life after death. Yet the biblical text attributes to God an unconditional commitment to a world where the inclination of the human heart is judged to be evil from youth and where murder and capital punishment are envisaged. This is not to "sanctify" evildoing; evil may be with us always, human living invites us to struggle against it always. The view that the poor will be with you always (Matt 26:11; John 12:8) is not an endorsement of poverty.

We might ask ourselves how many people across the centuries have been convinced that God could not have created a world as imperfect as this one (minimally, imperfect means "could be better"). Perhaps so. Perhaps something went radically wrong somewhere. According to the start of the biblical flood narrative, God clearly agreed; with sorrow and grief, God almost entirely destroyed this imperfect world. Then at the end of the narrative, without specifying any conditions but acknowledging human realities (even if a bit jaundiced), God is portrayed making the decision not to destroy this world again (8:21–22) and making a solemn promise not to do so (9:11, 15). Having demonstrated the capacity to destroy, God's decision never to destroy again, no matter what, is as good as a new creation in its own right, but the creation of a world as imperfect as this one. For many people, the world as it came from God of necessity had to be "very good" as it was described in Genesis One. To see the miseried mess of our present world coming from God's decision would, in such a view, be unthinkable. In Genesis 8:21–22 (and 9:2–6, 11), however, the unthinkable has been thought — and turned into biblical text.

Further, the self-contradiction in the heart of God ("I will do it; I will not do it") has to be faced and reckoned with. Such contradictions are easily accounted for in a polytheistic universe; god A says, "I will do it" and goddess B says, "Oh no you won't." In a monotheistic universe it is devilishly difficult. As noted, it is not a case of hating the sin and loving the sinner; unfortunately, the sinners have just been drowned, all of them.

There are two stories combined in the flood text, as we will see shortly. The transition in God from a "with regret, yes" to a "never again, no" is present in both. The way it is handled in the composition of the two is admirable. The transition is retained, but put in a context where it is somewhat less abrupt.

It is almost of the essence of one understanding of myth (i.e., that involving the interaction of gods [including semi-divine beings] and that involving gods and humans in direct interaction) that the action usually takes place in mythic time where gods and humans and spirits mingle and share and influence life. The drift of the flood story in folk memory has long been that eons ago, in distant time, God caused a flood because of human wickedness. Narrators and listeners have always known that we are here, less-than-perfect though we may be. What interpreters of this story do not seem to have given adequate weight to is that this present human existence of ours is given its guarantee of coexistence with God because of a decision attributed to God and, above all, that this occurs in the mingling of mythic and historic time.

Coexistence with God. For atheists, coexistence with God is not a problem. Because there is no God, there is no coexistence. The Bible, naturally, does not take this route. For many Christians, there is no problem because there probably was no flood; it is all part of that brand of Older Testament stuff, thought of as "primitive rot" and dismissed as ancient rubbish! Other believers in God systematize in multiple ways. For those of a deistic cast of mind, God does not interfere. For those with an eschatological bent, God will sort it all out at the end of time. For those with Christological convictions, God has already dealt with it in Christ. One thing alone is certain: we are here. In faith, we believe that we are here because of a decision by God not to destroy. Expressed more generally: we are here because of God's ongoing interest in and commitment to us human beings and the strange world we exist in. Ultimately, at a profound level, it is about the understanding of God, no matter how obliquely expressed.

Mingling of mythic and historic time. Myths are usually set in mythic time; all myths, however, are written in historic time. What is special about the biblical flood myth is that its story extends into historic time. Usually, a myth has its causes and effects contained within the myth story in mythic time. As we have seen, the biblical flood story does not. The wickedness of humankind after the flood cannot be contained within the story, not even as simple affirmation. It is the human race we know — with its history of violence we know all too well — that God has decided to coexist with. Nothing mythic here; sheerest history, the reality of who we are.

Small wonder that the exilic prophet in the book of Isaiah turned to the myth and has God say:

> This is like the days of Noah to me:
> Just as I swore that the waters of Noah
>   would never again go over the earth,
> so I have sworn that I will not be angry with you
>   and will not rebuke you.

For the mountains may depart and the hills be removed,
but my steadfast love shall not depart from you,
and my covenant of peace shall not be removed.

(Isa 54:9–10)

God's commitment to God's earth is rock solid.
God's commitment to God's people is rock solid.
Yay for rocks.

It is not surprising that Noah and Job are cited as two legendary figures in Ezekiel 14:14–20. The Ezekiel text is from around the time of exile and the book of Job is hardly early; the figures of Noah and Job are cited as legendary. Early figures can feature in late texts.

Comparison with the ancient flood myths (in *ANET* or Heidel, for example) is difficult but very informative. Controversy raged in nineteenth-century Germany, the Babylon-Bible debate (in German: "Babel-Bibel"). It was probably inevitable in nineteenth-century Germany; it is unnecessary now. The similarities between the biblical flood accounts and the Mesopotamian flood myths are incontrovertible; the differences between them are equally incontrovertible.

The existence of the flood myth in various forms, lasting for at least a couple of thousand years in ancient Mesopotamia — from Sumerian and Old Babylonian times to the period of Israel's exile — indicates the massive importance of the myth, an importance yet to be fully explored. The various forms in which the myth found expression, even in Mesopotamia alone, indicate the different uses to which it was put. The differing roles of the gods is a pointer to an ambivalence inherent in the myth, perhaps an ambivalence inherent in human experience. (Apart from reading the texts themselves, a comprehensive initial introduction to this multiplicity of versions is given in Westermann, *Genesis 1–11,* 398–406; in brief: "a whole history of flood traditions within a single area" [398]. English texts of the Mesopotamian myths are available in *ANET.* In relation to the epic of Gilgamesh, Stephanie Dalley notes: "we cannot often use one fragment to restore another, because each period and area had its own version of the story" [*Myths from Mesopotamia,* 39]).

In some versions of the myth, a cause is given for the flood (e.g., a god deprived of sleep, whatever that may evoke symbolically); in others, no cause is given. In some versions, the flood is preceded by plagues and the like; in others, there is nothing equivalent. In some versions, the survivor is designated by the gods; in others, the survivor escapes against the will of the gods. Finally, in some versions provision is made for the repopulating of the earth; in others, no such repopulating is envisaged. Unfortunately, versions seldom survive extensively enough for interpretation. Most are represented by a fragment or two, enough to show differences but often not enough to support interpretation. A welcome exception is the flood account of the more than three hundred lines of the intact Tablet XI from one version of the Gilgamesh epic.

One outcome of such a survey of the ancient versions of the myth is the realization that differences of detail and emphasis in the biblical flood texts are to be taken seriously.

Two traditions of the flood myth have long been identified within the biblical text; their combination in one way or another to form the present text is brilliant. The evidence for the two can be quickly summarized:

Names: Two names are used for God, one in each version: *elohim* (the Hebrew common noun for god) in text A (formerly: P); *yhwh* (the Hebrew personal name for Israel's God) in text B (formerly: J).

Times: Text A treats time in 150-day blocks; text B treats time in 40-day blocks, with in some cases 7-day blocks.

Animals: Text A has all its animals in one class and takes one pair of each on the ark, described as "male and female," along with foodstuffs; fortunately, it has no final sacrifice (with only one pair of each available, any sacrifice would have been an ecological disaster). Text B, on the other hand, has two classes of animals (clean and unclean) and takes seven of the clean and two of the unclean (pairs probably, but the Hebrew is not specific), described as "the male and its mate," without any specification of foodstuffs; the surplus of clean animals apparently suffices for food and the final sacrifice.

Waters: In text A, the waters come from both below and above ("fountains of the great deep" and "windows of the heavens"); in text B, the waters come from above only ("rain").

More could be said, but that is enough. For a full presentation of texts A and B and their combination, see Campbell and O'Brien, *Sources of the Pentateuch*, esp. 211–23.

◆ ◆ ◆

Drawing on *Sources of the Pentateuch,* texts A and B can be listed here without further discussion. The combined text (Gen 6:5–9:17) can be found in any Bible.

FLOOD: Text A (*elohim;* formerly Priestly)

Genesis 6

[9]These are the descendants of Noah. Noah was a righteous man, blameless in his generation; Noah walked with God. [10]And Noah had three sons, Shem, Ham, and Japheth.

[11]Now the earth was corrupt in God's sight, and the earth was filled with violence. [12]And God saw that the earth was corrupt; for all flesh had corrupted its ways upon the earth. [13]And God said to Noah, "I have determined to make an end of all flesh, for the earth is filled with violence because of them; now I am going to destroy them along with the earth. [14]Make yourself an ark of cypress wood; make rooms in the ark, and cover it inside and out with pitch. [15]This is how you are to make it: the length of the ark three hundred cubits, its width fifty cubits, and its height thirty cubits. [16]Make a roof for the ark, and finish it to a cubit above; and put the door of the ark in its side; make it with lower, second, and third decks. [17]For my part, I am going to bring a flood of waters on the earth, to destroy from under heaven all flesh in which is the breath of life; everything that is on the earth shall die. [18]But I will establish my covenant with you; and you shall come into the ark, you, your sons, your wife, and your sons' wives with you. [19]And of every living thing, of all flesh, you shall bring two of every kind into the ark, to keep them alive with you; they shall be male and female. [20]Of the birds according to their kinds, and of the animals according to their kinds, of every creeping thing of the ground according to its kind, two of every kind shall come in to you, to keep them alive. [21]Also take with you every kind of food that is eaten, and store it up; and it shall serve as food for you and for them." [22]Noah did this; he did all that God commanded him.

Genesis 7

⁶Noah was six hundred years old when the flood of waters came on the earth.

¹¹In the six hundredth year of Noah's life, in the second month, on the seventeenth day of the month, on that day all the fountains of the great deep burst forth, and the windows of the heavens were opened.

¹³On the very same day Noah with his sons, Shem and Ham and Japheth, and Noah's wife and the three wives of his sons entered the ark, ¹⁴they and every wild animal of every kind, and all domestic animals of every kind, and every creeping thing that creeps on the earth, and every bird of every kind — every bird, every winged creature. ¹⁵They went into the ark with Noah, two and two of all flesh in which there was the breath of life. ¹⁶ᵃAnd those that entered, male and female of all flesh, went in as God had commanded him.

¹⁸The waters swelled and increased greatly on the earth; and the ark floated on the face of the waters. ¹⁹The waters swelled so mightily on the earth that all the high mountains under the whole heaven were covered; ²⁰the waters swelled above the mountains, covering them fifteen cubits deep. ²¹And all flesh died that moved on the earth, birds, domestic animals, wild animals, all swarming creatures that swarm on the earth, and all human beings. ²⁴And the waters swelled on the earth for one hundred fifty days.

Genesis 8

¹But God remembered Noah and all the wild animals and all the domestic animals that were with him in the ark. And God made a wind blow over the earth, and the waters subsided; ²and the fountains of the deep and the windows of the heavens were closed. ³ᵇAt the end of one hundred fifty days the waters had abated; ⁴and in the seventh month, on the seventeenth day of the month, the ark came to rest on the mountains of Ararat. ⁵The waters continued to abate until the tenth month; in the tenth month, on the first day of the month, the tops of the mountains appeared.

⁷And he [Heb; NRSV has no pronoun] sent out the raven; and it went to and fro until the waters were dried up from the earth.

¹³ᵃ In the six hundred first year, in the first month, the first day of the month, the waters were dried up from the earth. ¹⁴In the second month, on the twenty-seventh day of the month, the earth was dry. ¹⁵Then God said to Noah, ¹⁶"Go out of the ark, you and your wife, and

your sons and your sons' wives with you. ¹⁷Bring out with you every living thing that is with you of all flesh — birds and animals and every creeping thing that creeps on the earth — so that they may abound on the earth, and be fruitful and multiply on the earth." ¹⁸So Noah went out with his sons and his wife and his sons' wives. ¹⁹And every animal, every creeping thing, and every bird, everything that moves on the earth, went out of the ark by families.

Genesis 9

¹God blessed Noah and his sons, and said to them, "Be fruitful and multiply, and fill the earth. ²The fear and dread of you shall rest on every animal of the earth, and on every bird of the air, on everything that creeps on the ground, and on all the fish of the sea; into your hand they are delivered. ³Every moving thing that lives shall be food for you; and just as I gave you the green plants, I give you everything. ⁴Only, you shall not eat flesh with its life, that is, its blood. ⁵For your own lifeblood I will surely require a reckoning: from every animal I will require it and from human beings, each one for the blood of another, I will require a reckoning for human life.

> ⁶Whoever sheds the blood of a human,
>   by a human shall that person's blood be shed;
> for in his own image
>   God made humankind.

⁷And you, be fruitful and multiply, abound on the earth and multiply in it."

⁸Then God said to Noah and to his sons with him, ⁹"As for me, I am establishing my covenant with you and your descendants after you, ¹⁰and with every living creature that is with you, the birds, the domestic animals, and every animal of the earth with you, as many as came out of the ark. ¹¹I establish my covenant with you, that never again shall all flesh be cut off by the waters of a flood, and never again shall there be a flood to destroy the earth." ¹²God said, "This is the sign of the covenant that I make between me and you and every living creature that is with you, for all future generations: ¹³I have set my bow in the clouds, and it shall be a sign of the covenant between me and the earth. ¹⁴When I bring clouds over the earth and the bow is seen in the clouds, ¹⁵I will remember my covenant that is between me and you and every living creature of all flesh; and the waters shall never

again become a flood to destroy all flesh. **¹⁶**When the bow is in the clouds, I will see it and remember the everlasting covenant between God and every living creature of all flesh that is on the earth." **¹⁷**God said to Noah, "This is the sign of the covenant that I have established between me and all flesh that is on the earth."

FLOOD: Text B (*yhwh;* formerly Yahwist)

Genesis 6

⁵The Lord saw that the wickedness of humankind was great in the earth, and that every inclination of the thoughts of their hearts was only evil continually. **⁶**And the Lord was sorry that he had made humankind on the earth, and it grieved him to his heart. **⁷**So the Lord said, "I will blot out from the earth the human beings I have created — people together with animals and creeping things and birds of the air, for I am sorry that I have made them." **⁸**But Noah found favor in the sight of the Lord.

* * * [*Announcement of the flood and building of the ark*]

Genesis 7

¹Then the Lord said to Noah, "Go into the ark, you and all your household, for I have seen that you alone are righteous before me in this generation. **²**Take with you seven pairs of all clean animals, the male and its mate; and a pair of the animals that are not clean, the male and its mate, **³ᵇ**to keep their kind alive on the face of all the earth. **⁴**For in seven days I will send rain on the earth for forty days and forty nights; and every living thing that I have made I will blot out from the face of the ground." **⁵**And Noah did all that the Lord had commanded him.

¹⁰And after seven days the waters of the flood came on the earth. **⁷***And Noah went into the ark to escape the waters of the flood. **¹⁶ᵇ**And the Lord shut him in. **¹²**The rain fell on the earth forty days and forty nights.

¹⁷ᵇAnd the waters increased, and bore up the ark, and it rose high above the earth. **²²**Everything on dry land in whose nostrils was the breath of life died. **²³***He blotted out every living thing that was on the face of the ground, human beings and animals and creeping things and birds of the air. Only Noah was left, and those that were with him in the ark.

Genesis 8

6a At the end of forty days, **2b**the rain from the heavens was restrained, **3a**and the waters gradually receded from the earth.

6bNoah opened the window of the ark that he had made. **8**Then he sent out the dove from him, to see if the waters had subsided from the face of the ground; **9**but the dove found no place to set its foot, and it returned to him to the ark, for the waters were still on the face of the whole earth. So he put out his hand and took it and brought it into the ark with him. **10**He waited another seven days, and again he sent out the dove from the ark; **11**and the dove came back to him in the evening, and there in its beak was a freshly plucked olive leaf; so Noah knew that the waters had subsided from the earth. **12**Then he waited another seven days, and sent out the dove; and it did not return to him any more.

13b And Noah removed the covering of the ark, and looked, and saw that the face of the ground was drying.

* * * [*Debarkation from the ark*]

20Then Noah built an altar to the LORD, and took of every clean animal and of every clean bird, and offered burnt offerings on the altar. **21**And when the LORD smelled the pleasing odor, the LORD said in his heart, "I will never again curse the ground because of humankind, for the inclination of the human heart is evil from youth; nor will I ever again destroy every living creature as I have done.

> **22**As long as the earth endures,
>   seedtime and harvest, cold and heat,
> summer and winter, day and night,
>   shall not cease."

◆ ◆ ◆

The carpentry for the ark and the hydraulics of the flood do not engage me. What captivates me is the theology that opens and closes both accounts as well as their combination.

In order to focus freely on the theological aspects, it will help to deal with each text separately, and then to move to the combination of the two accounts. We will deal, therefore, with text B first, both beginning and end, then with text A, both beginning and end, and finally the combined text, both beginning and end.

Text B contains the abrupt reversal in the heart of God (*yhwh*); at the beginning in 6:5–7, contrasting with the end in 8:21–22. The formulation repays close attention; naturally enough, it is not as blunt as "I will destroy," "I will not destroy"; perhaps reality is not so stark. It opens, in 6:5–7, with a statement describing humankind, followed by a statement about the inner state of God, and finally God's decisions, first about the fate of humankind on earth and then about everything else. The text closes, in 8:21–22, with the same issues in a different sequence. God's decision about earth and humankind precedes a statement describing humankind, and God's decision about everything follows. This sequence, of course, is that of the existing present Hebrew text; however, all analyses alleging differing origins for different phrases in the text are inevitably hypothetical.

What is in fact a distraction needs to be dealt with and dismissed. The mention of the ground (*adamah*), associated with the preposition "because of," in both 3:17 and 8:21 makes it inevitable that 3:17 will be evoked when 8:21 is read. Any closer correlation of the two is rendered impossible, first, by the use of different verbs in each (despite some translations understandably rendering the two Hebrew verbs by one and the same verb [in English, "curse"]) and, second, by the different contexts of each. The context in 3:17 is the state of the ground in the present ("cursed is the ground"); the context in 8:21 is the state of God's mind concerning the future ("I will never again devastate the ground"; the Hebrew verbal root is *QLL,* here "to do bad things to" but usually "to say bad things about" = to curse). Genesis 8:21 does not revoke what, in another story, was done in the past; it promises that what has just happened, in this story, will not be repeated in the future.

The abrupt reversal in the heart of God (*yhwh*) is linked to the statements describing humankind and is easily presented.

The two descriptions of humankind are almost identical:

Opening: "*every* inclination of the thoughts of their hearts was *only* evil *continually*" (6:5).

Closing: "for the inclination of the human heart is evil from youth" (8:21)

The two divine decisions are the opposite of one another:

> *Opening:* "I will blot out from the earth [Heb.: *adamah*] the human beings I have created" (6:7).

> *Closing:* "I will never again curse [better: devastate] the ground because of humankind" (8:21).

In the second description of humankind, the "every" and the "only" have been omitted; the "continually" has been somewhat mitigated. Essentially, nothing has changed. In the divine decisions, "I will blot out" and "I will never again curse [devastate]" are flatly contradictory.

Text B describes Noah as finding "favor in the sight of the LORD" (6:8), who alone was righteous before God (7:1). In what is preserved for us in the combination of the two texts, nothing further is added on this issue. There is nothing about the building of the ark; there is nothing about the purpose of the ark. We may speculate as to how this gap may have been filled; however, the text of 8:21 imposes severe limits on such speculation.

Text A approaches the story differently. After opening with Noah and his sons, it deals with a global state of affairs and does not even mention humankind explicitly. The opening statement is: "Now the earth [*arets*] was corrupt in God's sight [*elohim*], and the earth was filled with violence ... for all flesh had corrupted its ways upon the earth" (6:11–12).

Note: the phrase "all flesh" occurs in text A eleven times and nowhere else in Genesis; it is apparently relatively late and can in many cases have much the same meaning as humankind. One odd little statistic cannot be without significance. "Living creatures" is the term of choice in Genesis One; "all flesh" is its equivalent in text A of the flood. Yet in Genesis 9:8–17, the two occur five times and four times respectively. A likely possibility is that the person responsible for 9:8–17 wanted to pull together Genesis One ("living creatures") and text A of the flood narrative ("all flesh"). Whether this was part of a larger project (P, for example) is a question that remains open.

In a speech to Noah, text A has God express the decision "to make an end of all flesh" (6:13). Instructions concerning the ark follow. A covenant with Noah is promised (6:18). This is not found in text B.

At the end of its flood account, text A has no need to take up the issue of God's decision; it has already been made with the announcement of the flood and the promise of a covenant to Noah. Particular to text A is the specification of a change in the divine dispensation given in Genesis One. Noah and his sons are to "be fruitful and multiply, and fill the earth" (9:1, 7) as was the role of the couple in Genesis One. Two changes, however, legislate to accommodate a less-than-perfect world. First, the vegetarian requirement is removed ("I give you everything"), with the result that "fear and dread" rests on the animal kingdom (9:2–3). Second, within prescriptions about blood, murder is foreseen and its punishment legislated ("Whoever sheds the blood of a human, by a human shall that person's blood be shed" [9:6]). Of course, both changes take the narrative outside mythic time. The altered divine dispensation is then followed by the unconditional covenant that God establishes with Noah and his descendants after him (9:8–17).

The combination of texts A and B is a remarkable achievement. Text B's almost perfunctory mention of Noah links with text A's greater emphasis on Noah and mention of his three sons. Already, early on and obliquely, the way is being prepared for life after the flood. Text B's emphasis on the wickedness of humankind is broadened in text A to describe the earth as filled with violence and corrupt. God's determination to destroy had begun text B; in text A, the repetition of this determination is linked with the command to build an ark and the promise of a covenant. From the outset, some sort of survival is in view. In text B, it was rudimentary, the mere mention of Noah finding favor (6:8; also 7:1); in text A, it is given weight in the promise of a covenant.

At the end of the story, text B's reversal of God's (*yhwh*) decision to destroy is required; it was not prepared for at the start of text B. The reversal is then followed by the change of God's (*elohim*) dispensation for the earth, from text A. In this way, the shock of the abrupt reversal in the heart of God is modified by the twofold change in divine dispensation for life on earth. Finally, then, the story of the flood can be brought to a close with the establishment of the covenant between God and all flesh (9:8–17). God has indeed come to terms

with a less-than-perfect world. Life can go on, freed from any unconscious or archetypal fear of annihilation, freed of any unconscious
doubt whether the universal God could be committed to imperfect
humankind. Imperfect though humankind may be, relationship with
a perfect God is possible.

Over against those who believe that God could not be associated
with the emergence of a world as miserable as ours, the biblical
flood text affirms a belief that God, having once destroyed such a
world, made a solemn decision to allow it to re-emerge unchanged,
guaranteeing, without any conditions, never to destroy it again. In
all the mysteriousness of its mythic expression, this is a remarkable faith affirmation. God is portrayed doing two things. First,
God is portrayed declaring of our human race that it is thoroughly
and intrinsically evil: "the inclination of the human heart is evil
from youth" (8:21). Second, God is portrayed guaranteeing the re-
emergence of such a human race, without imposing any conditions
for change: "nor will I ever again destroy every living creature as
I have done" (8:21). All this is text B; the same faith is expressed
in text A. The re-emergence of a less-than-perfect human race is
present in 9:2–6 (see vv. 2, 6). The divine guarantee never again
to destroy is given in 9:8–17. The fundamentalist suggestion that
God's guarantee is never to destroy by flood so that the next time
will be by fire is unworthy of God and in flat contradiction to Genesis
8:21–22.

Genesis One portrays a creation judged to be "very good" (1:31).
The flood narrative portrays God giving the go-ahead for a world that
will be very much like ours — far from "very good." The contrast
between the two is marked. Ancient Israel and we today scarcely
need reminding about the nature of our world; it is part of everyday
experience. What the biblical flood text offers discreetly is an insight
into the understanding of God. *After having entertained the prospect,*
faith can affirm that God will not abandon our world.

Noah's death follows in 9:29. His sons repopulate the earth, so
that the unit may conclude: "These are the families of Noah's sons,
according to their genealogies, in their nations; and from these the
nations spread abroad on the earth after the flood" (10:32).

~ MODERN FAITH ~

It is surprising that, to my knowledge, we have no reflective and thoroughgoing analysis of the flood myth. We have analyses of the Greek myths and how they reflect explorations of human behavior. We have nothing similar for flood myths that I know of. Yet the myth of a flood is perhaps the most widely spread of human myths. Westermann notes a 1924 comment that there are some "250 flood sagas scattered across the world" (*Genesis 1–11,* 398). Yet we fall short of knowing what aspects of human experience are at the core of such myths. For Westermann, "The flood is the archetype of human catastrophe, and as such has been formed into narrative. What the flood narrative aims at expressing is derivation [*das Herkommen* = origin] as a result of the preservation of the one amidst the demise of all others. It is precisely this that is the goal of the flood narrative" (*Genesis 1–11,* 398–99). In my view, this is nowhere near enough. The climatologist may speak of the human fear of the power of water; "nestled deep within the human psyche lies a primal fear of the awful power of water" (Flannery, *Weather Makers,* 142). The theologian may want to explore further. Certainly, biblical creation accounts with their emphasis on God's control of the oceans, keeping them safely in their place, coincides with Flannery's view that "in our subconscious we understand that the waters can rise over the land" (*Weather Makers,* 143). Well may we wonder what aspects of human experience are at the core of flood myths.

As we have seen, the biblical flood narrative (6:5–9:17) comprises a merging of two versions (text A and text B). There is a marked difference between them. Text B focuses on the wickedness of "man" (NRSV: humankind) and God's decision to destroy all that has been created, the destruction by flood, and ends with the abrupt reversal of that decision and the commitment never again to destroy. Text A focuses on the corruption of a wider entity, "all flesh," and the announcement of God's decision to destroy "all flesh" and at the same time to preserve life, then the destruction by flood, and ends with a change of divine dispensation (9:1–7) and God's commitment of an unconditional covenant (9:8–17). The combined biblical text preserves both focuses.

Both focuses of the biblical flood story have a surprisingly contradictory stance. One pole of the contradiction would be: a story of
God's elimination of human evil. The other pole would then be: a
story of God's guarantee of the continuance of human evil. The first
is to be found at the start of the text; the second at the end of the
text. The contrast is starkest in text B; it is also present in text A. The
theologically minded among us will not like the language of God's
guaranteeing "the continuance of human evil." But if God guarantees
the continuance of human life and if God affirms that human living
is evil, then guaranteeing the continuance of human evil is what it is
about (see "the inclination of the human heart is evil from youth"
[Gen 8:21]; fear and dread in the animal realm, killing and execution
in the human [Gen 9:2, 6]).

What modern faith must ponder is the inner aspect of human
fragility and survival that is being touched on here. Modern cosmological science, reaching into the origins of our world and exploring
the vastness of our universe, brings to awareness as never before
the infinitesimally small speck that human life is within the universe.
Why should God give a damn? Global communications have brought
home to us, perhaps as never before, the extent of violence, poverty,
depravity, and brutal cruelty all over our globe. Why should human
life exist? (Not quite the same question as "Why does human life
exist?") The biblical flood myth offers no answer beyond the simple
claim of faith: God has given it thought and it does exist. Does something in our being need an assurance of survival in the face of our
fragility? Does something in our being need a recognition that the
ideal, symbolized in Genesis One, lies out of our reach despite our
striving, but that God's dispensation for human life has settled for
recognition of human distance from that ideal?

Ultimately, does the biblical flood myth respond, in its own strange
way, to our human need to be loved and valued — first, by ourselves;
second, by others; third (but above all), by God? Does the biblical
flood myth give an assurance of meaning in the midst of so much
misery? To expand Psalm 8's question: What are human beings in all
their wretchedness that you care for them? The biblical flood narrative replies: what indeed, but God does care for them. That such care
should be expressed in a myth of universal destruction is strange.

Stranger still is the care that such faith expresses in this myth of guaranteed existence.

BABEL

An aspect of the Babel story that fascinates me is how totally out of place it is in the sequence of its immediate context, following Genesis 10, but yet it is perfectly in place as a conclusion to the unit Genesis 2–11.

"Out of place" because it is a story of a time when the earth "had one language and the same words" (Gen 11:1), but in the preceding chapter the progeny of the three sons of Noah had spread across the earth by lands, languages, families, and nations (see Gen 10:5, 20, 31). In the context, one language for the whole earth is out of the question.

"Perfectly in place" because the little story of Babel, its city and its tower, mirrors more than adequately the opening story of the Garden. As such, it brings closure to the unit constituted by Genesis 2:4b–11:9. A duality is latent in the text of the Babel story, but need not be developed here. The group's proposal to build a city and a tower "with its top in the heavens" is followed by the intention to make a name for themselves and to prevent them being scattered abroad. At the start of the Abraham story, in the next chapter, it is God who will make a great name for Abraham. In the Babel story itself, it is God who scattered them abroad "over the face of all the earth" (11:8). What is portrayed is an attempt to use human capabilities and inventiveness to thwart God and make a name for themselves without God. As such, it is another story of the human desire to push beyond the boundaries of reality. Such failure to accept human reality and remain within its boundaries leads to a lesser level of life.

All four stories — the Garden, Cain, the flood, and Babel — bring home the disastrous results of failing to control what "lurks at the door" (Gen 4:7). What lurks at the door in these stories is the temptation to human supremacy without attention to the place of God. Yet the flood narrative, while emphatic on the nature of human failure, is equally emphatic on the readiness of God to remain in relationship with this humankind. The stories to come will reflect on that relationship.

~MODERN FAITH~

Cities have been part of human life for a few thousand years. Skyscraping towers have more recently become a spectacular symbol of human arrogance, rivaling other human beings rather than rivaling God.

Global communications and modern travel have shrunk our world to knowable size. Concern over climate change and global warming gives a sharp focus to the human yearning for unity. A yearning for peace has emerged in ways unthinkable a century ago. War is still with us; at least it has been eliminated as the primary source of glory, the pinnacle of patriotism and human achievement.

The story of the group who came out of the East and settled in the place that came to be called Babel remains a reminder to us that human longings can be met destructively, that human fears can be countered counterproductively.

Insecurity is latent in so much of human living. How we cope with it without intensifying it is a constant challenge to human ingenuity.

SUMMARY

What is of particular value about all that has been said is that, instead of what is often perceived as a rather scattered plurality of stories and fragmentary traditions purporting to be about our human beginnings and in fact having little to do with the reality of today, we have four bases for storytelling that suggest reflection on human living and issues that are still very much part of reality today: on human limit (Garden), human violence (Cain), human existence (flood), and human ambition (Babel), prefaced by an ideal image of creation.

Whatever it may have been understood to have said about creation, Genesis One was and is a firm faith statement that the world we encounter is not the world as it needs must be. It could be otherwise. There is a pristine quality to the world as Genesis One portrays it at the origin of human life. It is the background against which reflections on the human condition unfold in story form. Biblically, it is the background against which the story of Israel unfolds.

The Garden story is a reflection on the human inability to remain within what sober judgment views as appropriate boundaries, leading therefore to the loss of innocence. As Thomas Friedman might say: we need to make sure we have an olive tree to park the Lexus under (*The Lexus and the Olive Tree*). The strong oppress the weak; they always have. Individuals seldom rest content with what has been achieved; growth is felt as a need. Empires expand; they need not, but they do. Alas, so it is; alas, so it has always been.

The Cain family stories move the issue away from the quasi-mythic situation in the Garden — where dialogue occurs with the snake and the LORD God walked in the garden at the time of the evening breeze — more toward the circumstances of ordinary life. What has been exemplified in the Garden can be seen in the course of more ordinary life. It can be seen on the personal level of individuals; it can extend beyond the merely individual to involve killing and violence spreading over generations.

Where the flood is concerned, meaningful analysis is not easy. Certainly, it has to be dealt with on the level of text rather than event. Given the differences involved (chronologies, number and kind of animals, origin of waters, etc.), it is difficult to envisage deriving the texts from some event. Viewed as mythic text, it may well be that some fear, deep in the human unconscious, is being brought to the surface by the story and then assuaged, in its own peculiar way.

If so, it is likely that the fear is with us still and the task of assuaging it is a part of healthy human growth today. The flood story is one approach; for Christians, the story of the crucifixion is another. The flood story affirms a value in human life, even viewed most pessimistically; that is one understanding of why the text has God decide not to destroy everything again. The story of the crucifixion affirms a value in human life, even if it is expressed in the most appalling image. God sees value enough to share such human life and die in the solidarity of that sharing.

The Babel story takes us back to the beginning in the Garden. There was one couple in the Garden; there was one group and one language at Babel. One element of the Garden story is the snake's affirmation, "You will be like God." One element of the Babel story is the longing to be like God, unable to be "scattered abroad upon the face of the whole earth." As we know our world, we are out of the Garden and we are scattered all over the face of the earth. We call it the human condition. There may be no need to appeal to some primeval catastrophe (traditionally, original sin). It may be the way we are. The flood story asserts that God has come to terms with it. The task of modern faith is to come to terms with it too. How do we move from the ordinary (Gen 2–11) back toward the ideal (Gen One)?

The Christian picture of humanity must take seriously the absence of a traditional understanding of "original sin" and the Fall from the stories of the Garden of Eden and the flood. Both texts accept a human propensity to push beyond appropriate boundaries (in the Garden story) and the exercise of that propensity resulting in serious evil (in the flood story). Both texts portray God's acceptance of that human propensity. In the Garden story, the announced death penalty (Gen 2:17) is not enforced; instead, God is portrayed ameliorating the symbol of the loss of innocence, replacing fig leaves with garments of skins (Gen 3:21). In the flood story, God's acceptance of humanity's state is emphatic in the "never again" of Genesis 8:21–22. The "never again" is explicit, no matter how development of the text is understood; the "no matter what" that is so important is implicit but clear. There is no condition placed on the "I will never again destroy": the absence of any condition makes the implicit "no matter what" quite clear. The "never again, no matter what" of 8:21–22 is reinforced by the unconditional and everlasting covenant in Genesis 9:1–17, despite the "fear and dread" of 9:2 and the "shedding of blood," envisaged both as crime and punishment, in 9:6.

The traditional view of original sin (for all it owes to late rabbinic, Pauline, and Augustinian thought) must be derived by theologians from their observation of the world around them (note Hellwig's comment earlier). The dominance of redemption over salvation in much Christian theology can be tempered by viewing the incarnation of Jesus, his death, and his resurrection, as the expression of God's love (John 15:13). Salvation may be appropriately understood as human awareness of God's love for humankind.

The authors of both Garden and flood stories were no strangers to the observation of their world. The human loss of innocence is central to the Garden story; the human capacity for evil is central to the flood story. Central to both stories is God's acceptance of the human state. In this context, it may be noted that while it is not uncommon even today to assume that "God is now the God who is angry with them" (see, for example, Schuster, *Fall and Sin,* 70), it is important to be aware that, in both stories, the Bible does *NOT* make this assumption. It may well be that the modern interpreter's emphasis should be on divine commitment rather than on human sin. God-awful our world may be, viewed from certain aspects; God-forsaken our world is not, viewed from any aspect.

What is quite possibly all-important for theological thought in this area is the realization of the impact of the garments God made in Genesis 3:21 and the impact of the promise God made in Genesis 8:21. In modern terms, both can be summarized as "we are loved by God as we are." The garments of skins have long been pointed to as an indication of God's graciousness and mercy; they are more than that. They are an indication of God's acceptance of the human state after the loss of innocence. According to the story, the human couple after the loss of innocence sewed fig leaves together. A benevolent God is portrayed doing better than that and, despite the loss of innocence, facilitating the continuation of human life as we know it now. After the flood, God is portrayed recognizing that human life is no better than it was before. Nevertheless, the God portrayed gives a guarantee without any condition whatsoever never again to destroy human life as the flood had done. The upshot of these two passages is to have Israel's faith affirm that God was committed to us as we are. Garments are given to the man and the woman, no conditions attached. A guarantee is given after the flood, no conditions attached. In modern terms, this spells out unconditional love, commitment with no conditions attached.

Minor observations on the compilation of the present text may be helpful. As we have seen, the Cain material does not fit the context of the Garden story: there are other people around. As Cain says: "anyone who meets me may kill me" (Gen 4:14); in the context of the Garden story, of course, there is no such "Anyone." The Cain material presumably reflected independent traditions. The composition would profit from including them. Nothing easier; a couple of bridge verses, Genesis 4:1–2, bring Cain and Abel onto the scene.

Another tradition was also presumably independent. It traced the human genealogy back to Adam, not through Cain and Abel but through Enosh and Seth instead (see Gen 5:3–11). In order to bring this tradition into the composition (and the flood story with it), two more bridging verses were needed. Genesis 4:25–26 filled the bill admirably.

As we have noticed, the Babel tradition is of a single group with a single language, in marked contrast to the picture preceding in Genesis 10. A simple juxtaposition was enough; any sort of bridge would be difficult to imagine.

Chapter 2

Israel's Traditions
about Its Ancestors

It can come as a shock to many a reader or user to realize how different the traditions of Abraham, Isaac, and Jacob are from what they might have expected for fragments of traditions from a three-generation family of immigrants, finding life in a new land and eventually becoming ancestors of a new nation. What we see may not be what we would have expected to get.

To allow this realization to dawn on us, we need to take a considerable step back from the text that is all-too-familiar for some of us. Three considerations come to mind. However, it is important to stress from the outset that these are not arguments brought in support of some particular proposition. They are attempts to identify the causes of a certain uneasiness — no more. What we find in the Genesis text is not what we might feel entitled to expect. That raises unanswered questions: What functions did the recording of these traditions have? What roles did these recorded traditions play?

First, the realization that there is no basic plot of land or basic region where the family settled or operated from, before branching out. Abraham settled at Mamre near Hebron (Gen 13:18) and resided also as a sojourner at Gerar and then at Beer-sheba (Gen 21:34). Apparently, Isaac was born at Beer-sheba (cf. Gen 21:14). The biblical text has nothing to say about his time there or of anything shared with his father.

When, in due course, Isaac and Rebekah show up at Gerar, it seems much more like a new beginning than a continuation of the family story. There is no reference to Abraham and Sarah having earlier caused grave problems for King Abimelech of Gerar (Gen 20), referred to here as King Abimelech of the Philistines (Gen 26:1). In a famine, Isaac went to Gerar; the text does not say where from (Gen 26:1). It can scarcely have been from Beer-sheba for that is the region toward which Isaac will move and where Isaac will settle (Gen 26:33). The references to the wells dug by Abraham hardly fill in the familial gaps; they scarcely seem a mere generation apart. In this Genesis narrative, the last mention has Jacob heading southward to a region "beyond the tower of Eder" (Gen 35:21), a region unknown to us. There the text has him available for junction with the Joseph story.

Jacob is presented as Isaac's son and is at Beer-sheba. There is a reference to Esau as a hunter and Jacob as a quiet man. Nothing is said of the life of father and sons on the land. In strife with his brother, Jacob leaves Beer-sheba never to return there. Outside the country, with Laban, he founds a family and acquires wealth. On his return, he settles at Succoth and Shechem, far to the north of Hebron or Beer-sheba.

Much may be made of nomadic status. These ancestors were not settling on land as immigrants in more recent times might have done; nomads moved with their flocks. For all that, difficulties remain. Among others, the narratives have no traditions of the nomadic journeyings or the experiences associated with them.

Second, there is the literary quality of the traditions. The differences among the three are remarkable. The Abraham and Sarah traditions are generally in shorter units, relating to disconnected places and covering a variety of topics. The places involved are, after Canaan itself, somewhere between Bethel and Ai, the Negeb, Egypt, the Negeb again, back between Bethel and Ai, Mamre near Hebron, Transjordan (unspecified), unspecified for Genesis 15–17 (the Hagar story ends in the south but its start is unspecified), Mamre again, south to between Kadesh and Shur, then Gerar, and Beer-sheba, and finally Mamre. These can hardly be said to follow the trajectory of a planned itinerary.

The trips involved would keep a good travel agent busy.

1. To Canaan, with Sarah, terminating between Bethel and Ai

2. To the Negeb (Gen 12:9 = arid south)

3. To Egypt

4. To the Negeb (Gen 13:1, "up from Egypt...into the Negeb")

5. Return to location between Bethel and Ai

6. To Mamre, near Hebron

7. To Transjordan, location unspecified

8. Return to Mamre (assumed)

9. To the Negeb (pronounced Negev), between Kadesh and Shur

10. To Gerar

11. To Beer-sheba

12. To Mamre for Sarah's burial and, in due course, Abraham's death and burial

For Isaac and Rebekah, the places and journeys are far more restricted. We may begin with Beer-lahai-roi and the south (recognizing the difficulties in the Hebrew of Gen 24:62 and 67). Famine drives them to Gerar; the final stage is to Beer-sheba. As narrative, it hardly exceeds one chapter. The location of its beginning has to remain unclear; there is no account of Isaac's death and burial. The birth of both Esau and Jacob has been narrated earlier in the text (Gen 25:19–28); no location is given, no story attached.

For Jacob, his flight from Beer-sheba takes him through Bethel to the house of Laban, among "the people of the east" (Gen 29:1), where he acquires wives, family, and wealth. He does not return to Beer-sheba or to Bethel. His territory, where he settles, is in the region of Succoth and Shechem. His story is a multi-chapter narrative. His journey is associated with important topics — Bethel, wives, children, wealth, return, reconciliation — but it is fundamentally a single coherent journey. The surprise: the journey does not return to its starting place.

The two chapters associating Jacob with Bethel (Gen 28 and 35) will not be dealt with here, despite their interest. In chapter 28, Jacob is made a promise concerning "the land on which you lie" (v. 13), and he makes a vow on condition that "I come again to my father's house in peace" (v. 21). In the narrative, he does not take possession of the land associated with Bethel; as to his father's house, he does not return there. In chapter 35, surprisingly, Jacob is instructed by God to "go up to Bethel, and settle there" (v. 1). He goes to Bethel but does not settle there. The Bethel traditions are obviously important, presumably in association with the northern kingdom; they do not play a major role within the narrative of the Jacob cycle.

To summarize succinctly: the extensive texts for Abraham are fragmented and widely scattered; the text for Isaac is brief and focused; the text for Jacob is extensive, but focused on a single journey.

Third, there is a need to take into account the very different Isaac in the book of Amos and the not-so-different Jacob in the book of Hosea.

Isaac's name occurs twice in the book of Amos, in both cases paralleled by reference to Israel. The first is in a speech attributed to the LORD:

> "The high places of Isaac shall be made desolate,
>   and the sanctuaries of Israel shall be laid waste."
>   (Amos 7:9)

The second is given to Amos in his controversy with Amaziah, priest of Bethel.

> "You say, 'Do not prophesy against Israel,
>   and do not preach against the house of Isaac.' "
>   (Amos 7:16)

This is eighth-century Amos, in the king's sanctuary and a temple of the kingdom, at Bethel. The encounter is on the southern edge of the northern kingdom, but still in the north and far from Beer-sheba in the south.

Whatever the explanation for Isaac here (Wolff: pilgrims from Beer-sheba [which is positively unhelpful]; the Amos school [*Joel and Amos*, 301–2]; Sweeney: "rather enigmatic" [*Twelve Prophets*, 1.255]), the word is clearly being used, in parallel with Israel, as designation of the northern kingdom. That the ancestor whom Genesis locates in Beer-sheba should be used as an eponymous ancestor of the northern kingdom is surprising, to say the least. For the moment we need simply to hold the surprise.

The figure of Jacob crops up twice in the book of Hosea, where the individual is clearly being identified with the eponymous ancestor of the northern kingdom. The two passages are worth quoting, without entering into discussion of the particular difficulties of the texts.

> The LORD has an indictment against Judah,
>   and will punish Jacob according to his ways,
>   and repay him according to his deeds.
> In the womb he tried to supplant his brother,
>   and in his manhood he strove with God.
> He strove with the angel and prevailed,
>   he wept and sought his favor;
> he met him at Bethel,
>   and there he spoke with him.
>   (Hos 12:3–5 [Heb.]; NRSV, 12:2–4)

The second passage, at the end of the same chapter, is:

> Jacob fled to the land of Aram,
>   there Israel served for a wife,
>   and for a wife he guarded sheep.
>   (Hos 12:13 [Heb.]; NRSV, 12:12)

The correlation with the Jacob cycle in Genesis is clear (see de Pury, "Le cycle de Jacob"). What is less clear but nevertheless likely is that, if there is dependence, it flows from the Hosea traditions to the Genesis cycle. The issue is mainly one of sequence. The Hosea tradition moves from womb to manhood, from the conflict at the Jabbok to the meeting at Bethel and then, at the end of the chapter, to Jacob's flight to Aram and his experience there. The Genesis cycle places these in a more coherent sequence: womb, flight, service for a wife, striving with God, and finally Bethel (Gen 35, with name change and major promise).

The conclusion which has to be hazarded, while in no way being conclusively demonstrated, is that the traditions in Amos (for Isaac) and Hosea (for Jacob) may be independent of the respective texts in Genesis and may, perhaps, be the sources on which the Genesis material depends, at least in part. Such a sequence, from the northern prophets to the Genesis narrative, would make eminently good sense in the situation where the creation of an originating ancestral cluster was desired.

The hypothesis has to be entertained — though as no more than a hypothesis — that later Israel, wanting to create the legendary status of an originating ancestral cluster, drew together whatever traditions were available around Abraham, painted a sketch for Isaac, and reframed older traditions into a narrative for Jacob. This would account for the fragmented and scattered state of the Abraham traditions; they were derived from what was available. Isaac was known as a major figure from the past, but needed to be brought south to be associated with Abraham. A coherent Jacob narrative could be easily enough put together from the older traditions, enabling a flight to Aram (flight from the south is not mentioned by Hosea; the episode at Bethel in Gen 28 is unlikely to be that mentioned by Hosea) and finally a return to Israel — but to Succoth east of the Jordan and Shechem west of it.

If it is accepted that Genesis 24 is post-exilic (see Rofé, "Betrothal of Rebekah"), that Genesis 27 is late (see Campbell and O'Brien, *Rethinking the Pentateuch*), and also that the Joseph story is diaspora literature and therefore no earlier than exilic (again, Campbell and O'Brien, *Rethinking the Pentateuch*), then the need to create such an originating ancestral cluster is not surprising.

The outcome of these reflections can be expressed in one word: caution. The Abraham traditions in Genesis 12–25 are clearly multiple, fragmented, and scattered. The traditions of Isaac in the south (mainly Gen 26) are undoubtedly meager. The Jacob traditions in Genesis are extensive and, in the main, form a single coherent sequence. Automatically, the instincts of most readers are to see these Genesis traditions as the base from which the prophetic texts derive. In the current revisioning of Genesis as a whole, it may make sense to reverse the direction of dependence. Until much more is clear, the watchword must be: proceed with caution.

If what has been suggested above as a possibility is given stronger credence in the light of the current revisioning of Genesis and much of the Pentateuch, the ancestral stories as they are now in Genesis, and have been understood traditionally, function precisely as their authors or compilers wanted them to. They function as the narrative of an originating ancestral cluster, the legendary group that gives an origin and an identity to the people of Israel as a single whole. The figures may have been known, the names had their place in early prophetic texts (Amos and Hosea). When the stories of humanity were being assembled (life as it is now and always was from the beginning) and placed at the beginning of Israel's story, it would have been entirely natural and necessary to pull together an account of Israel's ancestors to follow on these stories at the beginning. Traditions of Isaac and Jacob were known from the north. The south had been termed Judah; it was necessary from the various traditions available to provide a portrait of Abraham. Hence the unity of the people (above all, after 722) could find expression in the unity of the ancestral family. The unity may have been real rather than familial. The unevenness of the traditions argues against any suggestion of fiction; distortion yes (reshaped as a single family, for example), fiction no.

It as been claimed that, in later periods, where Israel's authors had traditions available they used them, but where they lacked traditions they filled the gaps with fiction. Such a claim is easily made, but it needs to be sustained. Close study of what is claimed as fiction needs to demonstrate that fiction is indeed the likely literary category. In the fragmented and scattered state of the Abraham traditions, it is clearly not. Any ancient Israelite author elaborating fictional traditions would have done a more coherent job. Quite possibly, at some point in the past, somebody else made up traditions felt to be necessary. It is highly unlikely that they were the fictional creation of the compiler of the present text.

STATISTICAL DISTRACTION (computer-assisted using Accordance 5.7)

Occurrences in the Hebrew Bible:

  236 occurrences for Abraham (including Abram)

  112 occurrences for Isaac

  349 occurrences for Jacob

2507 occurrences for Israel

   24 occurrences for all three ancestors together (the triad, Abraham, Isaac, Jacob = 19; Abraham, Isaac, Israel = 5). (It is

worth noting that tradition gave preference to the name Israel
[one who strove with God and prevailed] over the name
Jacob [biblically: heel-grabber, supplanter]; not surprising,
but interesting.)

Extent of influence on Israel's traditions, outside the Pentateuch:

For Abraham, there is hardly a single occurrence that could be
considered early (i.e., before the seventh century).

For Isaac, there are the two references in Amos (7:9 and 7:16);
apart from these, there is not a single occurrence that could be
considered early.

For Jacob, two occurrences in Hosea have been noted; there is one
other, 10:11. As expected, it is clearly a reference to the northern kingdom (in the course of the verse Wolff retains the reading
"Judah," giving the sequence Ephraim–Judah–Jacob [*Hosea*, 185];
Mays regards Judah as redactional [*Hosea*, 144–45]). In Amos,
two references to Isaac have been noted; there are six to Jacob.
All refer to the northern kingdom; two have "house of Jacob." In
Isaiah 1–39, the references to Jacob are mostly late. Isaiah 8:7 is
an exception. Isaiah 9:8 (Heb.; NRSV 9:7) and 17:4 refer to the
northern kingdom; neither are considered original by Otto Kaiser
(*Isaiah 1–12*, 221, and *13–39*, 79).

For Israel, Amos has twenty-six occurrences, Hosea forty-one; in
Micah 1–3 there are eight, and forty-three in Isaiah 1–39. These
occurrences will not be analyzed here.

For the triad (all three ancestors), the distribution, if minimal, is
striking. Of the nineteen occurrences using Jacob, seven are clus-
tered at the call of Moses and seven in the book of Deuteronomy.
None of the other ten occurrences would be considered early (Gen
50:24; Exod 32:13; 33:1; Num 32:11; 1 Kgs 18:36; 2 Kgs 13:23;
Jer 33:26; 1 Chr 1:34; 29:18; 2 Chr 30:6).

Dating for Deuteronomy can be assumed as late seventh century
(second half). Traditional source analysis attributed the occurrences
associated with the call of Moses to J, E, and P. With the dissolution
of traditional source analysis, these attributions can no longer be

sustained. In the first five cases (Exod 2:24; 3:6, 15, 16; 4:5), the names are in apposition to the phrase "God of ... father/ancestors"; later expansion is possible.

More probable is a reassessing of the date for the two attributed to E (Exod 3:6, 15) and the two attributed to J (Exod 3:16; 4:5). Early dates are unlikely. Among others, two factors militate against an early date.

1. Almost daily contact between Pharaoh and Moses is unlikely; Egypt's Pharaohs were remote and godlike. Heads of state do not have such contact with each other. Possible mitigating factors (such as the claimed numbers of the people [Exod 1:9, 12] or the extent of the plagues) do not eliminate the difficulty. Characteristics of diaspora literature are present.

2. The association of the three ancestors at an early stage in the texts and no further reference until Deuteronomy would have to be regarded as unlikely.

With these considerations in mind, it is time to turn to the texts and the individual cycles.

ABRAHAM AND SARAH

Fantastic words are given God in God's opening call to Abraham (Gen 12:1–3; Abram at this stage in the text, until changed in Gen 17:5). Three issues for pondering. First, the experience of God: leave all that is familiar and venture into the unknown. It is God's invitation. Is it Israel's experience of God? Is it ours? Second, God's promise to Abraham: a great nation, a great name, a blessing. Third, God's commitment to us all: all the families of the earth shall be blessed. It is truly fantastic.

It is a faith statement of the highest order: land unspecified, ancestor and nation both to be great, blessing to be shared universally.

Two oddities catch the eye of the observant reader. First, the land is not named; it is "the land that I will show you." Second, while a great nation is to come from Abraham, no promise settles them on this land he is to be shown — unless surprisingly late in the piece.

The journey to this new land is a highly ritualized one. Three stops only, all within the new land. Once again, two oddities catch the eye of the observant reader: (1) the land is not promised to Abraham himself until 13:15–17; (2) at Shechem, the first stop, the land is promised not to Abraham but to his descendants, "to your offspring." The message: this is not so much Abraham's journey as the journey of Israel's ancestor. He stops at only three places: Shechem, Bethel, and Hebron (oaks of Mamre), and he builds altars at all three. However, Abraham has nothing to do with Shechem; it will be Jacob territory. Equally, Abraham has nothing to do with Bethel; it will be a royal sanctuary of the breakaway northern kingdom of Israel. He settles at Hebron, pitches his tent there, builds an altar there too (tenting, altar-building, and calling on the LORD are relatively rare activities in Genesis [see 12:8; 13:18; 26:25; 33:19–20]); the events of Abraham's life, at first sight, will revolve around that southern part of the country associated with Hebron.

The first promise of settlement in this new land is made by God at Shechem, of all places. Quite rightly, the promise is not made to Abraham himself; God's promise is: "to your offspring I will give this land" (Gen 12:7). The offspring, of course, will be Jacob and the northern tribes. It is just as well that this is text and not event; were it event, poor Abraham would have been awfully disappointed.

The biblical text in Genesis 12:1–8 gives minimal detail about the journey to Canaan. It is basically: he was told to go and he went. Any storyteller could manage that; there is little point in trying to identify versions for the sequences. Two points are of interest. First, the blessing promised Abraham — to be great and blessed; to be a source of blessing to all the earth — is the only promise common to all three ancestors (for Isaac, Gen 26:4; for Jacob, Gen 28:14). Second, God's word to Abraham at Shechem is reported as "to your offspring [seed] I will give this land" (Gen 12:7). The offspring, as noted, is Jacob. Nothing so far has been given to Abraham. If he is going to settle deep in the south, "between Kadesh and Shur," this may not be so surprising.

With Abraham and the group with him having arrived in the land, the narrative runs into a number of difficulties. At this point, it may help to look at them globally before going into the details. From the outset, we should be aware that we are dealing with a context that is presumed to be nomadic. Nomadism may help a little with the difficulties, but only a little; difficulties remain.

Globally, the problems that the Abraham cycle holds for us can be reduced to two categories: duplication in the case of three important items and difficulties in two other cases.

The duplications:

1. Abraham and Sarah are located at Mamre/Hebron and also at Gerar/Beersheba.

2. Correlative with these, Abraham stakes a claim to permanence in the land in two different places (therefore, twice). He publicly purchases a burial cave at Machpelah, near Mamre/Hebron. He digs a well in the Gerar/Beersheba region and establishes his right to it by covenant with Abimelech, king of Gerar.

3. Twice, once in Egypt and later in Gerar, Abraham asks Sarah to say she is his sister — keeping silent about the fact that she is his wife.

The difficulties:

1. After arrival between Bethel and Ai, and from there to the Negeb, famine strikes and Abraham heads off to Egypt, leaving Lot high and dry. Genesis 13:1 partially resolves this by making Lot a member of the party. Alas, he has no role in the story in Egypt. This sudden detour is in the present text. To the best of my knowledge, modern scholarship has no solution to it.

2. With the land unable to support Abraham and Lot living together, so extensive were their flocks and herds and tents, Abraham makes Lot a most generous offer: take your pick of the land and go one way; I will go the other (Gen 13:9). So Lot chose the well-watered Jordan valley. Lot went there; Abraham stayed in Canaan. The difficulty: God is presented using this moment to

make Abraham the offer of giving him and his offspring "all the land that you see" (Gen 13:15). What Abraham had just given to Lot God now gives to Abraham. Relegating 13:14–17 to secondary status does not adequately overcome the problem.

These issues, and smaller ones, make close examination of the text essential. Some repetition in what follows will be inevitable. It is my hope that it will not be harmful.

In relation to these issues, we need to recognize that there are three "sequences" to be found in the present biblical text of the Abraham cycle; it will be helpful to outline them. I refer to these as sequences. They are not narrative texts, telling a particular tradition as it was held in a particular community. They are, in my judgment, better referred to as sequences reminding ancient storytellers of the way in which particular traditions might be linked together. They provided a base for the narratives that embodied the traditions held in particular communities. There are three such sequences, presenting respectively an Abraham associated with the Southwest (for me, it has been a surprise to discover how extensive this sequence proved to be), an Abraham associated with the East, and an Abraham associated with his nephew, Lot.

There are three points that need to be borne in mind when considering these sequences:

1. Intensive experience of narrative text may lead to the conclusion (assumed here) that the canonical text is not end-text to be expounded but rather precanonical material forming a base-text to be expanded. To account for "the brevity and layered quality of much narrative biblical text," it may be an appropriate assumption that "ancient narrative texts were often written initially [as bases] to be used by ancient storytellers and others" rather than being written with a view to later being read as Bible, as finished text. This "user-base" approach assumes the ability of ancient users to select from and expand a condensed base-text (Campbell and O'Brien, *Rethinking the Pentateuch*, 17). Such a base-text needed to remind storytellers or other users of the essentials; it did not need to spell out all the details and provide a complete and smooth sequence.

Dalley's observations are particularly significant here, because they come from the world of Mesopotamian literature, not the biblical literature world. She notes:

> Through the study of several versions of one story, it has become clear that one version may omit an episode crucial to the sequence, or it may be so elliptical or telescoped as to be unintelligible without the help of another, more explicit version.... We should probably understand some of the abrupt changes of theme as bare skeletons which were fleshed out in practice by skilled narrators, rather as early musical notation gave only the guidelines needed to remind the musician of appropriate melody and rhythms, leaving embellishments and flourishes to his own skills and to popular taste. (*Myths from Mesopotamia*, xvi)

2. There are unquestioned difficulties in the sequences proposed. They are about evenly balanced by the unquestioned difficulties already there in the present text.

3. There are unquestioned examples of editorial operations here and there. In this overall presentation, these are not taken into account so as not to complicate discussion.

First sequence, focused on the Southwest

Genesis 12:9 can be seen as a bridging verse taking Abraham to the southwest. In the present text, it serves to make possible the introduction of 12:10–20 (so Westermann, "transition verse"). However, the comment has been made by Martin Noth that the Negeb "is the territory where Abraham really lived out his life" and there is also the observation by Rolf Rendtorff that perhaps "the Negev was the original home of the Abraham tradition" (quoted from Westermann [*Genesis 12–36*, 157]). Mamre/Hebron, of course, is not Negeb. In the hypothesis of the Negeb being the original home of the Abraham tradition, it is not surprising that Genesis 12:9 should carry more weight than that of a mere bridging verse. It melds comfortably into

Genesis 20:1aβ ("and settled between Kadesh and Shur"), so that 12:9 and 20:1aβ combine to give the sequence: "And Abram journeyed on by stages toward the Negeb and settled between Kadesh and Shur." That means that, after the dislocation of the original sequence, 20:1aα is in fact the bridging passage: "From there [wherever that was] Abraham journeyed toward the region of the Negeb."

The vision of Genesis 15 can been placed here, following Abraham's settling between Kadesh and Shur. Frankly, given that chapter 15 contains no location, it could go anywhere. Placed here, it can serve to motivate Sarah's efforts to provide Abraham with a son, his "very own issue" (Gen 15:4), offering him the services of Hagar. It is worth noting that, when the text portrays Sarah saying to Abraham that it was *yhwh* who was preventing her from childbearing (16:2), then Abraham's going to Hagar is in fact portrayed as an attempt to evade God, taking matters into his own hands, and as a lack of trust in God to do what God had promised.

The beginning of the Hagar story is bereft of any indication of its location; the end, however, has to be deep in the southern region. Genesis 16, therefore, can belong satisfactorily with this Southwest sequence. The first meeting with Hagar is at a spring on the way to Shur (16:7). At the end of the story, "the well was called Beer-lahai-roi; it lies between Kadesh and Bered" (16:14).

It is important to be aware that, in all likelihood, there are two stories of Hagar and Ishmael in the cycle. In Genesis 16, Hagar is proactive and a survivor (she opted to leave an intolerable situation; she was by a spring on her way home, v. 7) until ordered by an angel to return (vv. 8–9). In Genesis 21, Hagar is passive and a victim (she was sent away; she believed her son was at the point of death [21:16]). In both cases, Ishmael is removed from the picture.

The famous Genesis 17 is equally bereft of any indication as to its intended location. Like Genesis 15, it could be placed in either of the first two sequences (or in the later combined text, for that matter). What favors its belonging with this Southwest sequence is the emphasis given to Ishmael (see esp. 17:20). It is possible that God's self-identification as El Shaddai in v. 1 was added at some stage during the combination of the Abraham materials.

The move to Gerar and Beer-sheba is clearly bedeviled by the dual location of Abraham: in the East, at Mamre, and deep in the Southwest as well, ranging between both Kadesh and Shur and Gerar and Beer-sheba. The NRSV's "While he was residing in Gerar as an alien, Abraham said of his wife..." (Gen 20:1b–2) makes the best of what is now in the present text. No ancient storyteller would have had much trouble with it. As noted, relocating part of the present text, the combination of 12:9 with 20:1aβ is fully appropriate: "And Abram journeyed on by stages toward the Negeb.... and he settled between Kadesh and Shur."

While it is necessary to have Isaac's birth following God's promise in Genesis 17, the story of Hagar's dismissal locates her wandering "in the wilderness of Beer-sheba" (Gen 21:14), so the move to Gerar/Beersheba may well have preceded both Genesis 16, Genesis 17, and the report of Isaac's birth. The report of Isaac's birth is here credited with only two verses (Gen 21:1, 7), which may seem most miserly. It reflects the facts of the text; the text gives no details on the youth of Isaac. Genesis 21:1 is compatible with Genesis 17, although in the combined text it echoes 18:14; its dual mention of Sarah provides the subject for what has become the following verse (in the present text, of course, it is v. 7). Put briefly, the sequence would then be: move to Gerar/Beersheba, Genesis 16 (including the return to Sarah), Genesis 17, Isaac's birth, Hagar's dismissal. Associated with the move to Gerar and Beer-sheba is Abraham's covenant, made with Abimelech king of Gerar, solemnly recognizing Abraham's digging of the well (Gen 21:25–34).

The story of Genesis 22 belongs here; it ends with Abraham living at Beer-sheba. Furthermore, the long (and probably late) story of the embassy to seek a bride for Isaac also ends in the Southwest, associating Isaac with Beer-lahai-roi and the Negeb (Gen 24:62).

Summarized, this Abraham–Southwest sequence is as follows:

Journey to Canaan (equivalent of Gen 12:1–8)

Journey south (Gen 12:9)

Settlement between Kadesh and Shur (Gen 20:1aβ [= "and settled between Kadesh and Shur"])

Sojourn at Gerar: "settle where it pleases you" (Gen 20:1b–18)

Possible. Vision of God: promise of descendants and land (Gen 15:1–21)

Hagar story: birth of Ishmael (Gen 16:1–21)

Possible. Vision of God: establishment of covenant; promise of Isaac (Gen 17:1–26)

Birth of Isaac; dismissal of Ishmael (Gen 21:1, 7–21)

Covenant at Beer-sheba (Gen 21:22–34)

Sacrifice/Binding of Isaac (Gen 22:1–19)

Marriage of Isaac and Rebekah (Gen 24:1–67)

Second sequence, focused on the East

A second sequence associates Abraham with Mamre, near Hebron, in the East rather than the Southwest. Naturally, it would have begun with the equivalent of Genesis 12:1–8, with or without the promises. Then it would be eminently appropriate to have 12:8 followed directly by 13:14–18. Abraham has journeyed to Canaan; it is appropriate for him to be assured of land. The symbolism of the location between Bethel and Ai is right. It is at the southern end of the central mountainous chain known as Mt. Ephraim. Whatever of reality, it is a spot where the possibility of a four-way vision is imaginable. A view to the far south would not be so imaginable. The text has God say: "Raise your eyes now, and look...northward and southward and eastward and westward, for all the land that you see I will give to you and to your offspring forever" (Gen 13:14–15). And Abraham settled at Mamre. This positioning requires a substantial relocation of text; in its favor, it avoids the major embarrassment of God's promising to Abraham what Abraham has just given to another.

The promise of a son to Sarah is made at Mamre (Gen 18:1, 3, 10–15). Its introduction is intertwined with the visit of the three, for reasons that escape us; the passage associated with this visit is also to be located at Mamre, close to the Dead Sea. The text of 18:1, 3 (reflecting the presence of the singular, The LORD, My lord): "The LORD appeared to him [Abraham] by the oaks of Mamre, as he sat at the entrance of his tent in the heat of the day.... He said, 'My lord, if I find favor with you, do not pass by your servant....' " The observant will notice in 18:1, the Hebrew has "oaks" (plural and species); in 18:3 the three are invited to rest under "the tree" (singular and genus). The promise of a son to Sarah is to be followed by its fulfillment with the birth of Isaac (Gen 21:2–6). Genesis 21:1–7 is recognized as a complex text. Verse 2, with its reference to "the time of which God had spoken to him," follows appropriately on the divine vision of Genesis 18:1, 3, 10–15. The absence of details on Isaac's youth has already been noted.

Sarah's death and burial and Abraham's remarriage, death, and burial are appropriately associated with this sequence. The public purchase of the burial cave at Machpelah is symbolic of Abraham's claim to permanence in the land.

Summarized, this Abraham–East sequence is as follows:

Journey to Canaan (equivalent of Gen 12:1–8)

Gift of land and settlement at Mamre (Gen 13:14–18)

Promise of Sarah's son (Gen 18:1, 3, 10–15)

Birth of Isaac (Gen 21:2–6)

Sarah's death and burial (Gen 23:1–20)

Abraham's remarriage, death, and burial (Gen 25:1–11)

Third sequence, focused on Abraham and Lot

Third, there is the text associated with Lot. The idea of an Abraham-Lot saga was stressed by Gunkel, perhaps to the detriment of other traditions (see *Genesis*, 158–61); Westermann is nuanced, but unduly complex and in the end unsatisfactory (*Genesis 12–36*, 127–28). With the deterioration of the pentateuchal source hypothesis, the texts need to be reexamined.

An Abraham–Lot sequence would have begun with the equivalent of Genesis 12:1–8. In the present text, the Lot traditions probably begin as a coherent sequence around Genesis 13:2; the surrounding verses enable the integration of the Egypt episode into the composition. The storyteller has to be allowed some freedom to develop and expand information that is clearly in the text. The mention of Lot in 12:4–5 facilitates what is to come; so too the reference to "their possessions" (12:5). Abraham is treated well in 12:16; the Hebrew is neutral as to whether the specific wealth referred to enumerates gifts ("he received") or reflects earlier possessions ("he had"). Either way, the mention prepares for the separation to come.

As will be emphasized shortly, the narrative's detour taking Abraham and Sarah to Egypt and back is an unquestioned embarrassment (Gunkel: "a disruptive excursus," *Genesis*, 168). It is also an unexplained one. It can be the equivalent of a loose cannon, brought into the narrative independently, when the need for it was felt (see the fuller discussion later). The presence of Lot, along with the reference to possessions, in 12:4–5 and Lot's mention at 13:1, may be pointers to a possible association of Lot with the storytelling of this Egypt episode. The episode stands on its own in Genesis 12; it is not essential to any of the sequences. Not much more can be said. Westermann comments that "the structure of the narrative is particularly neat and clear" (*Genesis 12–36*, 161). What is not made "neat and clear" is what this episode is doing here, with its associated detour, and what its meaning may be. Faced with the narrative detour, the best that Brueggemann can manage is the note that "the text is an independent unit and appears to be an interruption in the narrative which moves easily from 12:9 to 13:2" (*Genesis*, 126). Nothing more is said on this aspect. Brueggemann is right that the text is an independent unit. Two questions, however, remain unanswered: Why is it here? What does it mean? Frankly, until we understand the episode and its parallels better (Gunkel and Van Seters have not said the last word), not much more can be said about its inconvenient presence here.

Once back at the location between Bethel and Ai, following the detour to Egypt, Abraham makes his generous offer to Lot, and there is a peaceful parting of the ways. A similar parting (within the land!) is claimed for Esau and Jacob (Gen 36:6–8). Genesis 13:12 provides a suitable conclusion: "Abram settled in the land of Canaan, while Lot settled among the cities of the plain." Verse 13 then prepares for what is to come. Rather than being spread across J and P (sources), which of course can be done, the passage reads easily as an independent unit which a compiler has integrated with the earlier conclusion

of Abraham's journey, following on Genesis 12:8. This "earlier conclusion" allows for a coherent account of Abraham's journey into
Canaan in Genesis 12. It is, in my judgment, preferable to see 13:14–
18 as an earlier conclusion that has been relocated rather than seeing
it as secondary, viewing it as "a later insertion into an older narrative"
(Westermann, *Genesis 12–36*, 172).

The separation from Lot is appropriately associated with the location between Bethel and Ai; it is an ideal vantage point for Abraham's
offer and Lot's choice. As we have seen, the massive detour to Egypt
is an embarrassment. Abraham's compliance with God's instructions
to go to Canaan is met with a famine — a surprising embarrassment,
unless it somehow expresses a conviction from Israel's experience.
The long narrative delay while Abraham and Sarah go down to Egypt
and return is an embarrassment. Lot's association with their journey
is a puzzle (see Gen 13:1). However, the sojourn in Egypt is there in
the present text; it clearly meets some need that, to the best of my
knowledge, currently escapes us.

There is another embarrassment introduced with the separation
from Lot, as we have seen. Abraham makes his nephew a most generous offer: "Is not the whole land before you? ... If you take the left
hand, then I will go to the right; or if you take the right hand, then I
will go to the left" (Gen 13:9). When this is over and the two have
gone their respective ways, God promptly offers the whole land to
Abraham — north, south, east, and west. One can always say that, in
the narrative, Lot was not going to be around for long. Some may say
that God can do what God wants to do. For many, the embarrassment
remains.

What follows is the account of Abraham's rescue of Lot in the
strangely enigmatic Genesis 14, followed in turn by the Sodom and
Gomorrah narrative, in its multiple episodes (Gen 18:2, 4–9, 16–
33; 19:1–38). After that, Lot disappears from the Genesis narrative.
Genesis 14 is not unfairly described as "strangely enigmatic." For
Brueggemann, "the most enigmatic chapter in Genesis" (*Genesis*,
134); for Westermann, in its final composition, a product of "the late
postexilic period" with its purpose "the glorification of Abraham as
a great and powerful prince" (*Genesis 12–36*, 192–93). Central to
Abraham's glorification is his rescue of Lot. We will not linger on

the text here, analyzing its components and so on. It is suitable for a place in the sequence of Lot traditions; it is equally suitable for a place in the final combined text.

Lot is not involved in the text again until the Sodom episode (Gen 18:1–19:38 [prepared for in Gen 13:13]). For reasons unknown to us, in 18:1–9 the introductions have been combined, both to the announcement of Sarah's child (18:10–15) and to the episode of Sodom (18:16–19:29). The God of Israel is required for the announcement concerning Sarah; the God of Israel and two others (men or messengers/angels) are required for some of the scenarios associated with Sodom (see *Rethinking the Pentateuch*, 119–21, 135–36). The use of singular or plural in the introduction is not decisive but points to 18:1 (*yhwh* alone) and 18:3 going with the Sarah story and 18:2 (three men) and 18:4–8 going with the Sodom material. Abraham is not named until 18:6, so that considerable leeway is left to the storyteller. Verse 9 is editorial, blending the two accounts; otherwise, "Where is your wife Sarah?" would be a foolish question after "Abraham hastened into the tent to Sarah" (v. 6).

Although it is the men who ensure Lot's flight and *yhwh* who can do nothing until Lot is out of the way, the text credits Abraham with Lot's survival. "God remembered Abraham, and sent Lot out of the midst of the overthrow" (19:29). Traditionally, the verse has been attributed to P; for Noth, as P it was originally associated with 13:6, 11b, and 12abα. From our point of view, the use of the common noun "God" may be no more than a pointer to the overall summarizing role of the verse. The episode ends with Lot's daughters organizing to become pregnant by their father and so engender the Moabites and Ammonites.

The interest in bringing this Lot material into the Abraham cycle — at considerable cost in terms of coherence and clarity — is that it establishes Lot's indebtedness to Abraham, removes him from the scene, and creates both kinship and distance in relation to the Moabites and Ammonites.

Summarized, this Abraham–Lot sequence is as follows:

Journey to Canaan (equivalent of Gen 12:1–8)

Possible. (Journey to Egypt and return [Gen 12:10–20])

Separation of Abraham and Lot (Gen 13:1–13)

Abraham's rescue of Lot (Gen 14:1–24)

Sodom and Gomorrah story (Gen 18:2, 4–9, 16–33; 19:1–38)

Genesis 18:2, 4 = "He [Abraham] looked up and saw three men standing near him. When he saw them, he ran from the tent entrance to meet them, and bowed down to the ground.... 'Let a little water be brought, and wash your feet, and rest yourselves under the tree....'"

Before we examine some of the text in closer detail, the following synoptic view displays the content of all three sequences.

Abraham–Southwest	Abraham–East	Abraham–Lot
Journey to Canaan	Journey to Canaan	Journey to Canaan
		(Journey to Egypt/return)
		Separation of Abraham/Lot
Journey south		
Settlement between Kadesh/Shur	Gift of land/settlement at Mamre	
Sojourn at Gerar		
		Abraham's rescue of Lot
		Sodom and Gomorrah story
Vision of God: descendants/land		
Hagar story: birth of Ishmael		
Vision of God: covenant; Isaac	Promise of Sarah's son	
Birth of Isaac; dismissal of Ishmael	Birth of Isaac	
Covenant at Beer-sheba		
Sacrifice/Binding of Isaac		
Marriage of Isaac and Rebekah		
	Sarah's death and burial	
	Abraham's remarriage, death, and burial	

Two aspects of the text involved are worth examining more fully. The first concerns the three episodes in which the ancestor (Abraham or Isaac) does not disclose the truth about his wife but in which God can be trusted to protect. The second concerns complications in the Abraham text: the erratic itinerary in chapters 12–13 and the complexity in 18:1–9.

Nondisclosure

As is well-known, there are two episodes of Abraham's omitting to avow Sarah as his wife (in Egypt, with Pharaoh [Gen 12:10–20] and at Gerar, with King Abimelech of Gerar [Gen 20:1b–18]). Along with the similar episode for Isaac and Rebekah (Gen 26:6–16), these have been extensively studied by John Van Seters (*Abraham in History and Tradition*, chap. 8). It may be true to say that for Van Seters, these exemplify three versions of one basic story ("three variants of a folktale," 167); I would prefer to speak of three stories exemplifying one motif. At issue is the significance of dependence between the stories. The following reflections will be based on the narrative given in the present text, leaving growth of text issues aside. Closer study is likely to show that the concerns now portrayed in the present text had their role to play in earlier stages as well.

The importance of the theme is evident from its place in Genesis 12, before Abraham's separation from Lot and before Abraham's settlement at Hebron. (Note: the assumption here is that we are dealing with the creation of a narrative, not the report of events as they happened — which would give rise to a different set of questions.) Two aspects of surprise need to be registered. First, called by God to a new land, Abraham encounters famine. How odd of God to starve the ancestor. Second, the episode in Egypt is hardly to Abraham's credit. How odd of Israel to treasure it. What is going on? A psychoanalytic interpretation may be valid; I doubt that it accounts for the place of these stories in the narrative (see Exum, "Endangered Ancestress").

It can be captivating to search for the meaning of traditions that were important to ancient Israel and whose importance to a degree escapes us. That is the case here. Whether things *happen* by chance we do not know; we do know that they are not narrated by chance. We have three stories of Israel's ancestor concealing the status of his wife: two for Abraham and Sarah (Gen 12 and 20); one for Isaac and Rebekah (Gen 26). Two of them are associated with famine (Gen 12 and 26); there is a third story where famine is central and significant (the Joseph story, Gen 37–50). Is the commonality worth exploring?

Regarding the three stories of Israel's ancestor's silence about the status of his wife, the title given in much of the literature (variations on the "endangered ancestress") is misleading; it points the reader in the wrong direction (better Van Seters, "the beautiful wife"). The endangered figure is the ancestor (Abraham, Isaac) who believes his life is threatened. Abraham: "they will kill me, but they will let you live" (Gen 12:12; see also 20:11); Isaac: "I thought I might die because of her" (Gen 26:9). So the ancestor engages in deception. *The ancestor does not trust God.* God is portrayed telling Abraham that he is to be a great nation (Gen 12:2); that can hardly happen if he is killed in Egypt. God is portrayed promising Isaac numerous offspring (Gen 20:4); that can hardly happen if he is killed in Gerar. Both ancestors cover up and conceal the key fact that Sarah and Rebekah are their wives. Both are portrayed not trusting their God. *The ancestor does not trust others* (in the event, foreigners). For Abraham, it is the Egyptians (12:12) or the people of Gerar (20:11); for Isaac, it is the men of the place, Gerar (26:7). Both are portrayed not trusting others/foreigners. God, in the two stories about Abraham, protects both the ancestor and the others; in the Isaac story, it is rather Abimelech's observation instead of God's action that saves the ancestor. Is that the point of the stories: trust others and trust God? There may also be a subordinate motif running through the telling of these stories: if, instead of trusting God, you trust your own wits, you run the risk of serious trouble, but nevertheless you may come out of it very well — God willing. There may well be more.

The first version of the story about Abraham is told in the present text even before he has separated from Lot and settled in the land. The version with Abraham at Gerar (in the present text) is told when Lot has disappeared from the narrative and Abraham is on his own. The story of Isaac at Gerar is located pretty much at the beginning of the scanty traditions we have of Isaac. The story of Joseph and the famine is hardly at the beginning of Joseph's story and certainly not at the beginning of Jacob's; but it is at the beginning of Israel's story. Trust of God is to the fore in the story of Abraham and Isaac (Gen 22). Is trust of God central to the theology of some in ancient

Israel? If so, at what times in Israel's story? Is trust of God a motif associating these four stories?

A tentative suggestion may be hazarded here as to one possibility for understanding at least the first two, where God is involved. Whether the storyteller was aware of it or not, the two stories in fact put God to the test: is God able to protect the newly arrived immigrant? If Abraham had not concealed Sarah's status as his wife and had he been killed as he feared, God's promises would have come to nothing. "Restored-to-life" experiences are not part of the horizon of ancestral stories. Kept alive, however, Abraham the immigrant experiences God's protection. Pharaoh is alerted by great plagues (12:17); Abimelech is alerted by God in a dream (20:6–7). In both cases, Abraham is enriched (12:16; 20:14–15); in both cases, the immigrant ancestor deals directly with the top authority, the pharaoh in Egypt and the king in Gerar. Stories illustrating God's protection right from the start make good sense for Israelite communities. Genesis 12:10–20 is at the start of Abraham's sojourn in Canaan; in the present text, Genesis 20:1–18 is at the start of Abraham's sojourn in the region of Gerar and Beer-sheba.

Famine is somehow significant. Famine drove Abraham to Egypt (Gen 12:10). Famine troubled Isaac at Gerar (Gen 26:1). Famine is not mentioned in relation to Abraham at Gerar, but it is central to the Joseph story. Famine did not take Joseph to Egypt; the hatred felt by his brothers did. Famine took Joseph to the peak of power in Egypt and famine brought Jacob and the rest of his family into Egypt. Is there a commonality that holds all four stories in some form of relationship? Abraham is treated richly in Egypt (Gen 12:16) and in Gerar (20:14–16). After his episode in Gerar, Isaac became very wealthy (26:12–14). Joseph's wealth is, of course, legendary.

The tangled complications

Apart from the episodes with Sarah in Egypt and Gerar and the dual settlements in Gerar/Beersheha and Mamre/Hebron, two specific passages involve embarrassing complexity. They are the erratic itinerary associated with the Egypt episode (Gen 12:10–20) and the interweaving of texts in Genesis 18:1–9. We need to examine both.

The erratic itinerary of Genesis 12–13. As we have seen. Abraham's itinerary is disjointed: Bethel, Egypt, Bethel, Hebron. Lot's presence is puzzling: he receives sparse mention in 12:4–5; in 13:1, he is reported to be with Abraham coming up from Egypt, but he was not mentioned in Egypt at all nor going down there; he is not mentioned significantly until Abraham's return to Bethel, at which point both men are portrayed as substantial pastoralists (13:5, flocks, herds, tents). God's speech is out of place, solemnly promising the whole land to Abraham and his offspring (13:14–17 [categorized by many as secondary]), but made after Abraham has already given part of the land to Lot. To say the least, these factors are odd.

If, as avowed speculation, the Lot material and the episode in Egypt (Gen 12:10–20) are removed, the narrative of Abraham's journeying through Canaan becomes limpidly clear. The pause at Shechem is, as we have seen, in relation to Jacob's future sojourn there. God's promise to Abraham is entirely appropriate, "To your offspring I will give this land" (12:7). Shechem is not of concern to Abraham; it will be given to Jacob.

Bethel, too, is not of concern to Abraham; small wonder the text does not locate him precisely there but nearby, "between Bethel and Ai," with Bethel on the west and Ai on the east. It is a most appropriate location for God's speech to Abraham; but that speech is now found inappropriately at 13:14–17, where it comes after Abraham's generous offer to Lot and after his separation from Lot. Bethel is roughly central, if we reckon between Esdraelon and the Negeb; it is also atop the southern part of the hilly ridge that is Mount Ephraim. It is an appropriate spot, at least symbolically, for God to invite Abraham to look north, south, east, and west. It is an appropriate spot for God to give Abraham the land: "for all the land that you see I will give to you and to your offspring forever.... I will give it to you" (13:15–17). Following directly on Abraham's invoking the name of the LORD (12:8), it is the divine speech that this narrative has been building up to. After it, Abraham can move on down to Hebron and settle there.

The complexity in Genesis 18:1–9. If, again as avowed speculation, we leave aside momentarily the Lot traditions of chapter 14 and the independent unit that is chapter 15, much of the Hagar story, and finally the second independent unit that is chapter 17, then we come to the convoluted text in which three men (one of whom turns out to be *yhwh*) come to Abraham and Sarah at Mamre, with the promise of a son through Sarah and the discussion of the fate of Sodom (18:1–15). If we take up the thread of the three — two visitors and *yhwh* — needed for the Sodom episode (therefore text using the plural), leaving aside the promise of a son to Sarah (for which only *yhwh* is required), we have the traditions of Sodom: Abraham's words of intercession, the visitation of the two (angels/messengers/men [see 19:5, 8, 10, 12, 16]), Lot's departure from the doomed city, and the origin of the Moabites and Ammonites. For the complications introduced by 19:18–22 and 19:24–25, see Westermann, *Genesis 12–36*, 304–7.

Altogether, the two chapters (Gen 18–19) present a powerful case for seeing parts of the biblical text functioning as bases for story-telling. Apart from the blending in the introduction, other parts of the text need clarifying or developing by a storyteller. The text begins with three men, one of whom becomes the God of Israel. They (plural) ask about Sarah's whereabouts; an unnamed "he" (singular) addresses Sarah and in due course is twice referred to as *yhwh*; "the men," number unspecified, move toward Sodom. *yhwh* then ponders whether to tell Abraham what he (*yhwh*) is about to do. Precisely what God is doing, whether inspecting or punishing, is not specified in the text at this point. The same ambiguity will return. Given that Abraham intercedes for Sodom, God must have told him of the proposed destruction; the text has no mention of it, so it is entrusted to the storyteller. Similarly, *yhwh* proposes to visit Sodom and verify the accusations against the people or alternatively acquit them. The text ignores this proposal; it is an option that is available, but it is not developed in the text we have. Abraham's intercession for the doomed cities, his haggling with God, is well known.

Up until now, the text has mentioned "men." When it comes to the inspection of Sodom and the sexual assault involved there, the text speaks of "angels/messengers/men"; obviously, given the heinous nature of the episode, *yhwh* could hardly be a participant. The declaration by the visitors that they are about to destroy the place is not motivated in terms of the sexual assault, but in terms of the outcry that had reached God (18:20–21), who has sent them to destroy the place (19:13). It would appear that their mission was not inspection but destruction. Just as there is a fluctuation between the men and the LORD as to who is to destroy the city (19:13 and 14, but quite compatible), so there is fluctuation between the angels/messengers and the men (19:15 and 16). The presence of Lot's sons-in-law is addressed in 19:12–14; they are reported treating Lot's warning as a joke. On the other hand, 19:15–16 concerns Lot's wife and two daughters. The wife looks back later, and the daughters will be mentioned again. One last transition remains to be noted. The presence of the plural in 19:18 is a pointer to the presence of the men. The understandable switch to the singular at 19:19 (addressing one of the two) eases the appearance of *yhwh* on the scene in 19:24–25. All in all, it is a remarkable lode for storytellers to mine.

It would be important to look more closely at these traditions, but this book is not the place to do it; here we may note that not only has Lot been placed in Abraham's debt but the traditions have taken care of three of Israel's important neighbors: Moabites, Ammonites, and Ishmaelites. These are family, and they are distanced. A fourth will be similarly taken care of in the Jacob cycle: the Edomites.

It may be worthwhile spending a few lines on each of the three "closed" texts we have already placed in the Southwest sequence.

Genesis 15 is one of those timeless texts whose dating tends to reflect the subjectivity of the interpreter more than the objectivity of the text. Opinions range from quite early to quite late. Westermann comments regarding Genesis 15: "The present state of scholarship would regard a late stage in the history of the patriarchal promises as the probable period of origin of the texts — a period when the possession of the land (vv. 7–21) and the survival of the people (vv. 1–6) was in danger, and the old patriarchal promises were newly revived so as to give surety to God's promise in a time of national danger" (*Genesis 12–36*, 217). For Westermann, it is all about two central promises: descendants and land. "Everything else is decoration serving to shape the promise into a narrative" (*Genesis 12–36*, 216). This observation overlooks the identification of the descendant. Abraham will be the biological father of the promised descendant, "your very own issue" (15:4); the promised descendant will not be merely a slave born in

Abraham's house. This description would apply to both Ishmael and Isaac. In Genesis 17, it will be narrowed to Isaac alone.

Genesis 17, on the other hand, while it is one of the more majestic and treasured passages in the Abraham traditions, is concerned with the fates of both Ishmael and Isaac. Covenant and circumcision are, of course, to the fore but the attention given both Ishmael and Isaac cannot be overlooked. Promised a son by Sarah, Abraham disbelieves; he shifts the focus to Ishmael (17:17–18). In the text, God reiterates the promise of a son by Sarah and identifies the son by name as Isaac and emphasizes the covenant with Isaac and his offspring. God's address then turns most strangely to Ishmael, who is to be blessed and be the father of twelve princes (17:20). Beyond Genesis 25:12–16, this tradition is not referred to anywhere else in the Hebrew scriptures. A tension with the text of Genesis 21 is real, scarcely to be avoided by appeal to Ishmael's survival. In 17:20, an exalted future is promised for Ishmael; in 21:15–18, Ishmael's imminent demise is assumed (see v. 16).

Genesis 22, as with Genesis 15 and 17, is timeless and substantially placeless. Like Genesis 15 and 17, it is a "closed" chapter — free-floating, not located with regard to time or place, not moving the narrative forward ("Moriah" may be specific as a place name, but its location is unknown). Genesis 22 is appropriate where it is in the present text: God is portrayed in it echoing the action of Sarah. In Genesis 21, Sarah orders Ishmael banished — and has her way; in Genesis 22, God orders Isaac sacrificed — but holds back at the last minute. Two aspects are noteworthy. First, in portraying a threat to Isaac's existence (which of course is a threat to Israel's existence in the future), it may be evoking the reality of an actual threat to Israel's existence; such was posed in 722 or 701 or, above all, at the time of exile. The emphasis on trust, "the LORD will provide," would be appropriate. The deuteronomic character of the second intervention (22:15–18) cautions against too late an origin. Second, as it stands, the text has Abraham return to Beer-sheba and live there (22:19).

One further point should be noted. The triple enumeration in both 12:1 (your country, your kindred, your father's house) and 22:2 (your son, your only son whom you love, Isaac) is well-known. It is surely significant that both passages open with the terse two-word command: "Go you" (Hebrew: *lech lecha*). Abraham's faith is on display in the journey to an unknown land; Abraham's faith is under test in the episode with Isaac. Horrible as this last passage may be to many, Abraham's faith and his failures may have resonated and still resonate with many. The tradition holds the distrust in Egypt or Gerar, the turning to Hagar, and the dismissal of Ishmael among episodes that might well be reckoned among his failures.

The duality in the Abraham traditions

When the cloud of all this speculation clears away, there remains a core to the Abraham cycle. What meaning might it have had for Israel at some stage in its theologizing? What meaning does it retain for us? As long as we remain aware of the speculative nature of the reflections, ranging from the "quite probable" to the "at least possible," we are free to recognize that some extremely attractive vistas are opened up. These vistas relate to two possible collections or sequences of tradition from which the present Abraham cycle was compiled. They do not in any way derogate from the present text; they simply point to possibilities as to the relatively near origins of its traditions.

Acceptance of the fragmentary nature of the Abraham traditions gives freedom from an anxiety about history and allows for a focus on legend and its invitation to symbol. The legend holds up Abraham as figure of faith; it also holds Abraham as figure of failure. In Egypt and Gerar, there is an uneasy exploitation of Sarah; through the rest of the tradition, there is an unspoken fidelity to Sarah. As legendary figure, Abraham is called by God into famine and fear. His claims to permanence in the land have their own symbolic value; the well is a symbol of life and the tomb (to be resting place of the ancestors) is symbol of a permanence beyond death. Abraham is the deliverer figure, whether in Genesis 14 or Genesis 19.

Beyond these imaginative possibilities, of course, recognition of the separateness of the two original tradition sequences has other more concrete advantages. First, it accounts for the duplication of several elements, above all: the episodes of Abraham and Sarah in Egypt and in Gerar (the two "wife/sister" episodes); the two locations for Abraham (Gerar/Beersheba and Mamre/Hebron). Second, it allows for some smoothing out of the itinerary sequence and associated problems in Genesis 12–13. Third, it accounts in part for the odd textual interweaving in 18:1–9. The combination of the two original sequences and the integration of the Lot traditions and the three other chapters does not give rise to difficulties.

This process of combination that formed the present text is not difficult to envisage but the task needs to be addressed. It is desirable to move in two stages: first, recapitulating the Abraham traditions — stripped of Lot and the "closed" chapters — and discussing their combination; second, discussing the integration of the other traditions to form the present text as we have it.

Stage One: combining the two Abraham sequences. The attractive aspect of the vistas opened by these two collections or sequences is their simplicity. Abraham answered God's call, came to Canaan, and — establishing an appropriate precedent — built an altar at Shechem where the land was promised to "his seed" (i.e., Jacob), and established himself in the land, formalizing rights in the Beersheba region, alternatively purchasing a burial ground for his wife and himself in the Hebron region. The ancestor came to the new land and settled there. From two sets of narrative collections the present text is easily compiled. What appears complex is revealed as simple.

The combination would have been effected easily enough. As noted, the sojourn-in-Egypt text (Gen 12:10–20) is a self-contained unit. Without the Lot material, its obvious place would have been after Abraham's arrival in the Hebron region. It could have been added at almost any time. Exploration of all the possibilities would be cumbersome and is needless here.

The major texts from the Southwest sequence do not begin until Genesis 20:1aβ. The Abraham–East sequence can be left untouched until the birth of Isaac. Of course, to some extent this depends on the stage in the transmission and combination that the "closed" chapters (Gen 15 and 17) are introduced into the process. Introduced at a relatively early stage, they probably belong with the Southwest sequence, as noted above. But, if introduced at a later stage, they are quite possibly essential to the Abraham–East sequence, in which case they would need to include Genesis 16, the first Hagar story and the birth of Ishmael (Gen 16:3, 15–16 can be liberated from the

Southwest sequence but hardly needs to be, unless perhaps at an early stage).

For a combined text, the two accounts of Isaac's birth would need to be brought together, as they are in the present text. This brings in its train the dismissal of Hagar and Ishmael (Gen 21:8–21). While at first sight, this may seem to run against the geographical references, the location described as "the wilderness of Beer-sheba" (Gen 21:14) is central enough to allow its association with the Abraham–East sequence and, therefore, to find its place in the combined text. It may not be as deep in the south as the surrounding text suggests, but, for the purposes of combination, it will do. After that, the present text (the combination of the two sequences) is straightforward enough. Assuming that Genesis 15, 16, and 17 have been given their place in the Abraham–East sequence, all that is needed is the move in Genesis 20:1a, followed by the rest of the Gerar story (Gen 20:1b–18), the covenant at Beer-sheba (Gen 21:22–34), the sacrifice or binding of Isaac (Gen 22:1–19), the death and burial of Sarah (Gen 23:1–20), the marriage of Isaac and Rebekah (Gen 24:1–67), and finally Abraham's remarriage, death, and burial (Gen 25:1–11).

The Gerar episode and the settlement in the region of Gerar/Beersheba are juxtaposed alongside the Mamre/Hebron traditions rather than thoroughly integrated with them. That is the way it is in the present text.

Stage Two: adding the Lot traditions. The primary troubling question is why the Egypt episode was placed where it now is, before the separation from Lot. If competition for pastureland was to be proposed as the cause for separation (related presumably to the possessions of 12:5), coupled with the symbolic visibility made possible by the mountain location, the separation text would have needed to have its place before Abraham's arrival in the Hebron region. The sojourn in Egypt could still have been situated after that arrival.

Several difficulties are raised by the present placement of the Egypt unit, before the separation. First, it requires a massive zigzag in Abraham's itinerary to get him from between Bethel and Ai to Egypt and then back to that spot between Bethel and Ai. Second, from a narrative point of view, it has poor Lot marking time in the Negeb for an indeterminate period. Third, to be plausible it requires the business in Egypt to be completed within a relatively short time.

The Egypt episode is where it is, however, and the oddity of its placement requires our thought. There may be an importance attached to the issue of God's protection that escapes us (see above).

The rescue of Lot (Gen 14) could have been added at any time and need not concern us here. The combination of the Sodom and Gomorrah traditions (which required both God and messengers) with the promise to Sarah (which required God) has resulted in the strange complexity of 18:1–9. Why it should have been so, we do not know; that it is so, we have to accept.

The "closed" traditions. There is a grandness of vision in Genesis 12:2–3; otherwise, grandiosity (and especially the concern for heirs, covenant, and land) is largely restricted to Genesis 15 and 17. Both can be fairly characterized as closed and independent texts. Genesis 15 could have been added at any time; prior to combination, it would have been at home in either sequence. Genesis 17 could equally have been added at any time. With its emphasis on Isaac, prior to the combination of the two sequences, it would have belonged to the Southwest sequence. As has been said, Genesis 22 impacts on the total tradition. It may well reflect the time around the exile (587–538 BCE) when the threat to Israel's existence was greatest. Deuteronomic characteristics in 22:15–18 are cause for caution; they need not be determinative for dating. The chapter has Abraham living at Beer-sheba (22:19). Genesis 24 will be looked at in association with the Isaac traditions.

Documentary sources are not needed. The material traditionally attributed to P (12:4b–5; 13:6, 11b, 12*; 16:1, 3, 15–16; 17:1–27; 19:29; 21:1b–5) is the result of blending the two collections. These collections reflect the experience of migrants in all times: the ancestor comes to the new country, settles, and becomes established there. In the Beer-sheba collection, Abraham digs a well with all due formality (21:25–34); in the Mamre/Hebron collection, with equal formality, Abraham buys a burial ground (23:1–20). The Beer-sheba collection is concerned with some of the surrounding peoples: Moabites, Ammonites, even Ishmaelites; they are kin and they are distanced. Abraham's land is in Philistine territory (20:15; 21:34).

Isaac is not mentioned. The Mamre/Hebron collection is concerned with the enduring possession of land; in what is presumably a specific tradition, the cave of Machpelah will be the resting place of the ancestors of Israel.

What all this allows for is the existence of Abraham traditions associated with two regions, Gerar/Beersheba and Mamre/Hebron. When a need was felt to bring the Abraham traditions together and preserve them, naturally both collections were drawn on and arranged in some form of linear sequence. It may be this linear arrangement that led later interpreters into seeing history where fragmented tradition mingled with theology, generating legend, might have been more appropriate.

Before we look at the implications for modern faith, it is important to distinguish clearly between two stages in the ancient modification of the Abraham traditions. In a first stage, the diverse Abraham traditions we have been analyzing have been compiled to form what is basically our present biblical text as far as Abraham and Sarah are concerned. In what may well be a quite separate second stage, the traditions of Abraham and Sarah appear to have been blended with traditions of Isaac and Jacob to constitute a "legendary ancestral cluster" constituting the base of the people Israel.

The date of the first stage of the operation is most uncertain. The compilation could, at least in theory, have occurred very early in the piece; alternatively, the compilation could have been quite late. As far as I can see, at the moment we have no way of knowing. When it comes to the second stage, the constituting of a "legendary ancestral cluster," certain observations are relevant. The need to insist on the unity of all Israel might not have emerged before the fall of the north in 722 BCE. The need to insist on the unity of all Israel might have been strongly felt at the time of exile or afterward. As we have seen, the triad of three ancestors is marked at the call of Moses and in the book of Deuteronomy. These occurrences set a time for focus on the three. At the same time, a focus on the three is not necessarily a focus on the three as family. The concern for racial purity was strong in some quarters after the exile. Genesis 24, the search for a racially pure bride for Isaac, has been described by Alexander Rofé as "a very late composition, written in the fifth century BCE" ("Betrothal of Rebekah," 27, see below). A focus on the three as family may be surprisingly late.

It is important too to recognize the difference between diverse Abraham traditions and a unitary Abraham tradition. With a unitary Abraham tradition, no matter how fragmented, there is the possibility of arguing that the tradition faithfully records material concerning the arrival of a single individual that is consistent with itself. With diverse Abraham traditions, meaning by "diverse" traditions that are not self-consistent, this is no longer the case. Whether or not the traditions go back to the same single individual is not the issue. The issue is that the traditions involve duplications and difficulties (i.e., are not self-consistent) and are subject, therefore, to the same vagaries of memory that are part and parcel of all human experience — and the emergence of legend.

Once again, it is important to emphasize that what traditional interpretation has long maintained is precisely what potentially late compilers may have sought to set out clearly. The unity of Israel as a people, experienced in reality, can be illustrated by appeal to a restructuring of ancient traditions in order to establish from the outset what I have called here a "legendary ancestral cluster." The tension, in some writing, between Abraham as man or myth is a false dichotomy. Abraham is neither a historical figure nor a mythical figure; as presented in the Genesis texts, Abraham is a legendary figure.

It is important to be aware of the process of analysis that has led to these conclusions. The traditions are dealt with at the level of present text. The text is sifted according to subject matter. There is no preconceived ideological concern driving the analysis. There is no scholarly detective work discovering distant origins concealed beneath layers of later invention. The only thing that has prevented us from seeing what is there to be seen is our having been thoroughly convinced of the understanding advanced by the later blending, itself emerging from later experience.

It is helpful to be fully aware of what is being done here. It is not a return to the literary-critical practices of old, where analysis sought to provide complete and final narrative texts, resolving apparent duplications in the present text. The major difference is in that phrase, "complete and final narrative texts." What this approach has sought to do is to establish links and attachment points that storytellers might find helpful as a base from which to weave a narrative. It trusts the ancient storytellers and seeks to uncover the bases from which they might have begun. It does not claim to recover the actual stories that they told. (See *Rethinking the Pentateuch*, 15–20.)

~ MODERN FAITH ~

A shift is noted in *Rethinking the Pentateuch* from the Pentateuch as record of Israel's *remembering its past* to the Pentateuch as record of Israel's *pondering its present* (9). What we have seen in the Abraham traditions is an example of the revelation found in such pondering. That is what these following reflections are about.

Imagination can image revelation coming from a past time to communicate what is not known. The deepening knowledge of ourselves and our world that comes from our experience of what is now happening to us and around us can also open our eyes to what is rightly revelation.

Another way of seeing this is given us by William Schniedewind:

What a hypothetical author intended to say often is difficult (if not impossible) to recover for an ancient text like the Bible. More accessible (and perhaps more important) is understanding what the text meant to its ancient readers, which does not necessarily resemble an author's intent. For example, what the U.S. Constitution means is usually more a reflection of its readers than its authors. Consequently, the meaning of the Constitution keeps changing along with the changing generations of its readers. . . . When a text is central to a people or a nation, like the Declaration of Independence or the Constitution is, the history of its interpretation can serve as a window into the history of that people. . . . Similarly, the meaning of the Bible will be imbedded in the history of the people who wrote it, read it, passed it on, rewrote it, and read it again. It is closely tied to when the traditions were collected, written down, edited, rewritten, and finally coalesced into the book we call the Bible. (*How the Bible Became a Book*, 5)

"Imbedded in the history of that people" includes reflecting the experience of that people. It is an opening of the eyes of that people to what is rightly revelation. So it is rightly found in the book we call the Bible. In our time, it is an opening of our eyes to what is rightly revelation, the pondering of the present and a deepening understanding of our God.

Did the Israelites learn from contemplation of their origins that their fate on earth was intimately tied up with that of the Ishmaelites? I very much doubt it. Did they learn from current experience that the Ishmaelites were family and could not be dismissed? I rather think so. Our present experience can be massively revelatory of who we are and of the nature of our God. Revelation is to be found at least as much in the present as it is in the past — perhaps much more.

Did the Israelites learn from contemplation of their origins that their well-being was closely associated with that of the Moabites and Ammonites as well as with that of the Ishmaelites? Once again, I very much doubt it. Did the Israelites somehow learn from their current experience that other peoples in their neighborhood were family to them? Did that reveal to them something of the universality of their God? I rather think it might have.

Discovering from their experience in the present that Moabites and Ammonites, as well as Ishmaelites, were somehow as family to them, what did this reveal to thinkers in ancient Israel of the mystery of their God?

In short, do we learn from close study of these traditions and their development and combination that divine revelation is not so much a matter of the distant past revealing to us what we could not know as it is acknowledgment that often in their reflective experience people come to understand these realities and understand their God more fully? Is it a cause for scandal that Israel's ancestral traditions were subject to so much development and amalgamation late in the piece or does it bring home to us the reality of revelation in our day-to-day present?

In both sets of tradition, Abraham left home without any clear indication as to his destination. Is that how Israel experienced its God: launch out into the unknown, let go of what is familiar and follow my call into the unfamiliar? Did Israel's theologians treasure these traditions because of the echo they found in them of their own experience? Do we? Did they adjust them in the light of their experience? If so, were they in this process uncovering something of the mystery of their God?

Did they learn in their experience that although they had two sets of traditions about Abraham, Beer-sheba–based and Hebron-based, they were one people; they belonged together? As one people, their God was one God. Did that come out of the past or out of the present? It is seldom a clean-cut decision, but my experience says the present frequently predominates.

The question being posed by all these examples can be generalized simply:

In this given instance, did past faith/experience predominate in generating the present story?

or

In this given instance, did present faith/experience predominate in generating the past story?

However we may answer that question in any particular case, experience suggests that what we term "revelation" may come to us from the past and may also come to us from our experience in the present.

On the legendary value of figures such as Abraham or Jacob, see below in the summary concluding this chapter.

The benefit of the seemingly tortuous analyses of the Abraham traditions that we have been doing is surprisingly clear. The separation into a Gerar/Beersheba collection and a Mamre/Hebron collection brings clarity into what is otherwise a muddled cycle and brings clarity into the traditions in the corresponding sequences.

The Gerar/Beersheba sequence is fundamentally the traditions of a migrant, coming to a new country, establishing himself there, and setting up the legal formalities allowing his family to remain there (i.e., the wells; see Gen 26:26–33). The Mamre/Hebron sequence does much the same for traditions of a settlement in the Mamre/Hebron area. Associated with it are traditions affecting relationships with surrounding nations, Moab and Ammon. As we have been at pains to insist, these analyses are speculative. Should they be judged unacceptable, the same phenomena remain present in mingled form.

The two great covenant chapters, Genesis 15 and Genesis 17, are concerned with the twin issues of descendants and land on a grand scale (esp. Gen 15:18–20 for land; Gen 17:6–7 for descendants). Both chapters are generally regarded as later than other traditions in the Abraham cycle. The migrant traditions regarding Abraham are far from grandiose.

The most far-reaching of these ancestral traditions may well be the "promise of blessing" texts. The promise recurs three times for Abraham (Gen 12:3; 18:18; 22:18); it will repeated again for Isaac (Gen 26:4) and Jacob (Gen 28:14). The promise sets a clear stamp on the Abraham traditions: the blessing given Abraham is to benefit all the peoples of the earth. This is an enormous claim. In the absence of the promises of extensive lands and imposing descendants, it is an amazing claim. "What 12:3b is saying is this: God's action proclaimed in the promise to Abraham is not limited to him and his posterity, but reaches its goal only when it includes all the families of the earth" (Westermann, *Genesis 12–36*, 151–52).

This claim of universal blessing included in the promise is probably made relatively late in the history of Abraham traditions. What is particularly fascinating about it is that the more insignificant Israel becomes, the more significant this claim becomes. Who is this God of whom it can be said that, through the medium of Israel, this God will bless all the peoples of the earth?

Whether early or late, the claim is remarkable. If it were linked to the more grandiose of the claims for Abraham, we could play it down more easily. But it isn't, so we can't. The question that we have to ask ourselves is whether a claim of this magnitude about an individual migrant is a reflection on the significance of this migrant or a reflection on the significance of the God claimed to be making this promise. I doubt that these texts in Israel have any uncertainty: the claim speaks of the nature of God.

However, the wider context demands a caveat. In at least the first two "wife/sister" episodes, three elements verge on the grandiose — pointing, perhaps, to something of the symbol lurking near. First, the couple deal with the highest political figure in the region (pharaoh, king); for recently arrived migrants this is, at the least, unusual. Second, the ancestor is greatly enriched (Gen 12:16; 20:14–16). Third, God's intervention is on a grand scale: great plagues for Pharaoh and his house (12:17); barrenness for the house of Abimelech, noted at the end of the story (20:17–18). All three echo aspects of the narratives about Israel in Egypt.

The primary theological task of modern faith is reflection on the nature of God. These aspects of the Abraham tradition provide grist for the theological mill. According to the authors of Genesis 15 and Genesis 17, for example, God is overwhelmingly concerned for Israel. Concern for others is principally restricted to 12:3b, 18:18, and 22:18. In Genesis 15, Abraham's descendants are to be as countless as the stars on a clear night (15:5). At the other end of the chapter, the land promised these countless descendants was to extend from the Nile to the Euphrates (15:18). Concern for the rest of the world is absent. In Genesis 17, the extent of land in the future is greatly reduced; "all the land of Canaan" (17:8) will be enough. Rather than their number, it is the eminence of the descendants that attracts attention. Nations stemming from Abraham fit in well enough with the promised countless number. "Kings shall come from you" (17:6) is hardly surprising if "nations" are in view. On the other hand, in this portrayal of what God will do, other nations are not in view. The relationship between Abraham's line and these many nations and kings is not spelled out. The same promise of nations and kings is repeated in relation to Sarah (17:16). Ishmael gets into the act, "fruitful and exceedingly numerous...the father of twelve princes...a great nation" (17:20), but nobody else, no other nations. This God of Abraham is a God of Israel whose vision, with rare exceptions, does not extend much further.

Back at the start of the Abraham cycle, the picture is a very different one. To be sure, Abraham is to become a great nation and be blessed. But at this point, the blessing is to have a universal focus: "in you all the families of the earth shall be blessed" (12:3). The God of

Abraham is envisaged as a God of all. The universal focus is repeated but it is hardly dominant.

A task of modern faith is to build on this image of outreach. It is all too easy for nations and peoples to turn inward and look substantially to their own interests. One of the processes that has been visible in these Abraham traditions is the constant combining of more limited vision into broader vision. At the beginnings of biblical tradition as it now stands, God is a God of all.

ISAAC AND REBEKAH

In the book of Genesis, poor Isaac gets short shrift. Abraham has more than a dozen or so chapters associated with him; Jacob has eight or so; by contrast, Isaac is struggling to have one whole chapter; in Genesis 25:19–34 details of his sons, their birth and later, are reported before his own story is begun in Genesis 26. Yet it is possible that his figure in tradition is the oldest of them all. In the English version of Claus Westermann's massive three-volume commentary on the book of Genesis, totaling something of the order of fourteen hundred pages, Genesis 26 is given pp. 420–30 of volume 2; that is all! In Walter Brueggemann's *Genesis,* Isaac gets no more than a few pages in part 3, "The Jacob Narrative" (esp. 221–26).

There is no Isaac cycle. Isaac and Rebekah together come into the text with the episode at Gerar (Gen 26:1–11). Before that, the text is emphatic that Isaac is the son of Abraham (Gen 21:1–7; 25:19). After that, the text is equally emphatic that Isaac is the heir to Abraham's wells (Gen 26:17–33). Beyond that, the text at this stage has little to say. Yet even in the little text there is, the universal outlook is not lost. Isaac's offspring are to be "as numerous as the stars of heaven" and to have "all these lands" and through these offspring "all the nations of the earth shall gain blessing for themselves" (26:4). God is portrayed as God of all.

The idea that the Isaac figure is independent and old among Israel's ancestral traditions is certainly possible. Demonstrating it is well-nigh impossible. For Noth, "These Isaac stories give the impression of being even more original traditio-historically than the stories of the West Jordan Jacob. They stand, as a matter of fact, closer to the origin of the 'patriarchal' tradition than do the latter" (*Pentateuchal Traditions*, 106). Noth's context allows of assumptions we would no longer dream of making; nevertheless, his instincts may have been sound. Westermann comments that the purpose of Genesis 26 was "to gather together the few Isaac traditions that have been preserved" and the chapter "has been subsequently interpolated into an already existing sequence" (*Genesis 12–36*, 423). In brief, both scholars see traces of early fragments as well as late composition in the Isaac composition.

Early traces should not be surprising. Amos 7:9 refers to "the high places of Isaac," paralleled with "the sanctuaries of Israel" (cf. 7:16). In Jacob's dispute with Laban, Jacob twice appeals to the god of his father, the *paqad* (the Fear) of Isaac (Gen 31:42, 53). It is redolent of an ancient name, as is the *abir* (the Mighty One) of Jacob (Gen 49:24; but see Isa 1:24; 49:26; 60:16; Ps 132:2, 5). Jacob as individual is featured in Hosea 12; as nation, Isaac and Jacob feature in both Amos and Hosea (Amos 3:13; 6:8; 7:2, 5; 8:7; 9:8; Hos 10:11; 12:2).

What is surprising is that the sequence of Abraham, Isaac, and Jacob is not found in the Hebrew scriptures before the late seventh century BCE. We will discuss this in greater detail below, after treating the Jacob cycle. For now, it is important to recognize here that the figure of Isaac is the link holding the triad together. Isaac is named as son of Abraham; Isaac is named as father of Jacob. Yet both Genesis 24, in which Abraham sends a servant to seek a bride for Isaac, and Genesis 27, which has Jacob part from Isaac and head for his mother's house in Haran, appear to be quite late texts. As such, they allow for Isaac's role in the tradition as link holding the triad together, but they situate the unity of any family bloodline relatively late. Three stages in the development of the tradition can be named theoretically: the association of the three ancestors (see Deuteronomy); the family unity of the three, without emphasis on any unity of bloodline (before Gen 24 and 27); the family unity of the three, with the unity of the family bloodline emphasized (with Gen 24 and 27).

The spread of locations — Shechem to the north and Beer-sheba to the south, Gerar somewhat to the west and Hebron somewhat

to the east — hardly favors some ancestral grazing patch. The suc-
cinct and (in Hebrew) assonant reference to Jacob as a wandering,
or near-to-death, "Aramean" (Deut 26:5) does not sit easily at any
time with a tradition of a father and grandfather in Canaan. In
the Hebrew scriptures, the word "Aramean" unequivocally means
Syrian. In the absence of a personal name here, A. D. H. Mayes,
suggesting that "we have the old beginning of a text here brought
into a deuteronomistic setting," considers "the identification with
Jacob quite uncertain" (*Deuteronomy*, 334), but in the context it
can hardly mean any other. Richard Nelson's move to expand "the
Aramean Jacob so that he grows into a collective representative of
all the patriarchs" (*Deuteronomy*, 309) fails to explain why such a
collective figure in Deuteronomy, of all places, should be Jacob and
be designated Aramean.

In other words, there are difficulties with the place of Isaac as
the linking figure between the ancestors Abraham and Jacob —
Abraham's son, Rebekah's husband, Jacob's father.

Abraham's son

In both Gerar/Beersheba and Mamre/Hebron collections, Isaac is
without doubt Abraham's son, born of Sarah. Beyond the barest,
information on the birth and the boy is notable by its absence in
either sequence.

Traditio-historically, considerable weight falls on Genesis 25:19–
28. It is plainly said there that "Abraham was the father of Isaac"
(25:19). This comes under the heading of *toledot*. For many in the
past, the *toledot* formulas have been treated with great respect. In
my judgment, given the multiple roles the formula plays, this respect
has been excessive. Whatever of that, the *toledot* formula is now
associated with priestly writing and scarcely with an early date. The
understanding of Genesis 25:19–20 would be in accordance with
either sequence (Gerar/Beersheba and Mamre/Hebron collections).
Whether it has much likelihood of being original is another question
altogether.

Arguing against associating this passage (25:19–26) with the bulk
of the Jacob traditions that follow is the birth oracle. First, the oracle
looks to nations rather than individual sons. "Two nations are in

your womb, and two peoples born of you shall be divided" (25:23). The bulk of the Jacob traditions that follow concern two individuals. Second, the relative strengths of the two in the oracle do not reflect the relative strengths of Esau and Jacob found in the longer-term narrative ahead. "The one shall be stronger than the other, the elder shall serve the younger" (25:23). This is certainly not the case in the encounter of Jacob with Esau in Genesis 33. Verses 27–28 prepare most suitably for chapter 27. Verses 29–34 render the words of the oracle into the goods of human barter.

It would not be unfair to characterize the composite passage as late and uncertain. It certainly cannot validate the weight of the ancestral tradition. The Hebrew style of verses 19–20 is questionable. Verse 19b is surprisingly abrupt: "Abraham begot Isaac." The verbal form (*hifil*, 3rd masc. sing.) is found in Gen 11:27 and here; otherwise, the contexts are exclusively late (forty-six of sixty-two verses are in 1 Chr 2–9). Verse 20 is surprisingly overstuffed. The identification of Rebekah as "daughter of Bethuel the Aramean of Paddan-aram, sister of Laban the Aramean" is inserted between "his taking Rebekah" and "to be his wife." The identification overwhelms the verse.

None of the other references to Abraham as father of Isaac are reliable witnesses to an early tradition (e.g., Gen 28:4, 13; 31:42, 53; 32:10 [Heb.; NRSV, 10]; 35:12, 27; 48:15–16).

Rebekah's husband: Genesis 24

Where Genesis 24 is concerned, Alexander Rofé's primary article opens with the statement: "My contention is that Genesis 24 is a very late composition, written in the fifth century BCE" ("Betrothal of Rebekah," 27). There is widespread agreement with this position; recently, for example: Römer, Scullion, Seebass, Ska, Soggin, and Van Seters (references given in *Rethinking the Pentateuch*, 34, n. 14 and 56, n. 65).

It is through Rebekah that the tie is made back to the old country. Rebekah, "born to Bethuel son of Milcah, the wife of Nahor, Abraham's brother" (Gen 24:15, cf. v. 24). When Jacob is to return there, it is to the family of his mother, Rebekah, that he is directed: "to the house of Bethuel, your mother's father; and take as wife from there one of the daughters of Laban, your mother's brother"

(Gen 28:2). Rebekah's significance is highlighted in those two desig-nations, Bethuel "your mother's father" and Laban "your mother's brother." This emphasis on Laban as "his mother's brother" is con-tinued into Genesis 29:10 (three times in the one verse). The emphasis on Rebekah as Bethuel's daughter is found in Genesis 24:24, 47 and 25:20.

Jacob's father: Genesis 27

Genesis 27 is that delightfully roguish story in which Rebekah, Isaac's wife, has her favorite son Jacob steal from his father Isaac the dying father's blessing — to firstborn brother Esau's utter dismay. It is a large-scale chapter that takes for granted that Isaac is the father of Jacob. It is highly probable that Genesis 27 is a late composition (no earlier than the seventh century BCE); if so, it presupposes Isaac as Jacob's father rather than being evidence for it. The bulk of the chap-ter provides one motivation for Jacob's flight to his mother's home, back in the old country. The possibility to be entertained, if the chap-ter is indeed late, is that a flight for Jacob has perhaps been grafted on to the front end of traditions about Jacob's coming from Aram to Canaan. An alternative would be to see the graft as an addition of the figure of Rebekah to an already existing narrative of Jacob's journey to Aram. The graft can be traced as far as Genesis 29:14.

Genesis 27 is in many ways Rebekah's story. She instigates Jacob's deceit; she instigates Jacob's flight. Jacob's dominant characteristic in much of the story is lack of gumption. Two motives are provided for Jacob's departure. First, Esau's anger, arising from the story of deceit. Second, Esau's wives, local women not of the family and causing irritation to Isaac and Rebekah (26:34–35; 27:46–28:5, 6–9).

The evidence for the age of Genesis 27 will not be given in detail here (it is laid out in full in *Rethinking the Pentateuch*, 58–59). The general result given there is: "Careful study of its language, however, leads to the conclusion that it is unlikely that Gen 27 is an early text; it is probable that it is not earlier than the seventh century" (*Rethinking the Pentateuch*, 58). The outcome from the point of view of the history of the text: "it may be that a Jacob tradition has been integrated with an Abraham tradition, the process facilitated by the Isaac and Rebekah traditions." From the point of view of theology:

"What does this quest for unity [the unification of Abraham, Isaac, and Jacob into one family] say of Israel's experience of itself and of its God? Who am I? Who are we? Who is God?" (*Rethinking the Pentateuch*, 59). These theological issues will concern us under the heading "Modern Faith" here and again later, after the study of the Jacob cycle.

The evidence for characterizing Genesis 27 as unlikely to be early is exclusively based on the study of its language. Some eighteen items of vocabulary are assessed; they feature in about twenty-four verses of the forty-five that make up the story. The overall impression is given above: "it is unlikely that Gen 27 is an early text; it is probable that it is not earlier than the seventh century." The precision "not earlier than the seventh century" is based on the absence of the triad, Abraham–Isaac–Jacob, prior to Deuteronomy (without assessing issues of levels in Deuteronomy). The dating of the chapter is not, at this point at least, a matter of demonstrable certainty; the terms are "unlikely" and "probable." In the face of such a conclusion, however, it would imprudent to conclude to an early text. The implications have to be looked at.

~MODERN FAITH~

For those of us who have been brought up over the years viewing Abraham, Isaac, and Jacob as the first family of Israel, it comes as a bit of a shock to realize that the three individuals may not have formed a family at all. The initial evidence has been sketched above. The clincher for a late date is the dating of Genesis 24 and Genesis 27. Neither can be early; without them, we have no evidence for the family structure.

For modern faith it is important to realize how much at any time the understanding of the past derives from an understanding of present experience. That is true today; it was true in past days. Israel's understanding of its present experience, at the different times that this was felt, deepened its understanding of its past traditions. As Israel became increasingly conscious of its identity as one people, one single people, one way of expressing this was to bring its ancestors into the unity of one family.

Awareness of this is important for us moderns because it helps to focus our own consciousness on the extent to which our present experience influences our understanding of our God. A couple of examples may help to bring this home. Belief in an intervening God — a God who intervenes in human history to reward or punish, for example — was a belief widely shared in communities of the past. Outposts hold to it still. For many, it is a belief that has been abandoned under pressure of experience: it just does not happen. Belief in a judging God, rather than a loving God, was a belief widely shared in communities of the past. Outposts hold to it still. For many, it is a belief that has been abandoned largely because of the realization in present experience of its anthropomorphic character, rendering it irreverent in respect to God. Put briefly: God has better things to do than to judge and condemn human beings.

In order to have a thorough grasp of divine revelation, it is this process of moving from present experience to an altered understanding of the past that we need to absorb. It is this process that is meant by speaking of the Pentateuch as a record of Israel pondering its present rather than a record of Israel's remembering its past. It is an important contribution that the Pentateuch makes to our own understanding today.

It is also significant for our own understanding to realize the roles given Sarah and Rebekah here in relation to the unfolding of Israel's past. Had it not been for Sarah, Ishmael and Isaac might have been on a much more equal footing. Had it not been for Rebekah, the same could be said for Esau and Jacob. Fascinating.

JACOB, LEAH, AND RACHEL

The ancestral figure of Jacob

Two preliminary remarks are in order. What has to be said in the next couple of pages is complex and highly speculative — i.e., the evidence is there to say that the conclusions drawn here *might* be so, but the evidence is not of such demonstrative power as to say that it *must* be so. What is said below necessarily presumes the conviction expressed that Genesis 27 is a late text. The evidence for this should be read first (see just above). What is to be said here is substantially deprived of energy if this view of Genesis 27 is not accepted. Because of the unavoidable detail, readers who are willing to trust others for the examination of evidence and accept their conclusions are advised to move on a little further to the Jacob cycle proper.

As has just been noted, the splendidly told story of Genesis 27 is, in my judgment, probably a late text. For me, this was a surprising discovery and one that I made most unwillingly a few years ago. This judgment is based exclusively on an analysis of vocabulary. The language used is predominantly late; therefore the text itself is very probably late. This will be reiterated below. In the light of this, the portrayal in our present text of Jacob's flight to Haran, and the reasons for it, needs reevaluation. It cannot be taken for granted. The first task will be to examine the texts in Hosea 12; the second to return to the text of Genesis 25:19–26.

Hosea 12

Hosea 12 holds two texts about Jacob that at first inspection seem to confirm the Genesis account; on closer examination, they are surprisingly troubling (for comparative purposes, see de Pury, "Le cycle de Jacob"). The first of the two is Hosea 12:4–5 (Heb.; NRSV, 12:3–4). It has three elements: (1) what happened in the womb; (2) the striving with God/the angel; (3) the encounter at Bethel. A literal translation of the first element is "In the womb he took his brother by the heel." Even that is an accommodation to the needs of English; the Hebrew, most literally, is: "he heeled his brother." All that non-Hebraists need to know is that the text is neutral as to what exactly the action was and who precisely the brother was. The second element, the striving with God/the angel, is pleasantly straightforward. All that we need to notice is that no location is given; it could have happened anywhere between Syria and Canaan. A river is not mentioned, much less the forthcoming confrontation with Esau. The third element is the more troubling one; it is the encounter at Bethel. The text has it in third place; it is actually tied syntactically to what precedes (i.e., the wrestling); no name is given. "He met him at Bethel, and there he spoke with him (Heb.: with us)" (12:5; NRSV, 12:4). In Genesis, of course, after the wrestling, Jacob first meets Esau and then establishes himself at Succoth, then Shechem, and in due course moves on to Bethel, but does not settle there despite orders from God to do so. The speech given God at Bethel (Gen 35:9–15) is demonstrably late. What, then, is the tradition that Hosea evokes?

The second of the texts is Hosea 12:13 (Heb.; NRSV, 12:12). Two minor puzzles. First, did Jacob flee to or from Aram/Syria? The text does not say. Both are linguistically possible. Second, the duplication in the second half of the verse is unusual: he served for a wife... for a wife he guarded. Odd! Odd enough that the NRSV, NAB, and JB, for example, supply an object, "sheep," an object which the Hebrew does not have (and neither do the LXX or the Vulgate).

The upshot of all this is pretty simple and not much at all. There was a tradition about Jacob — probably in Aram (noted only in 12:13/12) — that contains three of the elements found in the Genesis traditions: struggle in the womb, struggle with God/angel, encounter at Bethel. Who his brother was is not mentioned. Who his father was is not mentioned. Where it all happened is not mentioned. Esau, Succoth, and Shechem are not mentioned. The connection of Aram with a wife is clear; the sequence (flight, wife) suggests that the direction is flight to Aram. Does this confirm the Genesis traditions? Yes, it does, but only to a limited extent. Much the same elements could be situated within a quite different narrative framework. The elements are confirmed; a framework is not provided.

Genesis 25:19–26

The text of Genesis 25:19–26 is important, especially as it is a rather messy little conglomerate, as inspection of any competent commentary will reveal. However, only a couple of issues need trouble us. First and simplest: the primary oracle (v. 23) promises what the narrative does not provide. According to the oracle, "the elder shall serve the younger." Whatever of the history of Israel and Edom at various times, in the following narrative the younger is literally scared to death and the elder is definitely dominant (Gen 32–33). That in itself is ground for wondering whether this oracle is in place as introduction to this narrative.

The second issue is somewhat more complex; it concerns v. 24. The NRSV has: "When her time to give birth was at hand, there were twins in her womb." The NRSV has, perhaps wisely, totally omitted the problem. The problem itself is simple enough; the Hebrew has the little particle *hinneh* introducing the presence of the twins. The problem can be approached lexicographically. Can the particle *hinneh*, usually translated as "behold" or equivalent, be rendered by "indeed" or something like that? If so, this verse is probably the only place in a multitude of occurrences where the little particle has this meaning. Alternatively, the problem can be approached theologically. When God's oracle has been explicit ("two nations are in your womb"), is it theologically sound to be surprised to find that, lo and behold, *hinneh* "there were twins in her womb"? Either way, it does not look very good for faith in God. How should the *hinneh* be handled? "Lo and behold, there were twins in her womb" or "Indeed there were twins in her womb"? In either case, the *hinneh* seems to cast some doubt on God's oracle. Small wonder the NRSV did not translate it.

Put in slightly more technical terms: Does the text give us two answers to prayer: Isaac prayed and was heard; she inquired of the LORD and was given an oracle? Does the text give us two affirmations about her womb: two nations in your womb; twins in her womb? Certainly, two sons are born, but even the naming of one is odd. The first is red and hairy, preparing the way for one of two names: Edom (red) or Seir (hairy); instead, "they named him Esau." According to Westermann, "if vv. 19–28 are read without vv. 22–23, and this latter understood as an originally independent unit inserted here, then both are clearer and more comprehensible.... Only at the birth does it transpire that there are twins. It becomes clear yet again that vv. 22f. have been inserted later" (*Genesis 12–36*, 412–13).

The bluntest outcome of these observations is simply: the biblical text indicates that the present form of the Jacob traditions found in the Genesis text is not necessarily the only form that selections of those traditions may have taken in the past.

The Jacob cycle

Two issues were emerging at the end of the discussion of the Abraham traditions. First was the question of dating, sharpened by the realization that one collection of these traditions was focused around Gerar/Beersheba, with another at Mamre/Hebron. Second was the question whether traditions of three originally independent ancestors had been unified as members of one family — perhaps further unified as family without admixture of foreign blood — at a relatively late stage. Close study of the Jacob cycle is therefore essential.

We begin with the recognition that there is a clear Jacob cycle. It is radically different from the Abraham cycle with which we began this section on the ancestors. It demands of its users an openness to its past, and yet that past can only be reached by speculation for which there is not enough evidence to ground much in the way of certainty. The best we can hope to do here is to make an inventory of the elements involved, point to some of the possibilities indicated, and make sense of the process as best we can. We will not delve speculatively into the past, but will look closely at the present text. As a consequence, we will deal with an assessment of what is there and not of what might have been but that we do not have.

For a beginning to the present text of the cycle, there is no option but Genesis 25:19–26. Its opening couple of verses may present their problems. Its primary divine oracle proclaims the precise opposite of chapters 27 and 32–33 of the narrative (the chapters in the cycle in which both brothers feature): the elder does not serve the younger (25:23) but, despite the blessing, the younger flees for his life (chap. 27) and fears for his life (chaps. 32–33). The birth experience ("gripping Esau's heel," 25:26) prepares in its own way for chapter 27. Jacob's purchase of Esau's birthright (25:29–34) provides some form of legal justification for what is to come (see 27:36). As an introduction to the narrative to come, the passage may be unsatisfactory, but in the present text there is nothing else.

Jacob's journey from Beer-sheba to Haran is quickly covered; two sentences are enough (28:10 and 29:1). In between is the first Bethel episode. The complications of Genesis 28 are well known; the treatment in Genesis 35 is equally well known (see *Rethinking the Pentateuch*, 38–40). The primary problem of both chapters is that fundamentally Bethel and Jacob have next to nothing to do with each other. Bethel was "the king's sanctuary...a temple of the kingdom" (Amos 7:13), of importance therefore in the northern kingdom of Israel. It was scarcely important in the life of Jacob. In Genesis 28, he overnighted there; in Genesis 35, he was ordered by God to "settle there" (35:1). According to the text, he went there, built an altar there, experienced a theophany there, erected and sanctified a pillar there, and journeyed on (35:16). Settle there he did not.

Genesis 28, inserted or not, begins with a dream experience followed by a divine speech. *yhwh*'s self-presentation as "the God of Abraham your father and the God of Isaac" reflects a unified understanding of the ancestors as one family. The problematic relationship to Bethel is skirted by the promise to bring Jacob back "to this land" (28:15) — not to this place. It is in the solemnizing of this theophany — with a pillar erected, oil poured, and the name Bethel established — that Jacob balances God's promise with his own vow, naming as a condition "that I come again to my father's house" (28:21). Literally, of course, he does not.

Given the geographical position of Bethel, it is a natural stop on the outward journey from Beer-sheba to Haran. In any move south from Shechem, it lies along the route. For all that, the two episodes at Bethel have no impact on the narrative traditions. Both theophanies clearly assume a unified family portrayal of the three ancestors. An earlier report of Jacob's dream experience at "a certain place" (28:11–12) is certainly possible within an early narrative; its contribution to such a narrative is open to question. The complexity involved in holding the Bethel material within the narrative of the Jacob traditions can be seen in Noth's discussion (*Pentateuchal Traditions,* 79–87).

After the Bethel episode, the narrative brings Jacob to "the land of the people of the east" (29:1; cf. 28:10, "toward Haran"), his meeting with Rachel, and reception into Laban's house. One verse, 29:10, seems overly full, identifying Rachel as daughter of Rebekah's brother, Laban. Three times the one verse has the phrase "his mother's brother Laban," used first of Rachel, then of the sheep, and finally of the flock. We will return to this issue shortly.

With Laban, there follows the well-known motif of Jacob's serving twice seven years for his wives, Leah and Rachel. It is truly the stuff of legend. Following that is the account of the birth and naming of Jacob's eleven sons — Benjamin is left until later. The sons are born to four wives: Leah and Rachel, daughters of Laban; Zilpah and Bilhah, maids of the daughters. The family bloodline cannot have been an issue at this point, with no specifics given for Zilpah and Bilhah. What is truly surprising in this passage is that the names of the sons are given by Leah and Rachel alone and reflect the emotional states and domestic issues of these two women — the primary wives only.

Without detailing possible duplications, the names and reasons given are:

Reuben: *Surely now my husband will love me*

Simeon: *Because the* LORD *has heard that I am hated*

Levi: *This time my husband will be joined to me*

Judah: *I will praise the* LORD

Dan: *God has judged me*

Naphtali: *With mighty wrestlings I have wrestled with my sister*

Gad: *And Leah said, "Good fortune!"*

Asher: *Happy am I! For the women will call me happy*

Issachar: *God has given me my hire because I gave my maid to my husband*

Zebulun: *Now my husband will honor me*

Joseph: *May the* LORD *add to me another son*

With wives and children acquired, Jacob needs to acquire wealth to support them. Much of what follows is a storyteller's playground. At the start, Jacob asks to be sent home (30:25–26); at the end, Jacob escapes while Laban is away (31:19–20). It is not so much a question of competing traditions within the text as of competing options, with the principal option being who was to be portrayed as the primary agent of skullduggery. Was it Laban culling his flock and constantly changing Jacob's wages (30:35–36; 31:7, 41)? Or was it Jacob, with a little bit of help from God, stealing stock from Laban by manipulative breeding (30:37–43; 31:10–12)? Or were both practices involved?

However the story was told, the time for departure arrives. After "these twenty years" (31:38, 41) — twice seven years, four wives, and twelve children, as well as livestock — Jacob is to go to the land of his ancestors and to his kindred, to the land of his birth, "to his father, Isaac, in the land of Canaan" (31:18). He went to the land of Canaan; he did not go to his father Isaac or to his father's house. Jacob leaves while Laban is absent, leading to the narrative of pursuit and boundary negotiations (31:52), boundary negotiations that were hardly necessary if Jacob were heading for Beer-sheba in the far south. Finally they part. Laban is left behind; Esau remains ahead.

The prospect of the encounter with Esau fills Jacob with fear: "I am afraid of him; he may come and kill us all" (32:12, Heb.: NRSV, 32:11). We are not told whether Esau is still nursing a twenty-year-old grudge; the text gives no indication of Esau's move to Seir or how he became powerful and wealthy. Jacob's behavior hardly accords with the divine oracle, in which the elder shall serve the younger (25:23). The famous wrestling-with-God episode precedes the meeting with Esau. At one level, the reconciliation between the two is complete: "Esau ran to meet him, and embraced him, and fell on his neck and kissed him, and they wept" (33:4). At another level, measured mistrust seems to be in place, with Jacob true to form and lying: "until I come to my lord in Seir . . . but Jacob journeyed to Succoth, and built himself a house, and made booths for his cattle" (33:12–17). Jacob did not come to Seir, not then and not later.

Jacob settles in Succoth, east of the Jordan; then he moves to Shechem, west of the Jordan. Here, in my judgment, the Jacob cycle ends. The Dinah episode is in Genesis 34; Genesis 35 has the order to settle in Bethel, which Jacob visits and where he does not settle but journeys further southward; Genesis 36 is concerned with Esau's descendants.

Some general observations are in order. Above all, this cycle differs in at least three noteworthy ways from the Abraham traditions. First and foremost, while the Abraham traditions are fragmentary and with competing elements, this Jacob cycle is continuous and coherent. The diversity is deep; the coherence is there. As Noth comments, "These [Jacob-Esau and Jacob-Laban legendary stories (sagas)] are now artistically arranged into a massive coherent narrative, the 'Jacob-Esau-Laban saga cycle' " (*Pentateuchal Traditions*, 88). Second, there are passages of considerable detail in the Jacob cycle. Third, there is almost total domesticity in the Jacob cycle; this is intra-family stuff, not the stuff of migratory tradition.

Some subsidiary issues need to be kept in mind:

1. There is no account of Jacob's return to Beer-sheba.

2. There is no account of Rebekah's death.

3. There is no account of Esau's move and wealth.

4. There is no call from God.

5. There is no concern over blood lines and purity, given the four wives of Jacob.

All in all, the differences between this Jacob cycle and the preceding Abraham cycle and the material available about Isaac are remarkable. The Jacob cycle would fit quite comfortably into the period after 722, when the need was felt to integrate Jacob into the Abraham family. Some of the northern elite had come south; the unity of northern and southern peoples was experienced with renewed urgency; the need for this unity to be reflected in the ancestral traditions was clear. We can begin with this as a working hypothesis, aware of its speculative character.

Exploration of the hypothesis involves investigation at three levels: earlier, middle, and later. The main points can be highlighted; coverage of the details cannot be comprehensive here. At the earlier level, the question is what traces can be found of the earliest Jacob traditions. At the later level, it would seem that certain editorial adjustments were made at a relatively late stage to an already existing text. At the middle level, the task to be undertaken is the identification of this already existing text.

Where the earlier level is concerned, despite the best efforts of scholarship, nothing substantial concerning Jacob can be identified unambiguously as reflecting genuinely ancestral tradition. While the impression may be widespread — and right — that Jacob was the Shechem-based originating figure for the tribes of the northern kingdom, hard evidence sustaining this is not to hand.

Both the Hosea and Deuteronomy material can be interpreted as favorable to an ancestral understanding regarding Jacob. Unfortunately, neither is unambiguous. The sustained Genesis text is clearly portrayed as ancestral. Unfortunately, it cannot be accepted as such. While Jacob is portrayed leaving Isaac at Beer-sheba with the intention of returning there, he does not. While Jacob is instructed to settle at Bethel, he does not. From Genesis 27 to 33, the narrative is continuous, coherent, and straightforward. Leaving aside the Bethel episodes that are both, each in its own way, extraneous to or disconnected from the narrative, it enters into considerable detail; it is wholly domestic. It lacks the fractures and contrasts visible in the Abraham traditions and expected of traditions enduring from a distant past. It is not a story of transition from a place of origin (Beer-sheba) to a new location (Shechem). Overtly at least, it is portrayed as a story of departure from one location (Beer-sheba) with the intention of returning to the same location. It is primarily this disjunction between the overt intention and the actual implementation that most troubles the Genesis narrative.

Where a later level is concerned, the primary driving force is found in the late chapters, Genesis 24 and 27. If Rofé is correct, then Genesis 24 belongs most probably in the fifth century; if Campbell and O'Brien are correct, then Genesis 27 is unlikely to be earlier than the seventh century. Particularly relevant in this context is where the concern with purity of descent is found and where it is absent. It is found in Genesis 24. It is absent from the story of Jacob's wives. Leah and Rachel are specified as daughters of Laban; no such specification is mentioned for their maids, Zilpah and Bilhah. Where insistence on descent through Rebekah is found, the overly full verses give the impression of editorial activity (see Gen 25:20, "Rebekah, daughter of Bethuel the Aramean of Paddan-aram, sister of Laban the Aramean": 28:5, "to Laban son of Bethuel the Aramean, the brother of Rebekah, Jacob's and Esau's mother"; 29:10, "the daughter of his mother's brother Laban, and the sheep of his mother's brother Laban, . . . the flock of his mother's brother Laban"). If the impression of editorial activity (to bring the text into line with Gen 24) is correct, then a previous text already existed, somewhere in the middle.

Where the middle level is concerned, the possibility of Rebekah as wife to Jacob has to be entertained, without the emphasis on descent through her, at least at that level of the text. An alternative possibility is simply that Jacob's wife was unnamed in the text. The latter can be preferred; the occurrences of Rebekah's name in the few relevant texts are able to be understood as apposition or addition, in either case inserted later. For example: 25:21, Isaac prayed to the LORD for his wife (no apposition) . . . his wife (apposition: Rebekah) conceived; 29:12, "that he was her father's kinsman" (potential addition: "and that he was Rebekah's son"). A text with patrilineal descent through Jacob would probably be relatively early in the seventh century; a text with matrilineal descent, emphasizing the place of Rebekah, would probably be situated in the fifth century.

Motivation is needed for Jacob's departure. It can be provided by Genesis 27. Before that, it can be provided without Genesis 27 (noting instead Esau's awareness of Isaac's hostility to Canaanite marriages [see Gen 28:6–9]). Ultimately, it would appear that there was a Jacob cycle probably early in the seventh century (post 722), there may have been traditions before that but we do not have them, and there certainly was editorial activity later, which we do have. The working hypothesis, while still a hypothesis, provides a worthwhile base for further reflection.

Much is left undiscussed, above all the Bethel episodes (Gen 28:10–22 and 35:1–15) that are, however, not integral to the narrative (if desired, see *Rethinking the Pentateuch,* 38–40). Only in these is the promise of the land repeated. So too the attribution of 33:19–20 (for Noth, Elohist), which has the narrative's only account of the purchase of land, meager as it may be. The Dinah story is left alone (Gen 34) and the Esau traditions (Gen 36; note the peaceful parting within the land of Canaan of two wealthy pastoralists, Esau and Jacob, vv. 6–8). A tight focus on the ancestral character of the traditions of the Jacob cycle precludes our venturing into these areas here.

~ MODERN FAITH ~

For many the claim that the ancestral unity of Abraham, Isaac, and Jacob may be a construct of the seventh century is troubling. That this should be so is primarily the fault of an overemphasis on the "salvation history" and historiographic aspect of these early chapters. The importance of symbolic and theological thought has to be taken into account. In American tradition, for example, the names of figures like Jefferson, Lincoln, and Washington are highly significant. Historical issues are largely secondary; what often matters more is the symbolic value attached to such legendary figures. It is important, of course, to bear in mind that Jefferson, Lincoln, and Washington were never regarded as ancestral figures — legendary they certainly are. Real, of course; much of the stuff of legend is real. The boundaries of history and the real may overlap; the overlap need not be large.

In ancient Israel, in a somewhat similar way, the symbolic and theological values attached to such figures was of overwhelming importance. While descendants of Abraham and descendants of Isaac are hardly used to designate the people of Israel, and descendants of Jacob is used less than half a dozen times, descendants of Israel is commonly used (almost six hundred occurrences). Nevertheless, the ancestral traditions claimed for Abraham and Isaac are undisputed. The need to bring Jacob/Israel into this circle is theologically and symbolically of major importance. Where significant legendary figures are concerned in any culture, symbolic values take precedence over historical issues in almost all circumstances. On the legendary value of figures such as Abraham or Jacob, see below in the summary concluding this chapter.

There is a parallel with the early stories of Genesis, which reflect how human life is now rather than presenting the history of how it was then. In a similar way, rather than being a historical record from the past these ancestral stories were essential to an understanding of how it is now — in the Israel of the storytellers' own time.

A highly important consideration that surfaces here is the question where the revelation of God is to be located. One senior systematic theologian said to me once that the ultimate source of the revelation of God was to be found in the Older Testament prophets. It was a pity that he did not know the Older Testament prophets well enough to know that this was certainly not the case. The question recurs: Where do we best locate what we term the revelation of God? Almost certainly not in *one* area only. But the question remains: Where?

Revelation is one of those vast and complex areas that ought give full play to the life-force of theologians. Revelation can hardly be corralled into articles in encyclopedias or multiple nods in catechisms. "Through an utterly free decision, God has revealed himself and given himself to man" (*Catechism of the Catholic Church*, #50 [1994]); it is hardly necessary to add: in many and varied ways. Through scripture, of course; through tradition, naturally; through daily experience, not to be overlooked. "God's revelation takes place in history and the history of God with man is both the object and the means of his revelation" (*Sacramentum Mundi*, vol. 5 [1970]). The history of God with us did not stop with the death of the last apostle.

Our day-to-day experience, therefore, is one of the factors contributing to shaping our belief in God and therefore revealing to us something of the nature of our God. We can see this at work in much of our everyday activity.

One fundamental aspect lying behind many of the shifts noted is the change from imaging God as one who judges to imaging God as one who loves. As belief and sensitivity change, the understanding of God may change, and consequently what is read from scripture or emphasized from a scripture reading changes too. A simple example emphasizes this: Did God destroy Israel, justly punishing its behavior, or did Israel destroy itself, prey to the inevitable consequences of its behavior?

Few Christians today would spend their meditative time with the image of the Last Judgment and the separation of sheep from goats in Matthew 25, even when aware that it is illustrative of such good motives as care for the poor. Fewer today give their time to pondering passages about the "weeping and gnashing of teeth" (Matt 22:13) or the fearful image of the worm that never dies and the fire that is never quenched (Mark 9:48). "Bona Mors" (Good Death) societies have faded from the scene; novena patterns such as the Nine First Fridays (guaranteeing a merciful judgment) are moving into the past. Those who read now from the Older Testament tend to favor Second and Third Isaiah's promises and benign images of the future rather than other more gruesome passages. Tradition has it that prayer measures belief; *lex orandi, lex credendi*. The Roman Catholic Church, in a major Sunday liturgical reading, omits v. 7 from God's self-description in Exodus 34. The Almighty is censored in the light of modern belief! Not surprisingly, the Roman Catholic breviary omits the last three verses of Psalm 137.

This behavior pattern (the role of present experience in self-understanding and in the understanding of the past) is extremely important. We need to be fully aware of the pattern as a practice today. Experience of life may affect our understanding of God. As a result, today, how we understand God and relate to God affects what we read in scripture. In ancient Israel, experience of life affected their understanding of God. As a result, in those distant days, how they understood God and related to God affected what they read in scripture, of course, but also sometimes what they *wrote* in scripture.

Our present experience leads us to a fuller understanding of ourselves, our traditions, and our God; *the ancients' experience* led them to a fuller understanding of themselves, their traditions, and their God. For us, this reality controls our reading of scripture; for some in Israel, it also controlled their writing of scripture, from major creations to minor revisions. This experience leading ultimately to the understanding of God is one of the sources where we rightly locate revelation.

Our recognition of a process of revelation happening in ourselves allows us to recognize the process of revelation happening for others in the past. Those who had known themselves as belonging within a particular community claiming allegiance to Abraham or Isaac or claiming allegiance to Jacob came to recognize themselves as belonging to a wider community that rightly claimed allegiance to all three. The merging of two communities led to a merging of ancestors. The merging of ancestors needed to be reflected in the scriptures of the community.

When the traditions of an ancestor are being assembled, some merging and blending have to occur. So the traditions of Abraham and Gerar/Beersheba are blended with the traditions of Abraham and Mamre/Hebron. Equally, as people from the northern kingdom (claiming as ancestors Jacob/Israel and Joseph) recognize themselves as worshipers of the same one God as people from the southern kingdom (Judah), traditions of Abraham and Isaac are blended with traditions of Jacob. Experience expands the understanding of God; tradition goes along with the expansion. More puzzling for interpreters of the text is what it means that Genesis associates Isaac with the southern region of Beer-sheba while, on the other hand, eighth-century Amos refers to "the high places of Isaac" (7:9) and "the house of Isaac" (7:16) in relation to the northern kingdom.

As we know well, the Bible reflects developing as well as different understandings of God. Differences or developments in culture or social existence affect these understandings of God. For some among us, they may sometimes affect what we read. For some in ancient Israel, they may have sometimes affected what they wrote.

JOSEPH

Storm clouds have been gathering around the Joseph story for a while, both as regards its date and its meaning. On the matter of its date, we may sample a few specialists: Donald Redford, mid-seventh to mid-fifth centuries; Alberto Soggin, late but not post-Maccabean; Konrad Schmid, after 720 at the earliest but not as late as post-priestly; even Hermann Gunkel, for whom its very late form accounts for the lack of historical information (for bibliographical references, see *Rethinking the Pentateuch,* 61, n. 71); add to these Albert de Pury, extremely late ("Le cycle de Jacob," 81–83). Two of the late stories in Genesis are on the longer side: Genesis 27 with forty-six verses and Genesis 24 with sixty-seven verses. While length need not be indicative of age, with at least nine chapters the Joseph story's place in the chronology of Israel's literature has to be subject to reflection. Along with that, of course, its place in Israel's theology, binding the ancestral traditions to the traditions of exodus is equally subject to reflection.

The Joseph story specializes in dreams. Dreams of his ascendancy over his family have young Joseph murderously hated by his brothers. Disposed of by them, he ends up in Egypt. Imprisoned on a charge of attempted rape, his skill with dreams brings him to Pharaoh's notice. Success in interpreting Pharaoh's dreams — a success that is assumed without waiting for verification (see Gen 41:25–40) — brings him to the summit of political power in Egypt. With control of the Egyptian food supply, he has control of his brothers when they come to Egypt in need of grain. Recognizing in confrontation with Judah that the revenge he is taking on his brothers is causing much the same pain to Jacob, his father, as their brutality to him did in the first place, Joseph breaks down and is reconciled with his brothers. As part of the reconciliation, the aged Jacob and his family are established in Egypt. (For more detail, see *Sources of the Pentateuch,* esp. 223–37.)

Three stages can be discussed in relation to this text. In the last stage, Joseph is not only controller of the food supply (chap. 41) but the text extends his powers to include control of money, flocks, land, and even the Egyptians themselves (chap. 47). Such supreme power is perhaps imaginable in an absolute dictatorship; from what we know of ancient Egypt, it is unthinkable there. If 47:13–29 is regarded as a later addition to the story, an earlier stage would portray Joseph as second-in-command to Pharaoh (see Gen 41:37–45), with full control of Egypt's grain supply. This second stage is basically the present biblical text, without 47:13–29. A first stage, earlier than this, can be imagined as a hypothesis; its text would have to be matter for speculation. At such a stage, Joseph might be credibly envisaged being revealed as a competent administrator, achieving a high place in the administration of the Egyptian grain supply, and ultimately being brought into reconciliation with his family — without necessarily being brought into close contact with Pharaoh, the supreme leader of the great nation of Egypt.

Genesis 35 last had Jacob journeying south to what might be termed an undisclosed location, "beyond the tower of Eder" (35:21), about which we know nothing. The story of Abraham in Egypt (Gen 12:10–20) introduced the motif of famine causing a move to Egypt in search of food. Against this background, it is easy to understand how a Joseph story would have been used to bring ancestral Israel into Egypt, available for the potentially older exodus traditions.

Joseph's two sons, Ephraim and Manasseh, bear the names of the two major tribes constituting the northern kingdom of Israel. The reconciliation is effected in confrontation with Judah, eponymous ancestor of the principal tribe of the southern kingdom. Small wonder, then, that the suggestion is made that some form of the Joseph story might have had a role to play after the northern kingdom of Israel's incorporation into the Assyrian empire in 722, when some of the northern elite, from the Joseph tribes, migrated south and may well have needed reconciliation within the kingdom of Judah.

Composition of some form of the Joseph story could well go back to around this time, i.e., early seventh century. The context would be much the same as for the Jacob cycle, already discussed. It is unlikely that any form of the story would have been earlier. It is clear that what may have begun as a story focused on reconciliation, set on the stage of Egypt, was available for easy association back to a narrative focused on family migration, leading to national beginnings, and forward to the exodus traditions.

The more any dates discussed for the Joseph story creep into exilic and post-exilic periods, the more they approach the era of what we may call "diaspora literature." By the term "diaspora literature" is meant texts that deal with figures such as Daniel, Esther, Judith, and possibly Joseph. In such literature, an Israelite achieves great power and eminence in a foreign country. The stories mentioned involve two men and two women. The men, Daniel and Joseph, achieve eminence through their interpretation of dreams; the women, Esther and Judith, achieve eminence through their beauty. Where Daniel is concerned: "King Nebuchadnezzar fell on his face, worshiped Daniel.... Then the king promoted Daniel...and made him ruler over the whole province of Babylon and chief prefect over all the wise men of Babylon" (Dan 2:46, 48). In the Hebrew text of the book of Esther: "the king [Ahasuerus, who ruled over 127 provinces from India to Ethiopia, Esth 1:1] loved Esther more than all the other women...so that he set the royal crown on her head and made her queen" (Esth 2:17). By the end of the book, her uncle Mordechai was second in the realm, "next in rank to King Ahasuerus" (Esth 10:3). In the deutero-canonical book of Judith, Holofernes, chief general to King Nebuchadnezzar, is portrayed saying: "If you do as you have said, your God shall be my God, and you shall live in the palace of King Nebuchadnezzar and be renowned throughout the whole world" (Jdt 11:23). In due course, ravished by her beauty and his passion aroused, Holofernes foolishly got dead drunk (Jdt 13:2) so Judith "struck his neck twice with all her might, and cut off his head" (Jdt 13:8), so the poor chap was both drunk and dead — and, of course, Judith had saved Israel.

The Joseph story is little different. The language of the story in Genesis may be more restrained, but thematically the distance is not great; the role of God is clear. Joseph, a foreigner, an Israelite, jailed for allegedly attempting the rape of a royal official's wife, becomes the equivalent of vice-pharaoh over all Egypt. Says Pharaoh: "Only with regard to the throne will I be greater than you.... See I have set you over all the land of Egypt.... I am Pharaoh, and without your consent no one shall lift up hand or foot in all the land of Egypt" (Gen 41:40–41, 44). Readers are entitled to a dose of skepticism.

Of course, for the God, then or now, believed to sustain all the vastness of the universe, such involvement in human affairs would have to be considered a mere trifle. In the dispersion and depression of the Diaspora, whether in the time of the Exile or after it, such literature is believed to have found an audience. Hope could be engendered when it seemed wholly out of human reach. The question interpreters are obliged to ask is not whether God is considered capable of such achievements. Those who believe in God surely answer in the affirmative. The question to be asked, however, is whether such believers experience God becoming involved in human affairs in this way. At stake is the nature of the literature. Does it reflect the reality of large-scale famine and migration? Does it reflect the unreality of despair?

An alternative understanding poses the question of whether the Joseph story and the sojourn in Egypt are in some way integrating the experience of exile into the story of Israel? In such a view, composition of the Joseph story around the time of Israel's exile would make good sense, with the "fiddling" of 47:13–29 as probably post-exilic. Such a view is possible, whether proposed as the originating impulse for the composition of the story or as a further setting for its telling. It can never be more than a speculative possibility.

It is not my intention here to go into the technical details of the Genesis–Exodus discussion. Suffice it to say that the verses are there that show the Joseph story's use as bridge to locate the family of Israel in the land of Egypt. This has long been recognized in scholarship as a possibility. (The precise attribution of specific verses to pre-priestly,

priestly, and post-priestly origins is debated; see, for example, the contributions of Schmid and Gertz in *Farewell to the Yahwist?*) What needs to be done here is to reflect on the implications of this recognition and the late date given to the bridging role for the understanding of scripture in modern faith.

◆ ◆ ◆

Excursus:
Embracing Legend, Valuing the Legendary

The late linking of Genesis with Exodus enhances the likelihood of Exodus 1–2 being seen as legend (cf. *Rethinking the Pentateuch*, 69–71).

It is an age-old human longing, and understandable enough, to get our human hands on tangible evidence for the existence or action of God. It is a longing that usually needs to be respectfully resisted. Such is the case for aspects of Israel's foundational experience of God. We have no unchallengeable information about the origin of Moses. Scholars have no unchallengeable information about the location of either Mount Sinai or Mount Horeb or whether they are one and the same (J. L. McKenzie, a generation ago: "while the two names are the scene of the same events, it is not certain that the different sources localized the event in the same place" [*Dictionary*, 369] — perhaps one mountain and two locations). Tradition may be sure enough; scholars sometimes need to be cautious. Moses, Sinai, and Horeb are all hugely significant in the story of Israel; it is significant and right that we have no hard-and-fast information about the origin of one and the location of the other two.

As with most nations, ancient Israel had its appropriate share of fabled figures. In the almost mythical distant past, there were Enoch and Noah. "Enoch walked with God; then he was no more, because God took him" (Gen 5:24; cf. Sir 44:16; 49:16). Noah too walked with God (Gen 6:9); Noah alone was righteous before God in his generation (Gen 7:1; cf. Sir 44:17–18). In the past of legend, there was Job, from the land of Uz, "blameless and upright" (Job 1:1); for both Noah and Job, see Ezekiel 14:14–20 (early figures in a late text). In historical time, there was Elijah, who "ascended in a whirlwind into heaven" (2 Kgs 2:11; cf. Sir 48:1–11). Somewhere between legend and history, there was Moses: son of two pairs of parents (Exod 2:1 and Exod 6:20), with two sets of siblings (Exod 2:4 and Exod 6:20), with two women as wives (Zipporah, Exod 2:21; and the Cushite, Num 12:1), with two men and three names as fathers-in-law (Jethro, Reuel, and Hobab), and buried by an anonymous figure, presumably God, in an unmarked grave (Deut 34:6). Enoch and Noah walked with God; upstaging them both, Moses is portrayed as having talked with God (Exod 34:29; Sir 45:5). Moses is par excellence the man of God and man of mystery.

These facts — and the statistics for verses referring to Moses (Exod, Lev, Num: some 557; Deut–Josh: 86; Judg–2 Chr: 61 [i.e., overwhelmingly late]) — are well-known and have been for a long time. It is therefore worth stating bluntly that I do not know of any serious argument put forward expressing doubt about the reality of Moses. Historical details we may not have; reality we accept.

Neither the Exodus 2 nor the Exodus 6 traditions inspire confidence as historically sound. Starting with Exodus 2, the story is well-known. Two nameless Levites marry; she conceives and bears a fine baby son. One would assume that the son was their firstborn. Wisely it is not said in the text, because a couple of verses later there is an older sister on the scene. The woman hid her son for three months (Exod 2:3). The hiding of the son has, as background, two earlier scenes. In the first, the oppressed Israelites became "more numerous and more powerful" than the Egyptians, so that "the Egyptians came to dread the Israelites" (Exod 1:9, 12). To call such a situation "unlikely" is to be unquestionably moderate, if not unduly so. In the next scene, two women are alone portrayed filling the role of midwives to the Hebrew women, these same Hebrews who were more numerous than the Egyptians. It is lovely legend; to call such a situation "unbelievable" is to understate matters mildly. All of this casts doubt on the story of Moses' early months. Added to this is the similarity of the motif of placing the infant Moses in a basket among the reeds by the Nile with the story of Sargon of Akkad (c. 2300, but a mid-seventh-century Assyrian text; for more, see Propp, *Exodus 1–18*, 155–59). Propp's judgment may stand for many: "The historical Moses is most unlikely to have endured so traumatic an infancy" (*Exodus 1–18*, 155).

The alternative information is given in Exodus 6:14–25. The passage is widely recognized as a secondary insertion in the priestly text (see Durham, Noth, Propp [esp. *Exodus 1–18*, 267–69]). The tradition's concern is less with Moses than with Aaron (his elder brother by some three years according to Exod 7:7). To some degree, harmonization is possible and has been tried; it remains harmonization and the text itself does not attempt it. Historical evidence this is not.

As with Elijah, the exemplar figure of the prophet, the origins of Moses are unknown to us and this is probably how they should be. The same is true for detailed knowledge of Moses' end. The text is within Deuteronomy 34:1–8. It specifies that Moses' death was "according to the mouth of *yhwh*" (*al pi yhwh*, v. 5), which can be understood as word or command or will. It is unclear whether this refers to the fact of his death or to his having died outside the land. It remains unclear and, in its own way, shocking. P. D. Miller expresses this shock:

> All these facts — the frequent references to his death coupled with the equally numerous indications of his denied access to the land, the obvious lack of fairness in Moses' being deprived of that opportunity toward which his whole life had been set by God, and the varying and indeed conflicting reasons put forth to give justice to the reality — seem to suggest an inability finally to account adequately for what has happened. . . . (*Deuteronomy*, 242–43)

Who buried Moses? Literally, the text says: "He buried him" (Deut 34:6). For Nelson, "*Yahweh* buried him" (*Deuteronomy*, 396); so too Mayes, "it is doubtless intended that the subject of the verb is Yahweh" (*Deuteronomy*, 413). Not so von Rad, for whom it was not *yhwh* from the preceding sentence; it is more natural that one of Moses' companions buried him, for "Moses is not likely to have climbed the mountain without companions" (*Deuteronomy*, 210). Fancy von Rad favoring the event over the text; in the text, no companions are mentioned and the location of the grave is unknown (Deut 34:1, 6). Unclarity remains, as it should. Moses died outside Canaan; beyond that, the details of his end are unknown to us. His burial place is unknown. This is probably how it should be.

~MODERN FAITH~

When exploring modern faith in relation to biblical text, a couple of principles come into play. One was expressed in *Rethinking the Pentateuch*, as we have already seen: there is "a shift from the Pentateuch as a record of Israel's *remembering its past* to the Pentateuch as a record of *Israel's pondering its present"* (9). This applies to much of the Pentateuch and elsewhere too in the Older Testament. The second principle impacts solidly on the understanding of revelation as coming exclusively *from above and from the past,* an understanding that still influences many. As we ponder our lives and remember our past, in all the rich variety it involves (family, schooling, religion, culture), we come to a deeper understanding of ourselves and our world and a correspondingly deeper insight into our understanding of our God. That is surely an aspect of revelation, not the whole but an aspect — coming also *from below and from the present.* These two thoughts, already adumbrated, will bear repeating from time to time in the unfolding of this book.

Without any doubt, passion can blind us. History is full of examples. Sexual passion may predominate; it is certainly not alone. Passion for prestige, power, money is seldom far away. Biblical scholarship has for some centuries been blinded by passion, a passion for history, a preoccupation with history. In the Older Testament, Wellhausen's famous study, setting up the sequence of pentateuchal sources for a century or so, is entitled *Prolegomena to the History of Ancient Israel.* In the Newer Testament, the quest and new quest for the historical Jesus has occupied volumes. Until recently, in biblical scholarship the concept of symbol was shunned; it held overtones of the Middle Ages and medieval thinking. Modern faith may have to think again. Modern understanding has moved beyond its past.

History does not ignore the logic of chronology, and stories of a people's ancestors usually precede stories of the people's liberation (i.e., Genesis before Exodus). Symbolism does not ignore psyche; being free may take priority over being one (i.e., Exodus before Genesis). Symbolism and history can coexist. The language of competition is being used by some today; the language of complementarity may be more appropriate.

Until recently, concordances kept proper names to the back of the book; computer programs, thank God, do not. Nevertheless, it was hardly news to biblical scholars to find that, as an independent ancestral figure, Abraham only rated a couple of mentions outside Genesis, and these were late; Isaac much the same but earlier, and Jacob rather more, especially as name of the people. The exodus, on the other hand, bulks large. In 1 Samuel 12, even though a late and idiosyncratic chapter, the recital of the LORD's saving deeds begins "When Jacob went into Egypt...[and the LORD] brought forth your ancestors out of Egypt, and settled them in this place" (12:8). In Hosea 12, immediately after Jacob and Aram there is the exodus reference "By a prophet the LORD brought Israel up from Egypt, and by a prophet he was guarded" (Hos 12:14, Heb.; NRSV, 12:13).

Well before our present Genesis and Exodus texts were being composed, prophets were at work in eighth-century Israel. As we have seen, Isaac rates a couple of mentions in Amos ("the high places of Isaac shall be made desolate," 7:9; "do not preach against the house of Isaac," 7:16). Jacob gets what we might call a couple of moments in Hosea 12. The theme of exodus is common in both books; for example: from Amos, "the whole family that I brought up out of the land of Egypt" (3:1), "Did I not bring Israel up from the land of Egypt" (9:7); from Hosea, "as at the time when she came out of the land of Egypt" (2:15), "out of Egypt I called my son" (11:1), "I am the LORD your God from the land of Egypt" (12:10 [Heb.; NRSV, 12:9]), "I have been the LORD your God ever since the land of Egypt" (13:4).

What biblical scholars have always known is that traditions can flourish before texts are composed. This is surely the case for both the ancestral traditions and the exodus traditions. What biblical scholars are less eager to avow is that texts can be composed for other purposes than the equivalent of history. The exodus texts celebrate the power of Israel's God and the freedom of Israel. The ancestral texts celebrate the commitment of the ancestor's God and, in a first instance, the ancestor's acquisition of rights in a new country, in a second instance, the unity to be found among the descendants of the ancestors. As we noted earlier, the grandiose claims among the ancestral texts are largely restricted to Genesis 15 (a text that arouses the suspicions of many a critical reader) and Genesis 17 (a text that manifests a special breed of priestly concern).

The ancestral texts are not to be lumped together as though differing expressions of one history, with much the same historical concern. While the Abraham texts have several points of focus, primary is arrival in a new land and establishment there (a burial ground in

Mamre/Hebron; wells in the Beer-sheba region). The Jacob texts look to the issue of unity; the ancestors are of one family. The Joseph texts are different again; there the issue of reconciliation is to the fore. It would be unseemly to lump these so different texts into the one catchall of ancestral history.

There is a clear danger to be avoided: the harmonization of ancestral and exodus traditions into one record in some form of the historical sequence of the experience of a saving God. It is arguable as to whether the biblical text itself has fallen victim to this. The texts are there: Genesis 50:14, 22–23; Exodus 1:6–8, etc. The issue is interpretation. Should one assess twentieth-century anatomy in the light of Picasso's paintings, or should one assess Picasso's paintings in an appropriate light and leave anatomy to fend for itself?

David Carr speaks — and close attention to the Genesis texts bears him out — of a new consensus "sharpening our sense of the separation of ancestral and Mosaic traditions and the lateness of their literary connection with each other" (*Farewell to the Yahwist?* 180). When one balances the *major* differences against the *minor* similarities, the differences win hands down. The concerns are *different*; nevertheless the texts are now *combined*. From the point of view of history, this does create problems. From the point of view of symbol (i.e., ahistorical), it does not create these problems. The minutiae of attribution of textual connective tissue to putative strata or authors may be of high interest for speculative reconstruction; such minutiae are of low interest for the generation of meaning that is nonspeculative.

People have and have always had a need to belong. As a matter of community, we can call it family; on a larger scale, we call it tribe or nation. As a matter of place, we call it home; on a larger scale, we call it country. At base, Israel's exodus story is the story of its establishment as people and nation, with as end product its establishment in a country. As a matter of Israel's ancestral story, family mattered, tribe and nation mattered, place mattered. Logical priority goes to families before nations, to localities before countries. Psychological priority may be dependent on a variety of factors. For example: the security of possessing a country may be necessary before attention can be given to the needs of family — and so on.

Where much of Genesis and Exodus are concerned, the interplay of forces can be relatively complex. Psychologically, within a people, there may have been a need to develop the stories of exodus, the attainment of nationhood, the reality of land. Logically, families precede peoples; ancestors precede nations. The concerns of family livelihood may be felt as a matter of distant past to be given precedence chronologically. In another context, the concerns of nation — above all, freedom of existence — may take pride of place. It is hardly surprising that compositions that began with creation, as does the present text, and moved on from there should have been ordered logically rather than in terms of the time of composition. It is hardly surprising that the sequence chosen for the ordering of such compositions should have given rise to appearances that may have masked issues of their concerns or their interrelatedness.

◆ ◆ ◆

Excursus:
Egypt, Israel, and Exodus

Considerably later in the writing of this book, I found myself between a rock and a hard place and I come back to this spot to ponder. The rock: there is no archaeological evidence that there was an exodus from Egypt; there is biblical evidence that there was no journey from Sinai to Moab associated with the sanctuary complex, and there is biblical evidence that there was no entry into Canaan on the Joshua model. The hard place: the theme of exodus is evident early in Israel's traditions. By "early" I mean, for example, in the books of the eighth-century prophets Amos and Hosea and in the possibly tenth-century Ark Narrative (1 Sam 4 – 6; 2 Sam 6).

As to the absence of archaeological evidence for Israel's exodus from Egypt: while there is no archaeological evidence for the Exodus, there appears to be evidence for the possibility that the relevant period in Egypt's history allowed for presence in Egypt, oppression there, and flight from Egypt — what might be called "limited plausibility for something of the kind." To quote again from the summary of the 1992 Brown University conference on the Exodus and the Egyptian evidence:

Despite the suggestive title of this conference, there is no Egyptian evidence that offers direct testimony to the Exodus as described in the Old Testament. There are hints here and there to indicate that something like an exodus could have happened, though on a vastly smaller scale, but there is not a word in a text or an archaeological artifact that lends credence to the biblical narrative is it now stands. (see Frerichs and Lesko, *Exodus,* 105)

As to the existence of biblical evidence against a journey from Sinai to Moab (with the sanctuary complex) and the existence of biblical evidence against an entry into Canaan (on the Joshua model), full discussion will come later in this book.

So much for the rock. As for the hard place, references to the Exodus in the eighth-century prophets Amos and Hosea (Amos 3:1; 9:7; Hos 2:15; 11:1; 12:10 [Heb.; NRSV, 12:9]; 13:4) have been mentioned above. The Ark Narrative has two references to the Exodus. I do not see a valid case for dating its completion any later than the existence of Solomon's temple; Miller and Roberts (*Hand of the Lord*) date their substance of it a fraction earlier. The references to the Exodus (both within speeches, 1 Sam 4:8; 6:6) could be later insertions, of course. A case can be made for this; however, it has to rely more on prejudice than on evidence. With or without the Ark Narrative, the hard place is there; the Exodus is present in early tradition.

Pondering can focus attention on *text* rather than *tradition* and can require remodeling or transformation of the landscape. The transformation can begin when thought focuses on Exodus 15, reinforced by awareness that crowd numbers are not counted until the census that begins the book of Numbers and that, while the sanctuary complex goes no further, Israel moves on.

For me, the landscape was remodeled when the focus on text brought Exodus 15 into view. The rock moved, the hard place softened, and the landscape was transformed. The experience at the Sea (Exod 14, in part) was followed by entry into the land (Exod 15, in part). Sinai could be bypassed; the book of Joshua set aside. References to the Exodus did not depend solely on texts that might be late.

Tradition has the picture of Israel coming out of Egypt, being delivered at the Sea, journeying to Sinai for law-giving and sanctuary-making, then on to Kadesh-barnea; after a failed attempt on the land from the south, the picture has Israel bypassing Edom and Moab and arriving in the plains of Moab, across the Jordan from Jericho (Num 22:1). After that, it is over to Joshua.

While much might be said about this picture, primary is the fact that it passes over the chapter following the deliverance at the Sea, Exodus 15. In that chapter Moses and the Israelites celebrate triumphantly the victory over their foes and the destruction of the Egyptian forces: "Who is like you, O LORD, among the gods?" (Exod 15:11). The exultation over God's victory is followed promptly by praise for God's action: "In your steadfast love you led the people whom you redeemed; you guided them by your strength to your holy abode" (15:13). The journey across the wilderness is reduced to two verbs: you led, you guided. For a fuller study than is possible here, see Childs, *Exodus,* 240–53; note also: "The 'mount of heritage' must have originally meant the hill country of Canaan as Yahweh's special heritage" (Clifford, *Cosmic Mountain,* 139).

The itinerary is made clear by the list of peoples affected: the inhabitants of Philistia, the chiefs of Edom, the leaders of Moab, and all the inhabitants of Canaan (15:14–15). The nature of the destination is spelled out: the mountain of your own possession, the place that you made your abode, the sanctuary that your hands have established (15:17). In some five verses, the song celebrates the departure from Egypt and the entry into Canaan.

"The lack of unity in the account of the sea event has been recognized for well over a hundred years" (Childs, *Exodus,* 218; for texts and discussion, see *Sources of the Pentateuch,* 238–54; the alternative, reflecting a narrative and its redaction, is discussed by M. Vervenne, "The 'P' tradition"). Two accounts of Israel's deliverance and God's victory at the Sea, interwoven in Exodus 14, precede the song in Exodus 15. The version appropriate to Exodus 15's triumphant song is the one in which the sea is blown back by God's wind and God tosses the fleeing Egyptians into the returning sea. The wind, as God's agent, features prominently in the Exodus 15 song. At the blast of God's nostrils (the wind), the waters piled up, stood up in a heap (v. 8); God blew with God's wind and the sea covered them (v. 10). The deliverance account (within Exod 14, with the wind as God's agent) has the Egyptians fleeing to meet (literal meaning) the returning sea and God shakes them (literal meaning) in the midst of the sea. The picture is not clear, but it fits relatively well with the song's imagery of God throwing the Egyptians into the sea (15:1 and 4). The song specifies "horse and rider" and "Pharaoh's chariots and his army" (15:1 and 4). In the wind-version of the account, Pharaoh and his army are specified at the start, while afterward it tends to refer simply to "the Egyptians"; in the version where the waters are parted by the intermediary of Moses' hand, the Egyptian forces are itemized with terms such as horses, chariots, chariot drivers, and army (14:9). Given the undoubtedly complex history of the song in Exodus 15, any move beyond possible hints of association would be futile.

◆ ◆ ◆

The two accounts of deliverance interwoven in Exodus 14, one with Moses' hand as God's active agent and the other with the strong east wind as God's active agent, are short enough to be listed here. For further discussion, see *Sources of the Pentateuch*.

DELIVERANCE AT THE SEA — Agent: God's Wind

Exodus 14

⁵ᵇAnd the [Heb.; NRSV, The] minds of Pharaoh and his officials were changed toward the people, and they said, "What have we done, letting Israel leave our service?" ⁶So he had his chariot made ready, and took his army with him. ⁹*The Egyptians pursued them. ¹⁰*And the [Heb.; NRSV, The] Israelites looked back, and there were the Egyptians advancing on them, and they were in great fear. ¹³But Moses said to the people, "Do not be afraid, stand firm, and see the deliverance that the LORD will accomplish for you today; for the Egyptians whom you see today you shall never see again. ¹⁴The LORD will fight for you, and you have only to keep still."

¹⁹ᵇAnd the pillar of cloud moved from in front of them and took its place behind them. ²⁰It came between the army of Egypt and the army of Israel. And so the cloud was there with the darkness, and it lit up the night; one did not come near the other all night.

²¹*The LORD drove the sea back by a strong east wind all night, and turned the sea into dry land. ²⁴At the morning watch the LORD in the pillar of fire and cloud looked down upon the Egyptian army, and threw the Egyptian army into panic. ²⁵ᵇThe Egyptians said, "Let us flee from the Israelites, for the LORD is fighting for them against Egypt." ²⁷*And

at dawn the sea returned to its normal depth. As the Egyptians fled before it, the Lord tossed the Egyptians into the sea.

³⁰Thus the Lord saved Israel that day from the Egyptians; and Israel saw the Egyptians dead on the seashore. ³¹Israel saw the great work that the Lord did against the Egyptians. So the people feared the Lord and believed in the Lord and in his servant Moses.

DELIVERANCE AT THE SEA —
Agent: Moses' Hand

Exodus 14

Then the Lord said to Moses: ²Tell the Israelites to turn back and camp in front of Pi-hahiroth, between Migdol and the sea, in front of Baal-zephon; you shall camp opposite it, by the sea. ³Pharaoh will say of the Israelites, 'They are wandering aimlessly in the land; the wilderness has closed in on them.' ⁴I will harden Pharaoh's heart, and he will pursue them, so that I will gain glory for myself over Pharaoh and all his army; and the Egyptians shall know that I am the Lord. And they did so.

⁸The Lord hardened the heart of Pharaoh king of Egypt and he pursued the Israelites, who were going out boldly. ^{9*}And they overtook them camped by the sea, all Pharaoh's horses and chariots, his chariot drivers and his army, by Pi-hahiroth, in front of Baal-zephon. ^{10*}As Pharaoh drew near, the Israelites cried out to the Lord.

¹⁵Then the Lord said to Moses, "Why do you cry out to me? Tell the Israelites to go forward. ¹⁶But you lift up your staff, and stretch out your hand over the sea and divide it, that the Israelites may go into the sea on dry ground. ¹⁷Then I will harden the hearts of the Egyptians so that they will go in after them; and so I will gain glory for myself over Pharaoh and all his army, his chariots, and his chariot drivers. ¹⁸And the Egyptians shall know that I am the Lord, when I have gained glory for myself over Pharaoh, his chariots, and his chariot drivers."

^{21*}Then Moses stretched out his hand over the sea, and the waters were divided. ²²The Israelites went into the sea on dry ground, the waters forming a wall for them on their right and on their left. ²³The Egyptians pursued, and went into the sea after them, all of Pharaoh's horses, chariots, and chariot drivers.

²⁶Then the Lord said to Moses, "Stretch out your hand over the sea, so that the waters [Heb.; NRSV, water] may come back upon the Egyptians, upon their chariots and chariot drivers." ^{27*}So Moses

stretched out his hand over the sea. [28]The waters returned and covered the chariots and the chariot drivers, the entire army of Pharaoh that had followed them into the sea; not one of them remained. [29]But the Israelites walked on dry ground through the sea, the waters forming a wall for them on their right and on their left.

♦ ♦ ♦

Any move beyond, to identify either tradition or text preceding the deliverance and the song has to be sheerest speculation. The plague stories, with their frequent contact between Moses and Pharaoh, have strongly legendary features. A core account beginning with Moses' encounter with God at the burning bush presents an attractive possibility; it is no more than that. Even issues of servitude and oppression have to be recognized as possible development.

Integral to the text is a group's flight from the Egyptians, pursuit by the Egyptians, and deliverance by God. It is a reasonable assumption that the qualities required for membership in such a group (examples: courage, initiative, independence, enterprise, etc.) would be the qualities appropriate for leadership elsewhere. Should this group, coming from Egypt, have mingled with those settling in the hill country of Israel at the time, it would not be surprising if they took a prominent role in their communities and inspired people with their stories. The potential for the Exodus theme is there. The Exodus as concrete embodiment of what was otherwise the abstract vision of a God committed to liberation and life might well have been important.

SUMMARY

As we have seen, when exploring modern faith in relation to biblical text a couple of principles come into play. One was expressed in *Rethinking the Pentateuch*: there is "a shift from the Pentateuch as a record of Israel's *remembering its past* to the Pentateuch as a record of *Israel's pondering its present*" (9). The principle impacts negatively on the understanding of revelation as coming exclusively *from above and from the past*, a position that needs to be complemented by the understanding of revelation as also coming *from below and from the present*.

In the book of Genesis, the ancestral stories reflect the lives of those who have come to a new land, who seek to establish themselves there, who acquire land and children, who form relationships with those already there. Bringing these into unity, for Israel these are our ancestors and their God is our God. Predominantly, *traditions about them tell us something of who we are.*

In the book of Exodus, the stories of an ancient time reflect the emergence of Israel as a nation and the power of its God to bring the nascent nation out of its obscurity in Egypt, to assure its survival in what is the wilderness, and to bring it to a land to call its own. Predominantly, *traditions such as these tell Israel something about who God is.*

The appeal to ancestral figures, above all Jacob/Israel, in non-pentateuchal texts tells us little about how the portrayal of the ancestors touched the self-image of their descendants, beyond their belonging as nation. Promises matter, but it is the promise of land that predominates. The repeated promise of blessings to all nations finds its echo; it does not bulk large. Nonpentateuchal texts are largely from prophets and psalms. The impact of ancestral traditions on ordinary people has to be hazarded from the ancestral texts themselves. Little is said of Isaac. Of Abraham and Jacob, it is clear that, if these figures shaped the self-image of their descendants, the chosen are not above the ordinary. Both figures have their skeletons in their closets; if God writes straight, it is surely with crooked lines.

To the question "Who, then, are we?" the reply has to be: "We belong to the one people that claims these figures as ancestors and we acknowledge a single God who is faithful." As for any people that becomes intensely aware of its unity (perhaps in the aftermath of defeat or perhaps, threatened by dispersion, facing the possibility of the loss of its sense of unity), for Israel expressing that unity by unifying the ancestral traditions is natural. It may touch truth at its deeper levels.

The claim of "these figures as ancestors" raises the issue of the role of legendary figures in the life of Israel. In our own lives, legend can be larger than logic. Why not for Israel's? In some religious quarters, the misplaced craving for historicity can numb us to anything much more than the historically demonstrable.

For many, legends may contribute, however subtly, to our under-standing of ourselves. For many of us, though, that contribution is not often the subject of serious reflection. Reflection involves won-dering whether there is a part of our understanding of ourselves that is, perhaps subconsciously, reinforced by something in our family ancestry or our local or national past. A follow-up to that reflection is wondering whether something of the kind was present for people of Older Testament times. It probably was, but equally probably we will never know, because the reflective evidence is not provided to us.

In families, the impact of ancestral legend can on occasion be greater for people than the availability of evidence to sustain it. Sometimes no evidence is available beyond the family tradition. For example: "our family's origins are Latvian; the records of course are lost." Sometimes the evidence may conflict with the tradition. For example: "To our surprise, the family is not of Croatian stock; we left southern Italy ahead of a murder charge, and great-grandfather changed the family name and invented the family story." Sometimes the tradition simply goes beyond the evidence. For example: "The family legend is there, but it is very vague; the evidence is pretty minimal too, but the possibility is there."

Legends belong with various aspects of life: family, locality, nation. Legends can take the form of popular images, of ideal figures, or of actual individuals. Among the popular images: American democracy and drive, British sturdiness and common sense, French flair, German thoroughness. Among the ideal figures: John Bull, Marianne, Uncle Sam. Among the actual individuals: for Britain, Arthur (and the richly legendary Camelot), Boadicea, Canute; for France, Charlemagne or Napoleon; for Germany, Karl der Große ("Holy Roman Empire, Ger-man nation") or Bismarck; for the United States, Adams, Franklin, Jefferson, Lincoln, or Washington. These are only a few of the leg-endary influences that touch our lives. Some touch actuality; some may not be in touch with anything. What matters most is whether they touch us.

Detlef Jericke writes that Abraham is not to be understood as a historical person but only as a literary figure (*als historische Person nicht zu fassen...verständlich nur als literarische Figur* [*Abraham in Mamre,* 10]). At one level the language is unhelpful. It is perfectly possible that Abraham was an actual individual but, at the present time, it is certainly not able to be proved; it scarcely matters. Undoubtedly, it is highly likely that, for the ancient past, Abraham mattered as a legendary figure. History can be a loaded term unless due weight is given to the ambiguous and the contestable. Historian Inga Clendinnen remarks: "Social groups are held together through shared stories that sustain the preferred vision of the individual, of the group and of those others who exist beyond the group, defining its boundaries" (*Agamemnon's Kiss,* 156). The observant will note the "preferred" with its bow to ambiguity and contestability.

As the fortunes of Israel evolved and unfolded, national legend needed to be constantly refashioned and reshaped to keep pace with the unfolding reality of the nation. Not surprisingly, as the north–south separation collapsed and Israel became one nation, the figures of Abraham and Jacob might have needed to be merged. Not surprisingly, with Isaac firmly ensconced in the tradition, a place might have had to be found for him among the ancestors.

My ancestral heritage is Scots/Irish. In Scotland, we have traditions going back to Robert Bruce (thirteenth–fourteenth centuries). In Ireland, we have traditions from the time of Oliver Cromwell (seventeenth century), followed by a move to Spain and, a century or so later, to London. More recently, on both sides of the family, we were represented in India as part of the British raj (army and administration). Family trees provide some degree of verification; nevertheless, the evidence is fragmentary. However, that does not mean that the impact is unreal. Each of us needs to be conscious of the impact of legend on our lives, from surprisingly little to rather more than we bargained for. Only in the light of that consciousness are we in a position to understand the role of the ancestral figures in ancient Israel.

The move that brought the figure of Jacob into a unity with Abraham and Isaac probably occurred not later than the seventh century BCE. The move to make that unity into a family unity free of any foreign blood depends, in the present state of the text, on Genesis 24 and 27; it is therefore likely to be later by a century or more (see

Gen 24). These two moves imply the awareness within Israel that they are in fact one people, despite the centuries-old political division into two kingdoms, north and south. This awareness affects the self-understanding of the people, the "who are we?" question. At the same time, this awareness impacts on Israel's perception of the unity of God. If Israel is one people, then the God of north and south may indeed be one God.

The outcome here may be a deepened and more realistic understanding of God's revelation. As proposed earlier, in our today the encounter with God in present experience (fuller understanding of ourselves, our traditions, and our God) may lead to a selectivity in the passages of scripture that are read; in the past of Israel's people the encounter with God in their experience may often have had its influence on the passages of scripture that were written in their day, from major creations to minor revisions. As a result, the revelation of God is not shrouded in the mists of a distant past; the revelation of God is found in the clarity of an immediate present.

Awareness of how ancestral traditions were revised and amalgamated may bring us to a recognition of the many ways in which God's revelation may take place.

The combination of Genesis with Exodus may be best understood as a combination of people with God — that is, an association of this people's origins with their God's deliverance of them. The appeal to images of exodus reflects an understanding of God as endowed with power and committed to the freedom of God's people. "Let my people go" (Exod 5:1) is a primary statement. They are MY PEOPLE; they are to be LET GO. Our God has the power; our God has the commitment. How far back this conviction extends in Israel's traditions is a matter for study. It is certainly found in Amos and Hosea. It is present in the Ark Narrative (1 Sam 4–6; 2 Sam 6), but reflecting on the nature of Israel's God rather than on the nature of Israel; dating here is uncertain. Often, Israel's self-understanding is couched in terms of exodus; they are the people God brought out of Egypt, out of the house of slavery. Fundamental to this is, of course, the understanding of their God as the one who had the power and the commitment to bring them out.

Similarly, awareness of unity may have stimulated the editorial work that arranged ancestral and exodus traditions in an appropriately logical order. Such editorial work was almost certainly late (i.e., post-exilic). Such editorial work was most probably unwise or at least unduly risky. The risk is that the chain of episodes, ordered logically, may detract from emphasis on individual stories or clusters of stories that evoke the significance of the episodes.

The research that has emphasized the lateness of this editorial order in logical sequence enables users to view the text under at least two aspects. First, there is the significance of the episodes or clusters themselves. Second, there is the meaning to be derived from the sequence in which they have been arranged. Discretion is needed in discerning which of these should predominate in any given interpretation. It is to be hoped that the reflections to be found earlier here will help with this discretion.

Lurking discreetly in the background is the awareness that if the present apparently chronological sequence is given us by relatively late compilers of the present text, it may well turn out to be that the original formulations of tradition were more fragmented. A section on Israel's understanding of its ancestors might not have been preceded by the material now in Genesis 1–11; it probably was not followed by the traditions of Exodus, Sinai, and desert journey. The understanding of Israel and its God derived from the traditions of the Exodus might well have stood alone. If the organization of certain traditions to constitute a journey from the shores of the Sea to the banks of the Jordan is relatively late, the traditions of Sinai and Horeb may regain an independence they have lost and the stories of the desert wandering may take on a significance and individuality of their own.

As these possibilities are explored, it is likely that the revelatory quality of the text will be enhanced. As life was lived and understood, in its beginnings and in its later reflections, the enduring experience of God was available to be better known and more fully open to multiple understandings.

Chapter 3

Israel's Traditions about Mount Sinai

For Israel at Mount Sinai, there are two great blocks of tradition: the gift of the law in Exodus 19–24 (universally recognized as non-priestly) and the traditions of the sanctuary, begun in Exodus 25–40 and completed in Numbers 1–10 (universally recognized as priestly). About this there is no argument. Before exploring these very significant blocks of text, a preliminary observation needs to be noted.

There is only one itinerary given for Israel from the Reed/Red Sea to Sinai. This has been known for many years; its implications have not been unfolded. As we will see later, there is also no itinerary for Israel's sanctuary complex moving away from Sinai. There is a start to the journey, but no follow-up and no itinerary, not even implicit. In the light of these two observations, the issue needs to be looked at closely.

The classical position, represented by Martin Noth, attributed to nonpriestly origin (J = Yahwist) as itinerary the following only: "And they went into the wilderness of Shur. They went three days in the wilderness and found no water. . . . Israel camped there in front of the mountain" (Exod 15:22* and 19:2b). In between are the episodes of the water at Marah, the manna, the water at Massa/Meribah, and the battle with Amalek. There is no nonpriestly itinerary linking these episodes.

The itinerary texts in their totality are easily listed (from the NRSV):

Marah
Exodus 15:22: And Moses caused Israel to journey from Yam Suph and they went out to the wilderness of Shur

Elim
Exodus 15:27: And they came to Elim . . . and they camped there

Wilderness of Sin
Exodus 16:1: And they journeyed from Elim and the whole congregation of the people of Israel came [plural] to the wilderness of Sin

Rephidim
Exodus 17:1: And the whole congregation of the people of Israel journeyed [plural] from the wilderness of Sin . . . and they camped at Rephidim

Sinai
Exodus 19:2: And they journeyed from Rephidim and they came to the wilderness of Sinai and they camped in the wilderness. (Israel camped [singular] there in front of the mountain.)

When Mark O'Brien and I were working on this material some fifteen years ago, we commented that, where applicable, the J itinerary had been replaced by the P version (*Sources of the Pentateuch*, 144–45, nn. 127, 130). Interestingly, Noth himself does not make this affirmation; he simply says of the itinerary texts that they are P (with the exception of the two fragments noted above, Exodus 15:22* and 19:2b). Remarking on this, Childs comments: "Noth attributes the itinerary in vv. 22aa and 27 to P, even though the initial formulae are strange to P. It is equally possible that the earlier source had elements of an itinerary" (*Exodus*, 266). Reference to "the whole congregation" is an indicator of priestly origin; however, it is present here in two cases only. The two may speak for the five or the presence of only two may argue for an already existing formulation. Without that "whole congregation" there are no linguistic pointers suggesting an origin for the texts. The issue has to be left open: there may have been an existing itinerary that priestly writers took over with a couple of minor expansions ("the whole congregation"); alternatively, the itineraries were the work of priestly writers. In either case, the present biblical text has only one itinerary.

Three options are present:

1. There were two sets of itinerary texts that have been blended into one itinerary in the compiling of the present text.

2. An earlier text was taken over by the priestly writers to serve their own purposes, indicated by a couple of minor expansions ("the whole congregation").

3. The present text in its entirety is the work of priestly writers and any earlier itinerary either did not exist or was suppressed.

An option that we will not develop here would see the episode at Marah and the battle with Amalek as independent freestanding traditions, while the manna and the later water episode belong with Numbers 11 and Numbers 20 respectively, after Sinai. In this purely speculative hypothesis, an original text moving Israel from the Reed/Red Sea to Mount Sinai would have been the work of priestly writers.

It is fair to say that the itinerary issue is not extensively canvassed in current biblical scholarship. The more commonly encountered position reflects the third option in which the existing itinerary is priestly. From a traditional point of view, the least troubling option is probably the second, with an earlier text taken over by priestly writers. In this scenario, an earlier text moved Israel from the Reed/Red Sea to Mount Sinai; only fragments now remain (e.g., Exod 15:22* and 19:2b). The priestly texts concerning the sanctuary would then have been added to the earlier "gift of the law" capsule. Any pre-priestly account of Israel's moves after Sinai would been completely replaced by the priestly account of the sanctuary complex's departure. This last aspect, however, must be seen as problematic.

For the present, it is enough to recognize that only one itinerary is present in the text now to accompany Israel from the Reed/Red Sea to Mount Sinai.

In this context, there is one affirmation that needs to be made simply and clearly. Israel remembered a wilderness experience; the traditions are there. They include central issues such as food and water in the desert, survival and leadership on the journey. The absence of an itinerary is no more than that: the absence of an itinerary. It has nothing to say about the authenticity of the wilderness traditions themselves.

There is clear duality from Exodus 3 to Exodus 15 — two calls of Moses, two patterns in the plague texts, two texts for the Passover, and two accounts of the deliverance at the Sea; after the deliverance at the Sea, the duality ceases — just the one itinerary that leads from the Reed Sea to Mount Sinai ("the evidence is not there for two itineraries"; for details see *Rethinking the Pentateuch*, 79–83). There is no itinerary whatsoever leading away from Sinai for the great sanctuary complex envisaged there. Numbers 33, of course, includes a detailed itinerary extending from the edge of Egypt (Rameses) to the edge of Edom (Mount Hor). It is late in the book of Numbers; earlier in the book, Israel had arrived at Mount Hor in Numbers 20:22 and at the plains of Moab, "across the Jordan from Jericho," in Numbers 22:1. The need for an itinerary to be listed in Numbers 33 is mute witness to the absence of any such complete itinerary earlier. The Sinai experience and the sanctuary complex do not rate a mention in it. The itinerary says simply: "They set out from Rephidim and camped in the wilderness of Sinai. They set out from the wilderness of Sinai and camped at Kibroth-hattaavah" (Num 33:15–16). However, the list is pure itinerary; no other episodes are mentioned either.

The absence of an itinerary leading away from Sinai is significant. Despite *yhwh*'s detailed instructions on Mount Sinai for building a transportable sanctuary (Exod 25–31) and despite equally detailed reporting of the corresponding construction of this portable sanctuary (Exod 35–40) and furthermore despite highly specific instructions for the disposition of Israel's tribes around the sanctuary on its march (within Numbers 1–10), and with the detailed report of the sanctuary's departure in accordance with these instructions (Num 10:11–28), no equivalent report is given of the arrival of the sanctuary anywhere — not at the end of the first day, not at any further point. In my judgment, this can only mean that there is no march. Interpretation of these texts must confront the challenge of explaining why there should be such intensity of detail about organization and march when there is absolutely no mention of this sanctuary complex in the texts that follow?

"This whole complex, the deployment in camp and the order of march, is never heard of again ... it goes absolutely nowhere and is found absolutely nowhere" (*Rethinking the Pentateuch*, 91). A major consequence of this is that the whole complex may not be best understood as a report of what took place at Sinai in preparation for the move. It may be better understood in other terms than that of the journey from Sinai.

Nothing is new in seeking to understand Israel's traditions of Sinai outside the journey context. Half a century ago, Gerhard von Rad remarked: "It is thus obvious that the Sinai tradition has been secondarily inserted into already extant traditions concerning the Wanderings in the Wilderness.... Obviously it was only at a comparatively late date that this complex of tradition was inserted into the canonical picture of the saving history.... The Sinai tradition lived in independence longer than all the other traditional elements whose combination led to the construction of the canonical picture of the saving history" (*Old Testament Theology,* 1:187–88; for more extensive treatment of this issue, see von Rad, "The Form-Critical Problem of the Hexateuch," esp. 13–26, a view accepted by Noth, *Pentateuchal Traditions,* 59–62). For von Rad, the evidence was that "Kadesh traditions precede it, and Kadesh traditions follow it again" (*Old Testament Theology,* 1:187, presumably referring to Exod 17 and Num 20). His reasons may not have been right; his instincts may have been. More than half a century earlier, Julius Wellhausen had hazarded a similar conclusion: "one could be tempted to believe that the original form of this tradition did not have the digression to Sinai at all, but that it had the people get from the Red Sea/Sea of Reeds directly to Kadesh" (noting Judg 11:16, "when they came up from Egypt, Israel went through the wilderness to the Red Sea/Sea of Reeds and came to Kadesh"; "Judges 5 and Deuteronomy 33 provide no evidence whatsoever of Sinai as the mountain where the Law is given" [*Composition*, 108]). The present text of Exodus is clear on the place of the Sinai traditions in the narrative; at the same time, however, the journey context may not be essential to an understanding of these Sinai traditions.

To be credible, what follows is necessarily involved quite closely with the text. As noted occasionally earlier, those who are happy enough to take conclusions on trust, at least in a first reading, may be well advised to skip the sections on Law and Sanctuary and go to the Conclusion.

THE LAW

The nonpriestly material (Exod 19–24) needs to be considered carefully before moving to the extensive priestly text concerned with the sanctuary. Exodus 19–24 begins and ends with covenant. Theologically, the place of covenant here (and overall in Israel's relationship with God) is of major importance. Religious sensitivity in this regard makes it desirable to treat the text with delicacy and care. Its interpretation is for many enormously weighty. Honesty requires that the biblical text be given full and careful scrutiny.

Brevard Childs puts matters well: "Ch. 24 brings to completion the sealing of the covenant which had been first announced in 19.3. The repetition by the people of the same response (19.8 and 24.3, 7) marks the beginning and end of the one great covenant event" (*Exodus*, 502–3). The lawcode associated with the decalogue is called "The Book of the Covenant"; William Propp headlines Exodus 19–24 as "The First Covenant" (*Exodus 19–40*, ix, 101). John Durham speaks of what is "the important event of Exodus, and even of the OT itself," characterized as Yahweh's "coming to Israel at Sinai and entering into covenant with Abraham's descendancy" (*Exodus*, 265, 259).

The comments by Childs on 19:3–8 and 24:1–12 are completely accurate. Alas, however, I find myself uneasy with the total text described as "the one great covenant event." Quite frankly, if competent theologians wanted to put together a text celebrating so momentous an event as the sealing of the covenant between *yhwh* and Israel, I have grave doubts whether that text would be looking like Exodus 19–24. What is crucial theologically is whether the explicitly conditional quality of Exodus 19:3–8, described by Durham as "a poetic summary of covenant theology" (*Exodus*, 261), should be universalized as characteristic of what is understood as the covenant between *yhwh* and Israel. An inventory of the total text is in order.

After the arrival at Sinai, the text sequence is:

19:3–8	The "eagles' wings" passage
19:9–25	The preparations for the theophany and the theophany itself
20:1–21	The ten commandments known as the Decalogue and the people's reaction
20:22–23:19	The collection of laws known as the Book of the Covenant
23:20–33	The dispositions concerning the move to Canaan
24:1–11	The meal on the mountain itself (vv. 1–2, 9–11) and the covenant ceremony around the altar at the foot of the mountain (vv. 3–8).

Emerging from this inventory, certain points can be clearly affirmed.

1. Is there a relationship with *yhwh?* Definitely YES. "You have seen what I did to the Egyptians, and how I bore you on eagles' wings and brought you to myself."

2. Is there a covenant with *yhwh?* Definitely YES. A covenant is foreshadowed in 19:3–8; a covenant is explicitly celebrated in 24:3–8.

3. Is there an encounter with *yhwh* and the gift of the law? Definitely YES.

The question that is not so easily answered is whether Exodus 19–24 presents itself or can be interpreted as an account of covenant-sealing in which Israel becomes *yhwh*'s people. In my judgment, this has to be regarded as doubtful. The use of covenant language is exclusive to 19:3–8 and 24:3–8, 12. Israel gives its commitment, covenanting to obey God's word (Exod 24:3); this is not the same as covenanting to be God's people.

Terence Fretheim, for example, is rightly emphatic. First, "The law is a gift to an already redeemed community" and, second, "It has been claimed that Israel's election as the people of God took place at Sinai. . . . such an interpretation [is] unacceptable. . . . There is no 'election' of Israel in the book of Exodus; election is assumed" (*Exodus*, 22, 208).

In von Rad's presentation, God's giving of the Decalogue and the people of Israel's acceptance of it are two inseparable aspects of a single act with a single significance. "According to antiquity's understanding [claims von Rad], entry into a special relationship with a god was inconceivable without the acceptance and binding recognition of specific ordinances. Thus, only as Jahweh proclaimed his sovereign rights over Israel, and only as Israel accepted this will, was Israel's appropriation made complete" (*Old Testament Theology*, 1:192). Von Rad's reticence is regrettably evident; no references are provided to illustrate antiquity's understanding. More significantly, this understanding is not explicit in the biblical text here. Nor is it asserted in association with Deuteronomy's presentation of the Decalogue (Deut 5:1–33). At another end of the spectrum, Durham remarks that "without that affirmative response, indeed, there would have been only 'sons of Israel' the descendants of Jacob. With the affirmative response, 'Israel,' a community of faith transcending biological descendancy, could come into being" (*Exodus*, 262). I am afraid that I remain unconvinced. I would be more open to the acuteness of this logic had God earlier been reported as instructing Moses to tell Pharaoh: "Let the descendants of Jacob go." However, God did not. To the contrary, the word was: "Let *my people* go." Similarly, I might have been more open to conviction had Israel at the end of it all said, "As the LORD has spoken, we will be *yhwh*'s people" (cf. Deut 26:16–19; regrettably, the Jerusalem Bible here mistranslates badly). However, they did not. To the contrary, what they are reported as saying was: "All the words that the LORD has spoken we will do" (Exod 24:3). As any lovers know, obedience may accompany commitment, but obedience is not the same as commitment. According to the bulk of the Older Testament, *yhwh* is committed to Israel, whether they are obedient or not (e.g., Hos 3:1). See Deuteronomy 7:7–11, where God's choice of Israel is at the beginning (v. 7) and observance of the commandments is at the end (v. 11). Condition it is not.

Exodus 19:3–8 speaks clearly of a covenant and speaks clearly of conditions to be observed, "if you obey my voice and keep my covenant" (19:5). The outcome is equally clear: "you shall be my treasured possession out of all the peoples . . . a priestly kingdom and a holy nation" (19:5–6). Two aspects are unclear. First, is this covenant language describing what is to come in Exodus 20–23? Second, is this covenant establishing Israel as God's people or is this covenant taking the status as God's people for granted and going beyond it to an even higher status — treasured possession, priestly kingdom, holy nation? Without going into the minutiae of exegetical detail, it is enough to say that in this text these two aspects are unclear.

The language of Exodus 19:3–8 is close to that of Deuteronomy (see Deut 7:6; 14:2; 26:18; also 14:21; 26:19; 28:9); it is not identical with it. It is probable that Exodus 19:3–8 is a relatively late composition. More important, it is certain that Exodus 19:3–8 is one particular theology of covenant; it should not be universalized, an understanding to be imposed on all covenants. Furthermore, it is not at all certain that Exodus 19:3–8 should set the tone for what follows. It is prefaced to and outside the actual theophany and lawgiving, precisely where one would understand an alternative understanding to be situated. The concluding comment on this passage by Dennis McCarthy, who had as good a knowledge of ANE and biblical covenantal texts as any scholar of his generation, needs to be heard: "Thus in one way or another this tiny survey of the Sinai event departs from all the other traditions" (*Treaty and Covenant*, 273).

In relationships of ultimate commitment, relationships we call love, the interplay of behavior and belonging, expressed above all in terms of condition and consequence, is always intricate and delicate. In assessing the relationship of God and Israel, and the place of the term "covenant" within it, the concrete core issue can be whether right behavior is a condition for belonging to God or is a consequence of (the result of) belonging to God. In Exodus 19:3–8, the outcome (treasured possession, priestly kingdom, holy nation) is explicitly made a matter of condition, of right behavior that is required of Israel. Because the outcome here is dependent on the fulfillment of conditions, it is important to know whether that outcome includes Israel's being God's people. In my judgment, it is at least doubtful;

more accurately, it is unlikely. In my judgment, being "treasured possession, priestly kingdom, holy nation" is intended as a higher status
than simply "God's people." Explicit clarity, however, is not present.
The formal language, for example, of Deuteronomy 26:17–19 is not
present. I tend to believe the use of language such as "the one great
covenant event" needs to be considerably more circumspect. That is
one reason for the predominance of gift-of-law language earlier.

The structure of the book of Deuteronomy itself is revealing. Early
in the book, there is the Decalogue, beginning "I am the LORD your
God" and the Shema "THE LORD IS OUR GOD" (Deut 5:6; 6:4). Late
in the book, Israel is affirmed as God's "treasured people" (Deut
26:18). The commandments are there to be kept; even there, they
are a consequence, not a condition. The language of the Shema is
noteworthy. It is not YHWH ECHAD (= YHWH alone). It is YHWH ELO-
HENU, YHWH ECHAD (= YHWH *our* God, YHWH alone). The "our God"
makes all the difference. The relationship is there from the outset;
as a consequence of the relationship, the commandments are to be
observed.

The consequence or condition difference can be put bluntly:

Condition: *If* you keep my commandments, *then* you will be
                 my people.

Consequence: *because* you are my people, *therefore* you will keep
                 my commandments.

In relationships, there is no greater difference.

In the Older Testament, the theological stances in this relationship-
to-God area are surprisingly varied. A few examples will have to be
enough. Bad behavior: "I will blot out" (Gen 6:7); God's commitment
despite bad behavior: "I will never again destroy" (Gen 8:21); God's
commitment despite idolatry: "just as the LORD loves the people of
Israel, though they turn to other gods" (Hos 3:1); good belonging and
bad behavior: "You only have I known . . . therefore I will punish you
for all your iniquities" (Amos 3:2); bad behavior (and good belonging
all the same): "I will cast you out of my sight" (Jer 7:15, but like
Ephraim Judah still belonged); God's forgiveness of bad behavior:
"I, I am He who blots out your transgressions for my own sake" (Isa

43:25); God's forgiveness: "Why do you not pardon my transgression and take away my iniquity?" (Job 7:21). Given such a variety of stances, in these contexts issues of consequence and condition are never far apart and uncertainty is never far away. God's commitment is sure. In the Older Testament, in only one text is Israel "not my people" (Hos 1:9), a judgment promptly reversed in the verse that follows.

In the biblical text, Israel has been God's people since the beginning of Exodus. That is not in doubt. That the understanding of this relationship can unfold in a variety of complex theologies should not be in doubt either. Individual and community faith stances need to be identified. Such faith stances should not influence biblical interpretation. In my judgment, unfortunately they are often not avowed as such but allowed to impose on interpretation. In some objective matters such as syntax and translation this is eminently unforgivable; but it has happened.

Exodus 24 ends with a clearly combined text, combining what were probably an older and a more recent text. The older text (at the start and at the end): a "meal on the mountain" tradition, denoting a relationship between God and people (24:1–2, 9–11); the more recent text (in the middle): a tradition of a formal ceremony of covenant at the foot of the mountain (24:3–8). The people's response is not "*yhwh* will be our God and we will be *yhwh*'s people" (see *yhwh*'s statement of this and more, Deut 26:16–19). The people's response is "All the words that the LORD has spoken we will do" (24:3; note: 24:7 adds a verb, with the literal meaning hear, or hear and accept, or obey). This is what the people's response was at the beginning: "Everything that the LORD has spoken we will do" (Exod 19:8). The echo is clear; 24:3–8 means to solemnize something at least of what has preceded. That does not mean that it is not a later interpretation; nor does it mean that it is an incorrect one or, for that matter, a correct one.

Looking more closely, the nonpriestly report of the covenant in Exodus 24 is a surprisingly uneven text. First, it is an appendix to the lawcode, a lawcode that probably should be reckoned as ending with Exodus 23:19. Second, it is a combination of celebration by a meal up on the mountain and celebration by formalities at a twelve-pillared altar down at the foot of the mountain (Exod 24:4); the former account is a frame fore and aft of the latter. Third, "Moses wrote down all the words of the LORD" (Exod 24:4). A few verses later, however, it is the LORD who does the writing. "The LORD said to Moses, 'Come up to me on the mountain, and wait there; and I will give you the tablets of stone, with the law and the commandment, which I have written for their instruction'" (Exod 24:12). Decalogue written by the LORD and lawcode written by Moses is one approach to resolving difficulties. Of course, these latter verses are associated with the "meal on the mountain" scene, which began in the first couple of verses of the chapter (Exod 24:1–2). The book of the covenant, which Moses wrote (24:4) and read to the people (24:7), belongs in the altar ceremony at the foot of the mountain (24:3–8), inserted into the "meal on the mountain" passage. The combination of texts here is so fractured as to be thoroughly disconcerting. As Childs writes, the complexity of analysis brings about "the complete atomization of the chapter into a myriad of disparate and contradictory fragments" (*Exodus,* 500). The description of Exodus 19–24 as "the one great covenant event" (Childs, *Exodus,* 503) is scarcely reflected in the text; the description goes beyond the witness of the text. The covenant is of greater concern in Deuteronomy than it is here. The text here appears to be concerned primarily with the gift of law. In this light, the silence about the covenant on the part of the priestly text is less surprising.

~MODERN FAITH~

Emphasis on the language of "covenant" (*berit*), and the idea structure associated with it, as a term that articulates the relationship between God and Israel is relatively late. The use of covenant to describe relationships within this world is common enough and early enough (for example, 2 Sam 3:21; Hos 2:18). Not so between God and Israel. In Genesis through Numbers, for example, the *principal* nonpriestly uses of the term for the God–Israel relationship are Genesis 15:18 (probably as late a text as any in Genesis) and Exod 19:5 (which is unlikely to be early and concerns a conditional and probably special issue); book of the covenant and blood of the covenant are found in Exodus 24:7, 8 and references to the covenant in the inscrutable Exodus 34:10, 27–28. In Deuteronomy, twenty-six verses use the term; they are, however, predominantly from a relatively late stage in the evolution of Deuteronomy. Nothing changes in God's relationship with Israel, which has already been a long-term relationship; what changes is simply the language and ideas judged helpful for expressing that relationship. What matters religiously today is the understanding of the relationship more than the language in which it is expressed.

What is clear from the text is the tradition that Israel encountered its God and received from God the gift of the law. There is no reason why this should have occurred in the course of Israel's journey through the wilderness. Israel has been *yhwh*'s people since Egypt. The gift of God's law can be celebrated at almost any time. The location of Mount Sinai is, as specialists know, uncertain enough that it should not be used to determine the timing of the gift of God's law. The tradition of thunder and lightning, thick cloud and smoke, as well as the whole mountain shaking violently (Exod 19:16–18) is in stark contrast with the tradition of Elijah's encounter with God at Sinai, not in the great wind, not in the earthquake, not in the fire, but in the sound of sheer silence or sheer stillness (1 Kgs 19:11–13). The encounter with God should never escape the mysterious and the sublime.

The issue of behavior as a consequence of relationship with God or as a condition for that relationship is a matter for delicate and complex theological reflection. The biblical text respects both the delicacy and the complexity. Interpreters, of course, need to respect the biblical text.

THE SANCTUARY

The concern for the sanctuary begins with the priestly text's first words given *yhwh* at Sinai. Whether at the beginning of Israel's origins in the wilderness or in the time of Israel's exile, under threat of the end of that existence, they are of enormous significance. "Have them make me a sanctuary, SO THAT I MAY DWELL AMONG THEM" (Exod 25:8, emphasis mine). Nothing in the Hebrew Bible is more important than God's dwelling in the midst of Israel, with all that it implies (note three major textual moments: Exod 25:8; 1 Kgs 9:3; 2 Chr 36:23, the last verse of the Hebrew Bible). Nothing in the Newer Testament is more important than "the Word became flesh and lived among us" (John 1:14), with all that it implies. The sanctuary text is not concerned with the esoterica of ritual; it is concerned with the core of belonging.

The architect of the sanctuary is presented as none other than God: "In accordance with all that I show you concerning the pattern of the tabernacle and of all its furniture, so you shall make it" (Exod 25:9, see also v. 40). This is hardly surprising. First, it is to be God's dwelling, so it would be wise to have God design it. Second, it is a remarkably strange construction, so divine involvement with it is important. With some fifteen chapters, it has more text consecrated to it than any other construction in the Bible. One can assume, therefore, that important theological and emotional interests are vested in it.

It is best described as demountable: able to be dismantled, transported somewhere, and reassembled there. This dismantling and later reassembling is noted as the responsibility of the Levites, when the tabernacle is to set out and when it is to be pitched (Num 1:51); confirmation is offered at the end of the next chapter (Num 2:34). The movement of this demountable sanctuary was at the express command of God, symbolized by the cloud: "Whenever the cloud lifted from over the tent, then the Israelites would set out; and in the place where the cloud settled down, there the Israelites would camp. At the command of the LORD the Israelites would set out, and at the command of the LORD they would camp" (Num 9:17–18). In due course, with priestly precision, it is noted: "In the second year, in the second month, on the twentieth day of the month, the cloud lifted from over the tabernacle of the covenant [or: testimony; Heb. *eduth*]. Then the Israelites set out *by stages* from the wilderness of Sinai, and the cloud settled down in the wilderness of Paran" (Num 10:11–12, emphasis mine). It is worth quoting all this at length, because (beyond Paran which is unknown to us) it is *not what is reported later.*

Before returning to God's architectural instructions, there is one other area to attend to, namely: the absence in this priestly text of any reference to establishing a covenant.

"The fact of the matter is simple: there is no narrative in P language of a covenant at Sinai.... What Moses receives from God on the mountain are the instructions concerning the sanctuary. The two tables of the law [*eduth:* "testimony"] are mentioned (Exod 31:18; possibly 34:29–32); but there is no mention of any covenant" (Campbell, *Study Companion,* 72). Long ago, in 1993, O'Brien and I wrote of "Israel, splendidly and majestically organized around the sanctuary of God's presence in their midst, on the march toward the promised land" (*Sources of the Pentateuch,* 43, n. 55). When we realize that the text does not report any such march, it becomes less surprising that the text does not report any covenant either. Instead, it raises the question whether in fact it is this construction of a sanctuary that is the real core of the text.

While dealing with the absence of any report of a march, one other matter is worth mentioning: the guidance of Israel from Sinai to Canaan. Exodus 23:20 speaks of God's "angel" who is to guard Israel on the way and bring it to the place prepared. God's angel is also an option in the telling of the Reed Sea episode (Exod 14:19). Later, the priestly text has the Israel of the sanctuary complex guided by the cloud over the tabernacle (Num 10:11–12). Earlier, it had been the pillar (of cloud by day and fire by night); a harmonization is attempted in Numbers 9:16. In conjunction with this, there is the tradition of appeal to Hobab as guide (Num 10:29–32) and the tradition of guidance by the ark of the covenant (Num 10:33, 35–36). A multiplicity of traditions suggests a multiplicity of theologies.

Leaving all this, we may return to the priestly text concerned with the sanctuary complex. God's instructions for the sanctuary complex provide a detailed architectural blueprint for what is to be done. After the rest of the book of Exodus, all of the book of Leviticus, and the start of the book of Numbers, this completed sanctuary complex will be reported as moving out, in due and proper order, on its forward journey (Num 10:11–28). It will never be reported, in similar fashion, as arriving anywhere. It departs; it does not arrive. It starts; it does not stop. This observation makes it all the more important to be clear regarding what is said about the complex back at the beginning. Why is this strange "going-nowhere" construction so important?

The instructions for making the components of this sanctuary complex are given by God in an address to Moses. The address is introduced: "The LORD said to Moses" (25:1). The second-person singular address is used throughout (exception: 25:10, unless emended). Pointing perhaps to later expansion, the introduction to the address is not repeated until late in the speech and then repeatedly ("The LORD spoke to Moses," 30:11, 17, 22, 34; 31:1, 12).

The technical term "pattern" (*tabnit*) is used only three times in these chapters (i.e., 25–31; 35–40): in God's speech of instruction, at the beginning and end of chapter 25 (25:9 [twice]; 25:40). The occurrences encompass four articles: the ark of the covenant itself, its lid (cover, mercy seat), the table for the bread of the presence, and the lampstand. To contain these, the tabernacle (*mishkan*) is to be built (26:1–6) and also the frame over which it is to be draped (26:15–30). The fine fabric of the tabernacle is to be covered by a protective tent (26:7–14). When the tabernacle is to be erected, the command specifically notes that it shall be done according to what was shown "on the mountain" (26:30). All this so that God may "dwell among them" (25:8; cf. 29:43).

To be placed inside the tabernacle, hanging in front of the ark of the covenant, is the curtain (26:31–35), separating the "holy place" from the "most holy"; there is also to be a screen in front of the entrance (26:36–37); then there is an altar, overlaid with bronze and associated with fatty ashes (so presumably for burnt offerings), with rings for the poles by which it is to be carried (27:1–8). For the last time in these chapters, it is noted that it is to be made as "you were shown on the mountain" (27:8). These references to what Moses was shown on the mountain — all four of them (see 25:9, 40; 26:30; 27:8) — do not recur in what follows.

Other than the nature of the references back to God, what sets this text apart is its relative simplicity — about two chapters' worth of it, no more. Any experienced camper would recognize the gear: a frame to spread the tent over; the tent itself, with an inner and outer covering; the sacred paraphernalia to go inside — the ark itself, the curtain dividing the sacred space, and the table with its equipment for incense, drink offerings, and the bread of the Presence, the lamp-stand, and finally a screen for the entrance and a portable altar for the offerings. Any competent camper would have no trouble envisaging dismantling, transporting, and reassembling these. One might be extremely reverent in handling the sacred paraphernalia; nevertheless, they are eminently portable. More important, stripped of its wealth and its finery, this sanctuary allows God to dwell in Israel's midst pretty much anywhere or, if we prefer more precise theological language, to be symbolized among us pretty much anywhere. For ease of reference I will refer to this limited construction as the "sanctuary module." It is compact; it is simple.

What will be seen in what follows is that this relatively simple and compact "sanctuary module" in the text has been expanded by numerous items associated with its use. Interestingly, these expansions are less significant in the text of chapters 35–40 concerned with the construction of the sanctuary, according to God's instructions.

Following the instructions for this sanctuary module, the text goes on to list a number of varied items as commanded by God: a court surrounding the tabernacle, oil for the lamp, vestments for the priests, the rite of priestly ordination, the daily offerings, the altar of incense, the sanctuary tax, the bronze basin, ending with the anointing oil and incense for use exclusively in the sanctuary. Finally, Bezalel and Oholiab are commissioned for the task of implementing these orders. Appended to this is the law for the sabbath and, at the end of God's discourse, Moses is given the two tablets of the testimony (*eduth*).

A number of trace elements are pointers to the possibility of later concerns that are sanctioned by being added to God's speech here. The oil (27:20–21) is for the lamp that is to burn regularly in the "tent of meeting" (*ohel moed*). This is the first mention in this speech of any tent of meeting. There will be another dozen references in chapters 29–31 and a further dozen in chapter 40 alone. In all probability, the tent of meeting featured in a different approach to articulating God's presence in Israel and here is being blended with the idea of the tabernacle (*mishkan*). Second, in chapters 28–29, dealing with the priestly vestments and priestly ordination, the LORD is frequently referred to in the third person, despite the passages being part of a divine speech. In biblical text, it is not uncommon for this switch from first to third person to occur. All the same, it may be a pointer here to traditions that have been imported from elsewhere. Finally, it is worth noting that the use of the word "tabernacle" (*mishkan*) stops with the command for the court (27:9, 19); it is not resumed until Exodus 35:11. As noted, beginning with the oil for the lamp (27:21), the tent of meeting (*ohel moed*) appears to take the place of the tabernacle. Both are mingled in chapters 35–40, but with tabernacle predominating.

Where chapters 35–40 are concerned, the compliance phase or construction phase of the narrative, two aspects are worth noting. First, these chapters that seem to repeat so much of chapters 25–31 in fact deal principally with chapters 25–27, the "sanctuary module." Second, the tent of meeting (*ohel moed*), which was prominent in chapters 29–30, comes to remarkable prominence only in chapter 40 (references in the preceding five chapters are restricted to Exod 35:21; 38:8, 30; [and using both terms] 39:32, 40).

Where this construction phase is concerned, after a greatly reduced sabbath command, it begins with the collection of materials and next is the gathering of the workers. This is required before construction can begin. Then first comes the tabernacle, with its inner and outer layers; next the framework to support it as well as the curtain and screen. After the container, the contents follow: the ark, table, and lampstand. Up to this point, nothing is mentioned from outside chapters 25–26.

The incense altar (four verses) as well as the oil and incense (one verse) are inserted (in greatly reduced extent from their place earlier at 30:1–10 and 30:22–38) before the text on the altar of burnt offering, followed by the court, then an inventory of the materials used. Finally, the priestly vestments are made, the completion of the work noted, and erection of the whole described, including the cloud covering the tent and the glory of the LORD filling the tabernacle. The reference to what was shown Moses on the mountain (not extending there beyond the altar of burnt offering, 27:8) is replaced here by frequent reference to what the LORD had commanded. The tablets of the testimony (31:18) are not heard of again. No mention is made of the priestly ordination, the daily offerings, the sanctuary tax, or the bronze basin.

To summarize briefly: clear evidence allows the possibility that the original divine instructions concerned a relatively simple sanctuary, the "sanctuary module" of Exodus 25–27, which material has been — most understandably — subsequently expanded.

As to the second, the interplay of tabernacle and tent of meeting, it is important to recognize that these reflect different theologies of God's presence to Israel. The tabernacle reflects a theology of potentially constant presence: "so that I may dwell among them" (25:8). The tent of meeting is open to reflecting a theology of intermittent appearance: "I will meet with you, to speak to you there. I will meet with the Israelites there" (29:42–43). Nevertheless, the dwelling aspect is not far off: "I will dwell among the Israelites, and I will be their God" (29:45).

This fluctuation reflects the theological complexity of imaging the presence of God to an earthbound people. Theologians in ancient Israel were well aware of it. For example, in the prayer of consecration for Solomon's Jerusalem temple: "Will God indeed dwell on the earth? Even heaven and the highest heaven cannot contain you, much less this house that I have built!" (1 Kgs 8:27). The multiplicity of traditions has to be brought into account. The textual closeness of Exodus 29:42–43 to 29:45 prompts the reflection that perhaps one meets with God where God is symbolized as dwelling. The El Shaddai school of priestly thought, it may be noted, did not seem to share this view. When an appearance of God was complete, God departed: "And when he had finished talking with him, God went up from Abraham" (Gen 17:22); "Then God went up from him at the place where he had spoken with him" (Gen 35:13). This is appearance and disappearance theology.

Different traditions existed for the tent of meeting. In Numbers 1–10, it is right at the center of the camp of Israel (see Num 2, esp. 2:17). In another tradition, however, the tent of meeting was outside the camp, at a distance from it. "Now Moses used to take the tent and pitch it outside the camp, far off from the camp; he called it the tent of meeting. And everyone who sought the LORD would go out to the tent of meeting, which was outside the camp" (Exod 33:7). Some prefer to encounter God in the midst of the multitude; others prefer to encounter God in the solitude of the wilderness.

The differences of tradition in ancient Israel were many, at least as many as in modern Judaism or modern Christianity. So, for example, a tent of meeting is "set up" in Shiloh (Josh 18:1), about which the text tells nothing and nothing is said of any meeting with God — just the distribution of the land. A tent of meeting is reported at Shiloh in Eli's day (1 Sam 2:22); in the same period, a temple (*hekal*) of the LORD with the ark of God is also reported at Shiloh (1 Sam 3:3). On the ark's arrival in Jerusalem, David pitched a tent for it (2 Sam 6:17); in 2 Samuel 7, tent and tabernacle are mentioned in the same phrase (2 Sam 7:6). In the Jerusalem temple, the ark and the tent of meeting are installed within the same space in the temple but, unless the cherubim are represented there in two different forms, Solomon's ark is not the Sinai ark (1 Kgs 8:4, 6–7).

In Exodus 40 (as noted), the two symbols are juxtaposed, "the tabernacle of the tent of meeting" (Exod 40:2, 6, 29). Even here, however, a certain separation is apparent (see Exod 40:22, 24, 34–35). In Numbers 1–10, the two are largely mentioned separately, but not exclusively (see Num 3:7–8, 38); within these chapters, tabernacle and tent of meeting appear to be used interchangeably. The complexities can often be sorted out; nevertheless, they remain complex.

◆ ◆ ◆

Excursus:
Diachronic and Synchronic
(Process and Product)
in Numbers 1–10

Regarding Numbers 1–10, the discussion here will be at the level of the present text. Like many a text, this one is most probably the outcome of a *process,* the product of a period of development and augmentation; nevertheless, it will be dealt with exclusively as product, that is, at its final level, primarily for two reasons. First, the present text is the text we read and the ancient contributors to it were intelligent people whose contributions served a purpose. Second, I have found the most recent explorations of the process that may have produced the present text to be not overly helpful and, in some cases, to be advocating what may perhaps be possible but is unquestionably far from necessary.

The descriptions "not overly helpful" and "possible but...far from necessary" can be easily enough exemplified. Among the commentators, Martin Noth considers that Numbers 10:11–12 "belongs to the original P-narrative" while 10:13–28 "probably does not belong to the basic form of P" (*Numbers,* 76). Reversing this, Horst Seebass claims what is now Numbers 10:14–28a was originally P and belonged with 9:15–17 immediately before 10:11–12, equally P, but its position was switched by an editor, with the help of v. 13; there is a satisfying consensus that 10:13–28 is now an addition — he does not discuss what moving it contributed (*Numeri,* 7, 13). For Ludwig Schmidt, while vv. 11a and 12a are P, vv. 11b and 12b are secondary (they contradict Num 17:7 [Heb.; NRSV, 16:42]) and vv. 13–28 are even later (*Numeri,* 13). Baruch Levine, understandably, does not explore the diachronic (the process of growth), but does hint at mild unease: "it would be inaccurate to understand 10:11–28 as a record of actual marches, such as we find in chap. 33, for instance" (*Numbers 1–20,* 308). With "great caution and reticence," Noth might agree with the "actual marches" for the very late chapter 33, but for Sinai-bent pilgrims traveling a route that "could almost only be understood on the presupposition that Sinai lay in north-west Arabia" (*Numbers,* 243, 246). Great caution and reticence are certainly in order.

In the light of what we need to examine and also given that the treatment of the first part of Numbers in the commentaries of both Seebass and Schmidt was listed as "in preparation" (as of June 21, 2007), discussion here will be kept to the present text.

◆ ◆ ◆

Priestly theology

Of major moment for an understanding of aspects of priestly theology is the observation that this block of priestly text involved in the organization of Israel around the sanctuary of God's presence portrays a procession that begins with intricate detail and proceeds no further. Israel, surrounding this sanctuary, is left as it were en route, on the journey.

The apparent assortment of texts that comprise Numbers 1–10 has a certain sense of unity, though imperfect. It opens and closes with the Israelites as a numbered body, ordered for camping and marching, centered on the tabernacle. In association with these concerns, it has two passages on the Levites, dedicated to the service of the tabernacle (Num 1:47–53; 8:5–26). Between these are associated matters that were felt to need treatment before Israel left Sinai.

The body of Israel and the corps of Levites perform a combined function in regard to the tabernacle. The body of Israel is marshaled around the tabernacle in a highly systematic fashion. The corps of Levites provides an inner cushion of protection, ensuring that the cultically vulnerable Israelites do not endanger themselves by approaching too closely.

Intense conceptual energy is involved in the organizational planning outlined in the text of the disposition of Israel around this tabernacle. What interpretation (i.e., current interpreters) must not lose sight of is that, for all the language of setting out and marching, this vast phalanx is not followed beyond its setting out, ending with Numbers 10:28. The meaning of this text may not be found in movement. Interpretation must be wary of latching on to a surface appearance; the text speaks of movement but does not manifest it in any but the broadest terms (Num 10:12b only). The text's meaning may need to be sought elsewhere.

In this context, Noth's reflection on the role of itinerary in the book of Numbers needs to be kept in mind. With regard to the wilderness of Paran, he writes: "There is no certainty as to its location, especially as the P-itinerary only mentions isolated places and is scarcely based upon a definite concept of a coherent itinerary" (*Numbers*, 76). Movement may not be what matters.

The detail involved in these texts, unparalleled elsewhere in the Older Testament, is indicative of the intense energy invested in the idea of this organization of the people. Its beginning in the taking of a census is sourced in a command from God, delivered to Moses at the tent of meeting (Num 1:1, 19). The numbers involved appear to be vast; the total is in excess of half a million males of military age (options for understanding these are discussed by Noth, Mendenhall, etc.). The exception made for the Levites is precisely in relation to the tabernacle. Unlike David's census, carried out by the military and counting soldiers (2 Sam 24:1–9), this census is to be associated with the tabernacle and counts able-bodied adults.

Given that only the departure is reported for this complex (unless undue weight is given to 10:12b), it is worth noting that at the outset the role of the Levites is specified both for when starting to journey and when stopping to camp (Num 1:51). Beyond the task of dismantling and reassembling the tabernacle, a significant Levite role is to act as buffer between the tabernacle and the main body of the people. A prime reason for such a buffer is the presence of the tabernacle as dwelling place of God in the midst of Israel.

As the LORD's command opened the chapter, a note of Israel's compliance with that command closes the chapter (Num 1:1, 54). This is serious business.

The use of technical terms, such as "tabernacle" and "tent of meeting," is not such as to allow precise identification of the contexts they might come from. The fusion of Exodus 40 — with its "tabernacle of the tent of meeting" (40:2, 6, 29) and its use of both terms independently (tabernacle, 14x; tent, 9x; see esp. 40:34–35) — appears to be maintained subsequently. The tent of meeting, for example, is used in Numbers 1:1 and 2:2, 17; the tabernacle is used at Numbers 1:50–53, and not at all in chapter 2. Only the tent of meeting is used in chapter 8; only the tabernacle in chapter 9 and in 10:11, 17, 21. Whatever distinctions may be seen influencing the use of these, they do not appear to have bearing on the overall sense of the present text as explored here.

The command from God to Moses at the start of Numbers 1 gave a task to Moses and Aaron together ("you and Aaron," v. 3); the command from God at the start of Numbers 2 is addressed to both Moses and Aaron. Their task was to implement in detail what in 1:52 was commanded in general terms for the non-Levites: the Israelites shall camp in their respective camping units (*machaneh* or *degel*; NRSV: regimental camps), each in their smaller unit (*tsaba*; NRSV: companies). Each major unit (*machaneh* or *degel*) comprises three smaller units (*tsaba*). The leaders of the three units are named; the numbers are given for each smaller unit as well as for the major units. The camping order is primary; the marching order, or sequence on the move, is noted at the end of each major unit. From the outset, the camping location is given in respect of the tent of meeting (2:2);

immediately before, the language of tabernacle was used, the place where God dwells (1:48–54).

Camping order and marching order are combined in the one text; the focus is on the tent of meeting, the place of God. God is somehow at the center of the camp; God is somehow in the middle of the march. The tribes are listed in terms of their camping location in respect of the tent of meeting (the camping order: east, south, west, and north of the tent). After the summary for each major unit, its place in the sequence when Israel sets out is specified (the marching order: the sequence is clockwise around the camping locations; see 2:9, 16, 17, 24, 31). Judah camps on the east of the tent, with Issachar and Zebulun; they set out first. Reuben camps to the south of it, with Simeon and Gad; they set out second. The tent of meeting, with the Levites, is treated slightly differently, with setting out taking precedence: tent and Levites set out in the center, the camping location having already been established in 2:2; the correlation of camping and marching in v. 17b is general. Ephraim camps on the west of the tent, with Manasseh and Benjamin; they set out third. Camping to the north of it is Dan, with Asher and Naphtali, and in the order of march they are last. All this is laid out in exhaustive detail, with names and numbers. Total compliance with God's command is noted at the end of the chapter, both for camping order and marching order (2:34).

One might attribute the exhaustive detail to priestly obsession, if one were inclined toward such prejudice. Preferably, the exhaustive detail reflects the importance of the matter: God at the center of Israel. As has been indicated earlier, given the importance of the detail at this point and the absence of any of this detail once the march has got under way (i.e., after 10:28), the importance of the matter is probably not to be sought in the movement of the march — at least, by ancient Israel toward a promised land.

After attending to associated matters, the present text returns to the movement of the march with Numbers 9:15–23 and 10:11–28. The first passage places the journey under the sign of God's will: "At the command of the LORD the Israelites would set out, and at the command of the LORD they would camp" (Num 9:18, reiterated in 9:23). Echoes of earlier passages in Exodus (e.g., Exod 13:21–22;

24:15b–18; 40:2, 34–38) and foreshadowing of the journey ahead point to the likelihood that this passage is a secondary addition. If so, the need for it emphasizes the observation that, although a journey is the understood background for what is to come, the text is silent about the presence of this tabernacle/tent complex, so important in what has gone before. Only in a secondary addition at this point was it possible to underscore the issue of God's guidance.

Within the second passage (Num 10:11–28), verses 13–28 are judged to be probably secondary (Noth: "probably does not belong to the basic form of P" [*Numbers,* 76]; we have earlier seen the subjectivity of such positions). If these verses were secondary, it would not change what is being argued here one iota. It is *possible* to add this detailed departure at this point. It is *impossible* to add a correspondingly detailed arrival anywhere; the text to come is not concerned with one.

The arguments offered in support of the secondary nature of verses 13–28 do not carry weight. Seebass notes three (*Numeri,* 7). First, for Seebass, 10:12b already has the cloud in the wilderness of Paran. But Hebrew narrative frequently reports in general fashion what is then reported in detail (Knierim, *Numbers,* 157: "basically . . . specifically"). Second, for Seebass, 10:28b clearly blends into its context, repeating the initial verb of v. 13. Two points need to be made: one single verb ("and they journeyed") is a most miserable blending; alas, there is no context to be blended into. Third, for Seebass, the division of labor between the Gershonites and Merarites on the one hand and the Kohathites on the other reflects prescriptions in Numbers 3–4. The relationship is clear; whether the relationship implies secondary status for 10:13–28 is not clear. The general formulation in 2:17 is vague enough to accommodate something of the kind. The passages in Numbers 3–4 unfold it with precision. Whether the sort of understanding given in 10:13–28 depends on them is quite uncertain.

As so often in these speculative situations, the issue comes back to Martin Noth's observation that, from a source-critical point of view, often what is possible may not be necessary. With regard to the probably secondary status of Numbers 10:13–28, the first question is: "Is this source-critical move (i.e., relegation of vv. 13–28 to secondary

status) possible?" The answer is "Quite clearly: Yes." The next question should be: "Is this source-critical move necessary?" The answer
is "Quite frankly: No."

The argument being made here about the centrality of God's presence to Israel is valid, whether or not this passage is secondary. It
is possible to offer this detailed description of the departure at this
point. A correspondingly detailed description of arrival cannot be
offered later anywhere. The text to come is not concerned with what
has been central to much of the earlier priestly text at Sinai.

Finally, it is important to remember the significant differences
noted within much of the earlier priestly text at Sinai. A few examples
will have to suffice. Exodus 25–31 uses different language in several
areas from Exodus 35–40. A primary focus is visible in Exodus 25–
31 on the simple "sanctuary module" found in chapters 25–27; this
focus is partially respected in Exodus 35–40. Furthermore, in Exodus
40, the cloud covered the tent and the glory of the LORD filled the
tabernacle. In the Numbers material, the glory of the LORD is not so
much as mentioned. Different traditions and different theologies are
present.

Conclusions

Three major conclusions follow from these observations. In themselves, they are relatively simple. In their implications, they are
theologically significant.

Conclusion #1

If there is one single itinerary only from the Sea to Sinai, and it is
probably priestly, two inferences are immediate:

1. The duality that exists from the call of Moses to the deliverance
   at the Sea ceases after the Sea.

2. The priestly text at Sinai must deal with matters important
   enough to have all Israel brought there for that alone.

There are two reports of Moses' call, two accounts of the plagues
in Egypt, the Passover, and the deliverance at the Sea. Did the two
narrative sequences stop there? It is entirely possible that they did.

Alternatively, given the presence of Exodus 15, whatever its age, it is possible that one narrative sequence used the song to have Israel move directly to Canaan. "In your steadfast love you led the people whom you redeemed...to your holy abode." Philistines trembled, Edomites were dismayed, Moabites trembled, the inhabitants of Canaan melted away. God's people, whom God had acquired, were brought in and planted on God's mountain, God's abode and sanctuary (Exod 15:13–17). It is possible. That leaves the other narrative sequence free to have Israel move to Sinai — using an itinerary that is probably priestly.

If it is not essential for Israel to go to Sinai on its way to Canaan — not essential because one narrative sequence does not have Israel go there — the priestly text at Sinai must be of significant importance.

A further inference leads into the realm of high speculation. A signpost is enough; we will not embark on the journey here. Exodus 19–24 forms what we might call a capsule. It begins with the manifestation of God on the mountain, continues with the decalogue and lawcode, concluding with an appendix-like account of the celebration of covenant (24:1–11). If there is no pre-priestly narrative to take Israel from the Sea to Sinai, how did a pre-priestly Israel get there and what are the "capsule" chapters doing at Sinai? If the "capsule" has been prefaced to the priestly text, what kind of setting (whether institutional or literary) might the capsule have had before being "prefaced" to the priestly text? To follow this signpost would take us on a road that leads to high speculation. All that might be said here is that the primary point of the magnificent theophany of Exodus 19 appears to be preparation for the gift of the decalogue and the following lawcode.

The opening episode (Exod 19:3–8, "eagles' wings") is clearly about covenant and clearly conditional; whether or not the text is about Israel's becoming God's people in covenant is not so clear — in fact, far from clear. "Treasured possession," "priestly kingdom," and "holy nation" are three attributes that, at first sight, may be thought to go beyond being God's people. The explicit covenant aspect here and the explicitly conditional quality here create a level of uncertainty over covenant and condition in what follows. After the decalogue and lawcode (Exod 20:1–32:19), there is what might be called a first appendix that concerns the occupation of Canaan (Exod 23:23–33) and a second appendix then concerns the covenant, combining the meal on the mountain and the ceremony at the altar at the foot of the mountain (24:1–2, 3–8, 9–11 [12–14]). Enough!

Conclusion #2

Priestly Sinai is about God's dwelling in a tabernacle in Israel's midst. There is no covenant at all in the priestly text at Sinai. The text concerns a tent-centered sanctuary, God's instructions for it and Israel's construction of it. What gives that sanctuary the importance that its place in the narrative demands?

The opening statement given God is emphatically clear: "Have them make me a sanctuary, so that I may dwell among them" (Exod 25:8). The resonance is there with Jeremiah 7:3, 7 ("I will dwell with you"); it matters. It is important to notice that the explicit concern for this sanctuary to be made according to the pattern God showed Moses on the mountain is not repeated after Exodus 27:8. A relatively simple "sanctuary module" resulted. Additional items were naturally attracted to it in due course; the module itself is relatively simple. The insistence on the pattern shown on the mountain is motivated by the concern for God's presence in the tabernacle.

What the tabernacle involved was simple enough: a frame, a covering for it, the ark, a curtain before it, the table and lampstand, and a portable altar for burnt offerings. Given approximate dimensions of forty-five feet long by eighteen feet wide and fifteen feet high (c. fifteen meters by six meters by five meters = some fifty-six frames), the tabernacle itself is sizable, but not huge. Sizable, because naturally one would hardly want to envisage a chintzy pup tent for one's God. It may never have been real; in its dimensions, it is not unreal. Stripped of elaborate ornamentation, the idea is not unthinkable. This is not to claim that it was done; it is to claim that it could be thought. Thought-wise, it belongs within the realm of the realizable. The imagery does not detract from the faith-claim: God dwells among us.

An intriguing speculation that may be signposted here, but will not be explored, is whether this conception was retrojected into the past, significant for the present, or projected into the future — or embraced all three possibilities. The portrayal, with God and Moses on Sinai, certainly depicts the time of ancient Israel's past. Is there any evidence that the authors embraced this portrayal or that the situating of a later composition at such an early and significant time was indeed a retrojection? Around the time of exile and in the postexilic period, significance for the present or projection into the future are both evidently possible. The text mandating the sanctuary module portrays a God dwelling among the people outside Canaan and capable of movement with that people. Such presence of God to God's people is surely of supreme significance at almost any time.

Conclusion #3

Priestly dispositions for Israel's camping and marching in Numbers 1–10 are about the presence of God's sanctuary in Israel's midst, God's presence to Israel when Israel is no longer at the holy mountain (whether Sinai or Zion).

Driving this observation is the massive imbalance between what the text has Israel prepare for and what the text has Israel do. The issue is not the debated status of Numbers 10:12b; 9:15–23; or 10:13–28; the issue is the weight given to organization for the march when there is no mention of such organization or such a march later.

The intensity of thought and energy that went into elaborating and producing texts such as Numbers 1–2 and 9–10 can scarcely be underestimated. Yet those who expended this thought and energy knew full well that after Numbers 10:28, the complex they had so carefully elaborated would never be heard of again, not in any journey to the plains of Moab, not in any construction within the confines of Canaan.

The apparently obsessive expenditure of thought and energy in these texts about Sinai can be accounted for by the faith-claim that God was intimately associated with the tent of meeting or tabernacle and that the tabernacle or tent of meeting was central to Israel. The construction was made at God's command. The disposition of the people was made at God's command. God was present in the midst of God's people.

The narrative of the consecration of the Jerusalem temple has God reply to Solomon: "I have consecrated this house that you have built,

and put my name there forever; my eyes and my heart will be there
for all time" (1 Kgs 9:3). As the smoke rose from the ruined temple
(2 Kgs 25:9), such deuteronomic faith may have needed reformula-
tion. The confession embodied in Deuteronomy's "Shema" is central
for people's faith (Deut 6:4–9). The unity of their God in their lives
may have been reflected in the one temple in Jerusalem; it could survive without it. The priestly formulation of their faith was similarly
under challenge; the ark, the tent of meeting, and the holy vessels
had been in the temple (1 Kgs 8:1–11, without reference, however,
to Sinai). The temple was central to the exercise of priesthood. The
confession of God's presence, reformulated to be embodied in Sinai's
tabernacle, would have been central for priestly faith. Such a presence
could be with Israel in Israel's journeying; such a presence could be
with Israel outside the land, in exile from Canaan.

Beyond these three conclusions, one further observation is worth
emphasizing. As we have seen, a variety of traditions and theologians
have contributed to the texts of Exodus 25–31, 35–40, and within
Numbers 1–10. There can be no doubt that this is priestly literature.
However, language that reduces this multiplicity to an implied unity
is best avoided. Priestly Code, Priestly Document, Priestly Source,
Priestly Writing, just bare P, even Priestly redaction, all imply a certain unity. The evidence for that unity needs to be provided; in my
judgment, it is lacking. Scholars have claimed, for example, that the
extent of the Priestly source can clearly be demonstrated by its special
language, its overall structure, and the manifold literary references
between its texts. The claim has been made that there is indeed a
priestly source, assembled and unified from various priestly texts,
forming a composition with its own basic and formal unity, a unity
that is stylistic, thematic, and theological. Such views were reiterated by reputable scholars as recently as 2006; old myths die hard.
In my judgment, the evidence for the presence of priestly literature is
irrefutable; the evidence for the unity implied by language of a Priestly
source is lacking. As an analogy, being European does not mean
that Germans think like Italians or Spaniards act like the French.
As noted at the beginning of this book, Rolf Knierim has written:
"The expression 'Priestly writings' refers much more to a history of
ongoing priestly traditions rather than to a uni-level source, as in the

case of J or E" (*Numbers*, 7). I agree; so do many competent biblical scholars. The habits of scholarly language may not yet have caught up with such conviction. Observation reveals that E has already evaporated and that J is evaporating because the evidence for unity is not there; in my judgment, P will evaporate when the hold of tradition is loosened.

~MODERN FAITH~

Sinai is not a way station en route to the promised land. If source theory is not to be relied on in the Pentateuch, the arrangement of Israel's pentateuchal traditions along apparently chronological lines belongs to the final stages of editorial activity. Promptly enough, the human hankering to know about the past turned this arrangement into history. It may be worse. It may be a human hankering to bind God to the historically demonstrable. In recent years, much has been made of such yearning in terms of salvation history and the like. We may be much freer to encounter God in pentateuchal text when the shackles of history are thrown off.

In organizing Israel's traditions of Sinai as part of a journey from Egypt to Canaan, Israel's theologians ran a considerable risk. Their endeavor could be reduced to the almost mundane. Journeys people understand; mountains people encounter. The tangible can obscure the sublime. The risk is of focusing on what happened (the tangible) and losing sight of what it meant (the sublime).

Israel's memories of the experience at Sinai need to be balanced by and complemented by the memories of Elijah's experience at Sinai. Within Israel's traditions of Sinai, Moses on the mountain needs to be balanced by and complemented by God's presence off the mountain in the sanctuary, even while still at Sinai. The telling of Israel's experience begins with smoking fire and a quaking mountain. Elijah's experience began with much the same, but God was not in the wind or the earthquake or the fire. For Elijah, God was in the sound of sheer stillness; for Israel, Moses ascended into the silence of the mountain. For Elijah, God was not in the tangible, but in the stillness of the sublime. Stripped of the tangible, we are reduced to our human yearning for the sublime. For Israel, the risk is reducing the experience of Sinai to a moment in the middle of a journey; instead, it should stand mountainous at a high point in life, national or individual. Journey as mundane travel can be a spatial movement from Point A through possible intermediary stages to Point B. Journey as metaphor can be a spiritual movement from Stage A through possible intermediary points to Stage B. Sinai as intermediary stage in the middle of a spatial journey lacks the impact of Sinai as "mountain," a high point, in a people's spiritual development.

Once we have recognized the minimal nature of the journey aspect before the arrival at the mountain — perhaps more concerned with the stories of survival than with Sinai — and the absence of any sustained journey aspect for the sanctuary complex after the mountain, we may be better placed to focus on the meaning of the mountain. To help with that focus, we may realize that it would not be so very surprising if an analysis of the full wilderness tradition (a detour we cannot take here) revealed the possibility of a chain of significant stories, from the shore of the Sea to the bank of the Jordan, that did not necessarily involve the Sinai complex at all. As we have already noted, such a possibility would fit comfortably with a number of factors that attracted the attention of Gerhard von Rad: "It is thus obvious that the Sinai tradition has been secondarily inserted into already extant traditions concerning the Wanderings in the Wilderness.... Obviously it was only at a comparatively late date that this complex of tradition was inserted into the canonical picture of the saving history.... The Sinai tradition lived in independence longer than all the other traditional elements whose combination led to the construction of the canonical picture of the saving history" (*Old Testament Theology*, 1:187–88; also Wellhausen, see earlier in this chapter).

What may be the "meaning of the mountain"? For Exodus 19–24, the core is the gift of law. The event as portrayed is memorable; its meaning must not be forgotten. For Exodus 25–40, the core is the gift of presence, God's presence. The sanctuary as constructed is forgettable for most moderns; its meaning, in any age, must not be forgotten. Originally, the law and the sanctuary traditions were separate, just as originally the ten commandments and the lawcode were separate. Brought together, they articulate a high point in a people's development.

The interplay of what I have termed the logical and chronological is important here, even if these ideas need further refinement, a task that lies beyond my reach at the present time. It is a valid supposition that the text regarding the sanctuary at Sinai may have been put together *chronologically* after the collapse of 587 BCE, quite possibly in Babylon. If such a text was to have worth within the panoply of Israel's traditions, it was *logically* essential that it be situated with Moses and God, portrayed at the time of exodus and at Mount Sinai (*Jebel Musa*). As a late text, chronologically, it obviously drew on memories of the stone and timber of the Jerusalem temple. Much biblical scholarship has presented the sanctuary text at Sinai as a *projection* of the future temple. If the text is seen, chronologically, as a composition occurring after the destruction of the temple, *retrojection* is more likely. The text, situated now in the wilderness, presents features that were embodied in the Jerusalem temple.

What is the point of such a composition? As we have said, for the text to have worth and value, it needed logically to be situated in the portrayal of Moses and God at Sinai, especially in the supposition that it may have been chronologically late in its composition. Situated at Sinai, it was creating the potential for this conception of the sanctuary to serve as a symbolic image, allowing for the imaginative construal of the God–Israel relationship in the present (God has presence to Israel, Israel has access to God — anywhere) and so giving meaning to the world of Israel's exile, even without Jerusalem's temple.

Law, in one understanding at least, is a matter of how we live with one another. Biblically, "how we live" includes faith in God; biblically, "with one another" includes justice in society. Presence, in the understanding of Sinai, is a matter of how God lives with Israel — correlative: how Israel lives with God.

The two — God's law and God's presence; God and society; faith and justice — interact constantly. It is symbolically visible here, in the text complex associated with this mountain. In Exodus 19, there is fear and trembling: thunder and lightning, smoke and fire, violent trembling, with emphatic "keep off" limits set around the mountain. In Exodus 25–40, all is sweetness and light: the text opens with God's "that I may dwell among them" and ends with "the glory of the LORD" filling the tabernacle. In Numbers 1–10, both are there, sweetness and light but also fear and trembling. God's presence in the center of Israel echoes sweetness and light; the need for a surrounding buffer against the awesome nature of God's reality is a reminder of fear and trembling. As Israel's theologians knew, and any theologian knows, awe and love are potent words and inevitably are intermingled in any relationship with God.

Isolating Sinai as a high point in Israel's experience and self-understanding is therefore helpful. It frees us from the trap of reducing Sinai to a stage on the journey, even though a stage of massive importance. We are freed from the trap by realizing that in the biblical text, despite all its emphasis on the sanctuary complex, the further journey of that sanctuary complex spatially never happened. Sinai is freed for the recognition of its place as high point in Israel's spiritual journey. The sanctuary complex needs to be recognized as a symbol of God's presence in Israel's midst. Focused on the presence of God to Israel, the sanctuary complex too becomes a high point in Israel's spiritual journey — a journey that does not end with exile.

SUMMARY

As we have seen, when exploring modern faith in relation to biblical text a couple of principles come into play. One was expressed in *Rethinking the Pentateuch:* there is "a shift from the Pentateuch as a record of Israel's *remembering its past* to the Pentateuch as a record of *Israel's pondering its present*" (p. 9). This applies to much of the Pentateuch and elsewhere too in the Older Testament. This principle impacts solidly on the understanding of revelation as coming exclusively *from above and from the past,* an understanding that still influences many. As we ponder our lives and remember our past, in all the rich variety it involves (family, schooling, religion, culture), we come to a deeper understanding of ourselves and our world and a correspondingly deeper insight into our understanding of our God. That is surely an aspect of revelation, not the whole but an aspect — coming *from below and from the present*. These two thoughts are important for us to recollect from time to time in the unfolding of this book.

In the book of Genesis, *traditions about the ancestors tell people in Israel something of who they are*. In the book of Exodus, *the traditions tell Israel something about who God is*. In the traditions from the mountain of Sinai, in parts of the books of Exodus, Leviticus, and Numbers, Israel's thinkers and theologians have organized two blocks of text of major importance: the gift of divine law and the gift of divine presence. Predominantly, *traditions such as these tell Israel something about their relationship with God*.

What do we make of the gift of God's law and the gift of God's presence? Was the capsule of God's gift of the law brought out of splendid isolation somewhere to be situated at the absolute beginning of Israel's national existence? *God's law matters*. As we have seen, the observance of God's law need not be a condition of relationship with God; it can be a consequence of that relationship. Beyond the relationship with God, in biblical texts, the observance of God's law is a condition of good relationships between human beings in society; justice in society should flow from the observance of such law. *God's presence matters*. A God who is unconcerned is a God who need not concern us. A God who is present to us and who journeys in our midst in all the vagaries of our lives, that is a God we can call our own, who is concerned for us and who concerns us.

It is told of a Jewish community in Eastern Europe that in time of need a delegation would go to a sacred place in the forest and enact a special ritual. After a few generations had passed, when need arose again the delegation gathered at the place and realized that no one knew the details of the ritual. So they said a prayer instead. A few generations later, they again gathered in the forest and realized that, with the passage of the years, no one was left who knew exactly where the place was. So instead they told the story of the sacred place and the special ritual. Is something similar happening in these priestly texts? Is it possible that instead of the recall of an old tradition or the projection of a future program, the priestly Sinai texts on the sanctuary complex were a telling of the story? What was evoked in hearers was not remembrance of what was nor vision of what might be but pleasure in the telling of the story. "And God said to Moses,..." Was immersion in the text an approximation to immersion in the presence of God and awareness of the closeness of God, even when far from the Jerusalem temple? Did the telling of the story evoke awareness of God's presence? Did the emphasis on precious metals and luxurious appurtenances solace those living in the abject poverty of exile?

Genesis One on creation has to be a matter of faith and not of fact; too many other biblical portrayals of creation differ from it to allow of any contamination from thoughts about fact. Two narratives about the flood keep the focus on faith. The exodus narrative clearly has its legendary aspects, with a focus therefore on faith. If the priestly texts at Sinai joined with these, they would be in good company.

What matters, ultimately, is the role we expect past facts to play in present faith. In most cases, it is a subtle and delicate role.

What was said above may be repeated here. The outcome may be a deepened and more realistic understanding of God's revelation. Today, the encounter with God in present experience (fuller understanding of ourselves, our traditions, and our God) may lead to a selectivity in the passages of scripture that are read. In Israel's past, the encounter with God in their experience often led to a selectivity in the passages of scripture that were written in their day, from major creations to minor revisions. As a result, the revelation of God is not shrouded in the mists of a distant past; the revelation of God is found in the clarity of an immediate present.

The research that has emphasized the lateness of this editorial ordering in logical sequence enables users to view the text under at least two aspects. First, there is the significance of the episodes or clusters themselves. Second, there is the meaning to be derived from the sequence in which they have been arranged. Discretion is needed in discerning which of these should predominate in any given interpretation. It is to be hoped that the reflections to be found earlier here will help with this discretion.

Present in the background is the awareness that if the present apparently chronological sequence is given us by relatively late compilers of the present text, it may well turn out to be that original formulations of the tradition were more fragmented. A section on Israel's understanding of its ancestors might not have been preceded by the material now in Genesis 1–11; it may not have been followed by the traditions of exodus, Sinai, and desert journey — and vice versa. The understanding of Israel and its God derived from the traditions of the Exodus might well have stood alone. If the organization of certain traditions to constitute a journey from the shores of the Sea, by way of Mount Sinai, to the banks of the Jordan is relatively late, some of the traditions of Sinai and Horeb may regain an independence they have lost and the stories of the desert wandering may take on a significance and individuality of their own. Exodus 15, of course, provides witness to a passage from the Sea directly to Canaan.

As these possibilities are explored, it is likely that the revelatory quality of the text will be enhanced. As life was lived and understood, in its beginnings and in its later reflections, the enduring experience of God was and still is available to be better known and to be more fully open to multiple understandings.

Part Two

The Book of Joshua
and Enigma

*The book of Joshua is seen by many as purporting
to be about Israel's conquest of Canaan, which is what
it certainly is not. The enigma:*

What then is the book about?

Chapter 4

Israel's Traditions about Joshua and the Land

INTRODUCTION

Over recent years, the book of Joshua has been a source of considerable embarrassment to many Bible readers. Three reasons have predominated. First, the image of God found in the book of Joshua is not the image of God found by many in the ordinariness of their day-to-day lives. Massed Israelites delivered at the Reed Sea, massed Israelites numbered at Sinai, and massed Israelites crossing the Jordan, processing around Jericho and sweeping up the country from south to north — it does not fit well with the God many of us encounter in our lives. Second, it has been embarrassing that theoreticians and archaeologists have failed completely in their attempts to correlate the picture in the book of Joshua with what we know of ancient Israel in the land. Third, many today are massively embarrassed by the idea of a God ordering the killing of anything that was not Israelite — "men and women, young and old, oxen, sheep, and donkeys" (Josh 6:21); "that they might be utterly destroyed, and might receive no mercy, but be exterminated, just as the LORD had commanded Moses.... So Joshua took the whole land, according to all that the LORD had spoken to Moses" (Josh 11:20, 22). Even if we know that these passages are a small part of the book, probably about what never happened, and very probably quite late additions, they are still embarrassing.

Close reading of the text gives us a pleasant surprise. All these centuries, those who read the first part of the book of Joshua as an account that unfolded how Israel entered and took the land have been suckered. Maybe it is not such an account at all. Readers may have been misled all this time. Close reading, freed from preconceptions, reveals that anyone who thought the Bible claimed that Israel entered the land pretty much the way it is depicted in the book of Joshua has been taken for a sucker, all these centuries. Maybe ninety-nine-year traffic rights to bridges like the Golden Gate or the Verrazzano Narrows for a hundred dollars would be a bargain.

The introductory chapter, Joshua 1, should be the first item to set alarm bells ringing. While it is the lead-in to the book of Joshua, its concerns are far from identical with those of Joshua 2–12; its overwhelming concern is to place Joshua's activity under the authority of Moses and ultimately, therefore, under the authority of God. The Joshua traditions in chapters 2–12 are concerned with walled cities (Jericho, Ai, peace with Gibeon). In Joshua 1, walled cities and towns are not mentioned. "You shall put this people in possession of the land" (1:6). The compiler, responsible for the chapter, was very probably part of the deuteronomic movement. The unity so central to Deuteronomy (the Shema for the individual; the centralization of worship for the nation) was explicitly extended to embrace Israel in the land. Three figures are at the core of this unity: God, Moses, and Joshua. "As I was with Moses [says God], so I will be with you [Joshua]" (Josh 1:5). This unity is highlighted as the whole is wrapped up: "As the LORD had commanded his servant Moses, so Moses commanded Joshua, and so Joshua did" (11:15).

Was the compiler of the text convinced that, in bringing together the various traditions available, a picture was being shaped of the sequence of events in the time of Joshua? Or was the compiler of the text convinced that the traditions being brought together were worth preserving and gave insight into events that were significant to Israel, that may have been thought to reflect the sequence of events from Joshua's time, but that certainly brought meaning into aspects of Israel's life in the land? Possibly a bit of both; we almost certainly cannot know. But after Deuteronomy, a leader was needed; that leader had to be Joshua. Traditional texts are being used; of that we can be reasonably sure. They have been stitched together in a relatively logical sequence; the sequence does not portray the events of Israel's entry into the land. Of that we can be quite sure.

The first pointer is in the opening speech given to God: "From the wilderness and the Lebanon as far as the great river, the river Euphrates, all the land of the Hittites, to the Great Sea in the west shall be your territory" (Josh 1:4). This is an unbelievable stretch of territory, from the Euphrates to the Mediterranean. No credible politician in modern Israel or modern Palestine would dare make such a claim. Media outlets may talk of 1967 boundaries, the Gaza Strip, the West Bank; they do not put the Euphrates River and the Mediterranean Sea in the same sentence; that is something approaching half the Middle East. Ancient Israel, in its wildest moments, could not make such a claim as real. Earlier in the book of Exodus, at Sinai, the text at first is within the realm of the real: "I will set your borders from the Red Sea/Sea of Reeds to the sea of the Philistines"; then it moves into fantasy: "from the wilderness to the Euphrates" (Exod 23:31). The first bit is realistic enough; the second was never a reality. The claim to sovereignty over half the Middle East (Deut 11:4; Josh 1:4) is only a little less extreme than Ben-Sirach's mind-stretching "from sea to sea and from the Euphrates to the ends of the earth" (Sir 44:21). It is a theological ambit claim; it would be out of place at the beginning of a report that has Joshua only get as far as Hazor and northern Israel. Many Deuteronomists were great theologians; some were also great dreamers. Within the dream, of course, is an understanding of God — unique, universal, encompassing all.

The claim has been described as "a description of the territorial limits of Israel in the days of Davidic-Solomonic glory" (Durham, *Exodus*, 336); it is not. The territorial limits of Israel in the days of David and Solomon were never of that order. At best, it may be "an ideal projection" attributed by tradition to the glorious reign of Solomon (Childs, *Exodus*, 487; cf. 1 Kgs 4:21, NRSV; Heb., 5:1). Theoretical claims could be as unreal then as they can be now. Rather than even a theological ambit claim, these texts reflect a theological dream. It should be called for what it is: illusion on a grand scale. We can scarcely deride it. Memories of voices raised in lusty song, celebrating Britain ruling the waves, or Germany owning the world, or simply America being the beautiful are all too fresh — and none too different.

The second pointer is in the same opening chapter. Joshua sends officers through the camp to prepare people to cross the Jordan in three days' time (Josh 1:11 — when the spies will be back). A minor problem is that Joshua has not yet sent the spies to go view the land; technically, therefore, the timing of their return is as yet unknown. This is a compilation of traditions, not a running commentary on events as they unfolded. Harmonization, smoothing things out, would be easy; however, as in so many cases, the text does not do the harmonizing. It would have been simple to have the officers say: we will need to be ready to cross the Jordan "when the spies return"; the text, however, does not have them say this. Of course, it is perfectly acceptable for the text to be a compilation of traditions. This is simply a pointer indicating that the text's purpose may be other than providing an account reporting how Israel entered and took the land.

The clincher comes with Joshua 5, before any city has been taken, before the Jericho episode. The chapter has three items, all of which are thoroughly theological (circumcision, produce, army commander); none comes near to touching on the historical. Circumcision reflects the concerns of Genesis 17, late and priestly. No army commander would countenance the circumcision of troops on the eve of battle. No issue is made of it on those terms in the text. The ending of the manna is theologically symbolic. It symbolizes the ending of a period; the wilderness period is over. It is not looking at the realities of food procurement (requisitioned from others) or agricultural production (requiring seasons and years). The "commander of the army of the LORD" does not offer Joshua advice or assistance; his command is for Joshua to remove his sandals, because he is on holy ground. As the opening of the book made clear, accompanying the transition from the wilderness to the land is a transition in the leadership from Moses to Joshua; from Moses commissioned at the burning bush (Exod 3:5; wilderness) to Joshua, his succession affirmed before Jericho (Josh 5:15; land). As it was for Moses in the distant wilderness, so it is for Joshua in the promised land. Sandals off, Joshua is now in Moses' shoes, so to speak. The issues are theological; they are to be settled before any city is captured, any land taken.

Beyond these, the compilation of the texts has its trouble spots elsewhere. First, the two Ai passages (Josh 7 and 8) do not belong together. Joshua 7 is much more a storytelling appendix to the ban material in Joshua 6; Joshua 8 is a study in the tactics by which a town may be taken. Second, the traditions around Makkedah and the "extermination" sweep into the south do not fit together easily (cf. Josh 10:15, 10:21 balanced against the style of 10:27–41, unparalleled elsewhere). Third, the northern campaign (Josh 11:1–15) is bereft of traditions of movement given elsewhere (e.g., Josh 10:7, 15, 43); it is all-embracing, but bereft of significant geographic detail. Joshua 11:1–15 probably deserves to join Judges 17–21 in the "too strange" basket, to be left for later generations after us to deal with.

The book of Joshua has significant matters compiled in a logical sequence. It does not provide an account of the sequence of the events believed to have happened in Joshua's time, whether the compiler thought so or not. It does offer a theological understanding of what may have been thought to have been the events of that time.

Clearly the traditions compiled include the skeleton of a campaign attributed to Joshua, beginning with the spies (Josh 2) and mentioning Jericho (Josh 6:1–2), Ai (Josh 8:1), and the coalition of five (Josh 10:1–3). Equally clearly, the Jordan crossing and Jericho capture bulk large. Beyond that, there is the extermination sweep (Josh 10:27–41) and the northern campaign (Josh 11:1–15, incorporated into 11:16–20). For now, it is time we looked at some of these more closely. The ultimate invitation is to reflect on what meaning such traditions might have had for Israel once and might have for us now (further assistance can be found in Campbell, *Joshua to Chronicles*, 25–52).

In turning to these texts, it will help to focus on three aspects. Where Israel's campaign is portrayed, we may speak of a focus on Israel's doing. Where God is portrayed taking the major role, we may speak of a focus on God's doing. Where total extermination is reported, we had best be honest and speak simply of what is absolutely appalling.

FOCUS ON ISRAEL'S DOING
(The Campaign Traditions)

A series of texts relate to what we might call "campaign traditions." While the final composition has blended these with the great gateway liturgy (Jordan crossing) and empowerment liturgy or story (Jericho capture) and some other texts, the skeleton of campaign texts can be seen to have an identity of its own. It is probably not appropriate to think of these traditions as having once constituted an independent text. It seems more likely that a number of such traditions were available in ancient Israel and some have been gathered here and preserved. The sending of a couple of spies to explore the lay of the land, for example, is indicative of a military campaign that will be Israel's doing (Josh 2). The crossing of the Jordan text has a subordinate element (the two and a half armed tribes) that points in the direction of Israel's doing. Most of the story of the capture of Jericho is a portrayal of God's doing, but pointers at the beginning of the chapter, recurring again later in the book, indicate an understanding where the capture is Israel's doing (Josh 6:1–2). The success of the second attack on Ai reflects military and strategic skills that put it in the class of Israel's doing (Josh 8). The story of deception achieved by the Gibeonites (Josh 9) is portrayed not so much as Israel's doing as a case of Israel's going astray when it did not consult its God. It is a necessary lead-in to what follows, both the relief of Gibeon (Josh 10:1–15) and the killing of the five kings, hidden in the cave of Makkedah (Josh 10:16–27).

Reconnaissance: Joshua 2

Like so much of the book of Joshua, the passage has its complexities (see, for example, Nelson, *Joshua,* 36–52); fortunately, they seldom concern us here. The mission Joshua gave the two spies was: go view the land and Jericho (Josh 2:1). The implication is clear: a campaign is being planned with the whole land in view. God's role in it all is not ignored. The two spies head for the house of the prostitute; nothing more is said of Rahab's profession. We encounter a king of Jericho, who knows that the men have come to Rahab and, according to the text, "that they have come to search out the whole land" (2:3). When the king's enquiries have been fobbed off, Rahab is given the claim: "I know that the LORD has given you the land" (2:9). Negotiations are brought to a successful conclusion and the two spies head for the hills for three days. On their return to Joshua, they report: "Truly the LORD has given all the land into our hands" (2:24).

All other matters to one side, the primary focus of the narrative is on a military campaign planned by Joshua, and the whole land is in view. The LORD's role is acknowledged, but Joshua is going to have to do the job. We will meet the king of Jericho again (Josh 6:2; 8:2; 10:28, 30) and other kings as well (of Ai, 8:1–2; of Jerusalem, 10:1; the coalition of five, 10:3–5, 16–27 — also generalizing, 9:1). A narrative thread focused primarily on Israel's doing runs through these early chapters. It is important for readers to be aware of it. While it has conquest in view — with all that conquest may imply — there is no reference to be found there of any massacre of the locals. Even when Rahab is portrayed negotiating good treatment for herself and her family, mention is made of Sihon and Og (which may date these verses) but no mention is made of any forthcoming elimination of the locals. Military campaigns usually have most unfortunate consequences for the losers; they do not necessarily include ethnic cleansing.

Campaign: Joshua 6–10

The military campaign under Joshua is prepared for in Joshua 2. The liturgical procession intervenes in Joshua 3–4; Joshua 5 is concerned with other matters. The pointers to the campaign recur in Joshua 6:1–2; this southern campaign concludes with Joshua 10:42 ("Joshua took all these kings and their land").

The indications of this campaign are referred to here as "pointers" because it cannot be said that there is a full-fledged narrative of the campaign. Joshua 6 begins with reference to a siege of Jericho and to Jericho's king and soldiers (the soldiers are textually problematic, but they are there). The king and the soldiers are not mentioned again in the chapter. In 8:1–2, Joshua is sent against Ai, with the instruction or promise that he will do to Ai — king, people, city, and land — as he did to Jericho and its king. The kings provide the thread allowing us to trace the campaign narrative. A single clause in 8:2 differentiates the attack on Ai from the attack on Jericho: "only its spoil and its livestock you may take as booty for yourselves." The clause implies that what was narrated for Jericho — "men and women, young and old, oxen, sheep, and donkeys" were put to the sword (6:21) and "all silver and gold, and vessels of bronze and iron" went into the treasury of the LORD (6:19) — was different at Ai, where the treasure and the livestock could be taken as booty. It would have been very simple for the final editors, inevitably involved with the extermination level, to have inserted such clauses, with a condition here that might have rendered it more palatable to those who looked favorably on the idea of a bit of booty.

The analysis of the text concerning the capture of Ai (Josh 8) must unavoidably be fairly dense and detailed. Those preferring to dispense with such detail may be well advised to skip to the conclusions at the end of the discussion.

The "no survivors" claim that is typical of the dense extermination text of 10:28–41 is found as the concluding clause of 8:22; it refers to the defenders who had come out of the city. The massacre within the city is restricted to vv. 24–27, verses that come between the report of the King of Ai's being taken alive and brought to Joshua (v. 23) and the report of his fate (v. 29). Verses 24–27 could easily be an insertion by the final editors concerned with the issue of extermination (as in Josh 6:17–19). They could be; they need not be.

The situation of four verses between the capture of the king and his execution raises suspicion — no more — that they might be an insertion. What gives some substance to this suspicion is a certain tension between 8:24–27 and the earlier 8:16–17. It is reported earlier in the text that all the people capable of participation in the pursuit did so, leaving the town open, presumably undefended (Josh 8:16–17). On the other hand, the extermination verses (vv. 24–27) are in some tension with this. According to these verses, after the slaughter in the open country, all Israel turned back on Ai "and attacked it *with the edge of the sword*" (v. 24, as later). This juxtaposition of open country (where the slaughter has occurred) and town (to be attacked with the edge of the sword) does not fit well with v. 17's image of the city left open and undefended. The *signal* given in 8:18 (*kidon,* a rare word for sword or javelin; note v. 19, "his hand" only) has become a *symbolic action* in 8:26 (missing from the LXX). The suspicion that 8:24–27 may be an editorial insertion is strengthened.

The fundamental text of Joshua 8 is not straightforward; as Nelson puts it, "this narrative is rough and confused" (*Joshua*, 110). Three issues will make the point.

1. Three ambushes are mentioned (with thirty thousand troops, with five thousand, and "behind the city") where only two at most are needed.

2. Joshua "overnights" twice (v. 9: with the army/in the camp; v. 13: in the valley) which leaves the troops sent out earlier a long time in ambush.

3. The exit from Ai is portrayed as both spontaneous and succumbing to strategy. In v. 14, the king of Ai saw something and hurried out for battle, to attack (direction: east). In vv. 15–17, Joshua's stratagem lured away Ai's armed forces, in pursuit (direction: north).

The possibility of two texts here has to be explored.

Joshua 8:1 and the final sentence of 8:2 command both the attack and a strategy (an ambush behind the city). The first sentence of 8:3 has Joshua and the troops move against Ai; the first sentence of 8:9 has the ambush established. It would be desirable, ideally, to have the troops selected before they are sent; a competent storyteller, however, would have no difficulty with it. The final sentence of 8:13 has Joshua (with the rest of his troops presumably) pass the night "in the valley," presumably below Ai. According to 8:14, the king of Ai saw this (the troops below in the valley) and sallied out for battle, profiting from the upper ground. In 8:21, the ambush has done its job and smoke is rising from the torched city; Joshua's troops turn to the attack and the men of Ai are slaughtered. The king of Ai is taken alive and brought to Joshua in 8:23; 8:29 has him hanged and in due course buried under a great heap of stones, "there to this day." Putting these verses together (8:1, 2b, 3a, 9a, 13b–14, 21, 23, 29 — see the text given below), a bare-bones narrative emerges in which Ai is captured, its forces killed, and its king hanged. It could be a base within a campaign narrative.

The actual strategy is clear: the ambush is behind the town, to the west; the visible attackers are in the valley below the town, to the east. It is understandable that the king of Ai and its defenders should sally forth to the attack; they enjoy the upper ground and they can only see a part of Joshua's force. Joshua and all Israel "turned back" (v. 21). While the circumstances make this quite intelligible, the narrative is at its barest. Nothing is said about the forces from Ai seeing the smoke and hurrying back to their town; it may be presupposed, but the narrative would be more satisfactory if it were stated. However, it is not stated at 8:20 either. That Israel was falling back before the initial attack from Ai can be taken for granted; it is essential to allow the forces in ambush time to mount their attack and fire the town. When the smoke is seen, Joshua and all Israel can turn on the defenders. More emphasis on the slaughter would be more satisfactory; nevertheless, the needed verb is there, "they struck down" the men of Ai (v. 21). Is it perfect as a bare-bones narrative? I think not. Will it pass muster as a bare-bones narrative? I think so.

The resulting text, probably best understood as notes toward a campaign narrative, would be (NRSV text, but with "and" in place of contextual adjustments):

◆ ◆ ◆

8:1 And the Lord said to Joshua, "Do not fear or be dismayed; take all the fighting men with you, and go up to Ai. See, I have handed over to you the king of Ai with his people, his city, and his land.... **2b**Set an ambush against the city, behind it."

3aAnd Joshua and all the fighting men set out to go up against Ai. **9a**And Joshua sent them out; and they went to the place of ambush, and lay between Bethel and Ai, to the west of Ai. **13b**And Joshua spent that night in the valley. **14**When the king of Ai saw this, the men of the city hurried out early in the morning, to meet Israel in battle, he and all his people, to the meeting place facing the Arabah [sequence changed to mirror the Hebrew]; but he did not know that there was an ambush against him behind the city. **21**And Joshua and all Israel saw that the ambush had taken the city and that the smoke of the city was rising, and they turned back and struck down the men of Ai.

23And the king of Ai was taken alive and brought to Joshua. **29**And he hanged the king of Ai on a tree until evening; and at sunset Joshua commanded, and they took his body down from the tree, threw it down at the entrance of the gate of the city, and raised over it a great heap of stones, which stands there to this day.

◆ ◆ ◆

If the unchanged 8:2b is taken as an outline of strategy, it is adequate but terse in the extreme. If in any way it sets the tone for the whole, much of what follows it is positively verbose.

The concerns of the extermination level can be seen in 8:2a, comparing Ai with Jericho, and in 8:24–27 which spell this out. See below.

The additional text celebrates Joshua's strategy. What is implicit, perhaps, in the bare-bones version is carefully unfolded and all credit given to Joshua's cunning. The cunning of the strategy is sufficiently evident. The text itself, however, needs to be dealt with here.

Given an appropriate introduction, 8:3b–8 specifies an ambush and a strategy. At this point, the ambush is to consist of thirty thousand warriors. They are to move off under cover of darkness and position themselves near the city, behind it. (The best understanding of 8:12 may be a daylight alternative with a smaller force.) The strategy is spelled out: Joshua and the troops with him (*ha-am*, v. 5) will lure the defenders out of the city, those in ambush will seize the city and set fire to it — all this "as the LORD has ordered" (v. 8). According to 8:9b, Joshua spent the night with the main body of his troops (*ha-am*). The execution of this plan is narrated in 8:10–13a, 15–22. In the morning, the main body of troops is positioned before the city, to the north (this verse is not in the LXX, avoiding the second overnight stay; but the LXX also omits v. 9b, so no overnight stays by Joshua); the smaller force is in ambush to the west. The larger ambush has been set up the night before in v. 3; its precise function is obscure and must be entrusted to the storyteller's skills. As noted, perhaps the two — thirty thousand by night or five thousand by day — are alternatives, with only one to be utilized in a particular telling of the story. The movement of the rest, with Joshua in the morning, is specified in vv. 11–12; main body to the north in v. 11 and ambush to the west in v. 12. The general disposition of the forces is summarized in v. 13a. Verses 15–17 spell out the success of Joshua's strategy; Israel takes to flight and, following in hot pursuit, Ai's defenders are lured away from the town, which is left open and undefended (v. 17). This contrasts with v. 14, where the movement out of the town is initiated by the king and defenders, not leading to pursuit, but to meet Israel in battle and attack (in the sentence, the Hebrew sequence is preferable to that of the NRSV); the reference to the Arabah, the Jordan valley, suggests a move downhill, to the east, not an engagement with a force to the north.

Apart from any knowledge of the campaign text, a storyteller would have no difficulty filling out details needed here, especially given 8:5–8. Resisting a siege was apparently not envisaged; pursuing the Israelites was of the essence of Joshua's strategy. According to the narrative, at the appropriate moment commanded by the LORD, Joshua gave the signal or rallied his troops (v. 18), the forces in ambush did their job (v. 19), and the defenders of Ai were trapped between the two fronts and soon massacred (vv. 20 and 22, improved by the removal of v. 21). The final note concluding the story is given in 8:28.

The resulting text, detailing something of Joshua's strategy, would be (NRSV text, but with "and" in place of contextual adjustments):

◆ ◆ ◆

8:1And the LORD said to Joshua, "Do not fear or be dismayed; take all the fighting men with you, and go up to Ai. See, I have handed over to you the king of Ai with his people, his city, and his land...." 3bAnd Joshua chose thirty thousand warriors and sent them out by night 4with the command, "You shall lie in ambush against the city, but all of you stay alert. 5And I and all the people who are with me will approach the city. When they come out against us, ... we shall flee from them. 6And they will come out after us until we have drawn them away from the city; for they will say, 'They are fleeing from us....' While we flee from them, 7you shall rise up from the ambush and seize the city; for the LORD your God will give it into your hand. 8And when you have taken the city, you shall set the city on fire, doing as the LORD has ordered; see, I have commanded you." 9bAnd Joshua spent that night in the camp.

10In the morning Joshua rose early and mustered the people, and went up, with the elders of Israel, before the people to Ai. 11All the fighting men who were with him went up, and drew near before the city, and camped on the north side of Ai, with a ravine between them and Ai. [12]Taking about five thousand men, he set them in ambush between Bethel and Ai, to the west of the city. [13a]So they stationed the forces, the main encampment that was north of the city and its rear guard west of the city. [15]And Joshua and all Israel made a pretense of being beaten before them, and fled in the direction of the wilderness. [16]And all the people who were in the city were called together to pursue them, and as they pursued Joshua they were drawn away from the city. [17]There was not a man left in Ai or Bethel who did not go out after Israel; they left the city open, and pursued Israel.

[18]And the LORD said to Joshua, "Stretch out the sword that is in your hand toward Ai; for I will give it into your hand." And Joshua stretched out the sword that was in his hand toward the city. [19]And the troops in the ambush rose quickly out of their place and rushed forward. They entered the city, took it, and at once set the city on fire. [20]And when the men of Ai looked back, the smoke of the city was rising to the sky. They had no power to flee this way or that, for the people who fled to the wilderness turned back against the pursuers. [22]And the others came out from the city against them; so they were surrounded by Israelites, some on one side, and some on the other; and Israel struck them down until no one was left who survived or escaped. [28]And Joshua burned Ai, and made it forever a heap of ruins, as it is to this day.

◆ ◆ ◆

Something of this kind is present in the text. The texts recovered are not perfectly satisfactory to me; therefore, they are less likely to be perfectly satisfactory to others. Often this is due to the text that is there rather than to the process of analysis and recovery. The process does not fragment or atomize the text. What the analysis reveals, however, is that something is there present in the text, that there probably was some sort of campaign narrative, a text as a base for storytelling, and some sort of account of the details of Joshua's strategy. What the analysis further reveals to me is that the elimination level here (vv. 2a and 24–27) probably is later than the other two story texts, and is to be understood on its own terms and no others. In the meantime, it is good to be aware that the geographical topography in the text is unquestionably difficult. It is not important, however, that it should satisfy a critical modern observer on the spot; it is important for it to appear plausible to a listener in an ancient audience.

The chief conclusion from these reflections is that the extermination interest is restricted to no more than a few verses (vv. 2a and 24–27). Beyond that, the text contains notes relating to a campaign by Joshua and a more discursive treatment of Joshua's strategy. A reader might well ask what sort of text is here. Was there ever such an entity as a campaign narrative? Did the reflections on Joshua's strategy constitute a text in its own right? How should chapters 7 and 8 be related to each other? I tend to think in terms of notes as a base for storytelling or further reflection rather than completed texts. In my judgment, Joshua 7 (failure) and 8 (success) now belong together but originally they probably did not. The weakness of Ai's defenders is important to chapter 7; emphasis on it would detract from Joshua's exploit in chapter 8. The taking of booty (a mantle, silver, and gold) which was Achan's downfall in 7:21 is specifically allowed in 8:2, 27. The two little linking phrases, "as before" (8:5, 6), are editorial.

The campaign narrative notes continue. A coalition is noted in 9:1–2, but without details or names. It portrays a universal picture: all the kings beyond the Jordan, hill country, lowland, and coast. It coheres well with the universalism of 10:42; it goes beyond the restricted nature of other campaign notes.

Another coalition is noted in 10:1–5. In contrast to 9:1–2, the kings and towns are named, all five of them. The object of their attack is not Joshua but Gibeon. It leads into the account of Joshua's victory in delivering Gibeon. The text credits both Joshua's military competence and the LORD's miraculous intervention. Joshua marches all night from Gilgal and takes Gibeon by surprise (10:9). The LORD threw the enemy into panic (10:10) and even threw killer hailstones down on them (11:11). Joshua and the troops return to Gilgal (10:15). Gilgal has been Joshua's base for this campaign (see 10:43).

The universalizing conclusion to these campaign notes is given in 10:42–43. Joshua was victorious over the kings and their lands. All this Joshua did from Gilgal. What is envisaged appears to be a military campaign, not the settlement of a people. Historically, what actually happened probably has to remain out of reach of the modern interpreter.

Gibeon: Joshua 9

As a tradition, the story of Gibeon has a fascination of its own. It stands in a class of its own among these traditions of Joshua; perhaps it is best thought of as a cautionary tale. Its focus is not on what Israel can achieve for itself and it is not on what God did for Israel. Rather, its focus might be said to be on what happened to Israel when it did not involve its God. In the story, Israel takes matters into its own hands; there is no consultation of God. The outcome of the story has Israel tricked into a treaty with the Gibeonites that it would otherwise never have considered.

A theology of the "hardening of hearts" is invoked in a summary accounting for the extermination (Josh 11:20). As noted in the same context, the case of Gibeon did not come into this category (see Josh 11:19). It is almost as if an attempt is being made in the text to blame locals for their own extermination, with Gibeon noted as the exception.

The Jerusalem coalition: Joshua 10:1–11

The story is simple enough. Adoni-zedek, king of Jerusalem, is reported hearing about Joshua's exploits at Ai and Jericho and how the people of Gibeon had worked out a peace settlement with Israel. He is reported assembling a coalition of five kings: of Hebron, Jarmuth, Lachish, and Eglon, along with himself, king of Jerusalem. For reasons that are not fully disclosed, the coalition is to attack Gibeon and the people of Gibeon send to Joshua for help.

Credit is given to Joshua. He and his troops marched all night, coming up from Gilgal, and took the coalition by surprise. However, it is not merely Israel's action that is the focus of the text. It includes both God's words — "I have handed them over to you" — and God's action: "The LORD threw them into a panic before Israel.... The LORD threw down huge stones from heaven on them" (10:10–11).

The text notes that God's hailstones killed more than the Israelites did. "The LORD fought for Israel" (10:14).

Israel's participation is integral to the story. There is the forced march by night, the slaughter at Gibeon itself, and the pursuit "down as far as Azekah and Makkedah" (10:10). Joshua put in a word with the LORD to lengthen the day. At the end of it all, Joshua and his force returned to Gilgal (10:15).

A tradition that is separate from this one will take up the story, with the focus on Joshua, of the fate of the five kings who took refuge in a cave at Makkedah (10:16–27, see below).

Makkedah: Joshua 10:16–27

As with the other texts in this category, Joshua's action is paramount, but God's contribution is not ignored. The LORD has given the towns into Israel's hand (10:19). What is happening to these five kings, the LORD will do to all Israel's enemies (10:25).

Two aspects of these verses demand attention. First, they constitute an isolated fragment. Before this episode, Joshua and the troops are reported to have gone home to Gilgal (10:15). There is no equivalent note about returning to camp at the end of the passage. Second, two clauses — "Do not let them enter their towns" (10:19) and "when the survivors had entered into the fortified towns" (10:20) — suggest a campaign to eliminate the leaders, but certainly not a scorched-earth policy of total destruction.

The episode is set within the campaign against the coalition of five. In contrast with 10:15's return to Gilgal, there is a camp at Makkedah (10:21). As so often, Israel's traditions may be more manifold than we imagine. It is an interesting theology. "Thus the LORD will do" (10:25; note the echo of Josh 1:6) is asserted in the context of what the military commanders are doing, treading on the necks of their foes. The fate dealt out to these five kings parallels that claimed for the king of Ai.

~ MODERN FAITH ~

The observation that is surely primary for modern faith concerning these texts is that there was more going on in the traditions of the book of Joshua than the conquest of a land and the massacre of innocent locals. In the crossing of the Jordan, the presence of forty thousand warriors is noted in the middle of a liturgical celebration. In the capture of Jericho, the potential for solemn liturgy is prefaced by reference to military campaigning. In the capture of Ai, the brief noting of a military campaign has been mingled with the details of Joshua's successful strategy. Both texts, regarding Jericho and Ai, have been the object of the later extermination editors, inserting their concerns — but briefly.

Beyond that, what I find attractive in these texts is the opportunity to watch theologians in ancient Israel exploring the ways in which action in the human sphere can be portrayed, while consistently maintaining a role for God. In the texts where the focus is primarily on God's doing (see the next section), God indeed did it; in these campaign texts here, Israel does it, but God's role is not ignored. In the case of the Jordan flow or the wall of Jericho, what is attributed to God lies far beyond human power. In these campaign texts, humans do what humans can, encouraged by the conviction that God is with them. "God with us" is a phrase that, today (above all in military contexts), can have most unfortunate connotations. In the book of Joshua, the final context of extermination may help moderns evaluate their actions with extreme care before invoking God's approval.

Put in a sentence, the experience of these texts might be read as: extermination issues can be isolated as peripheral; human action is not wisely divorced from God.

What remains puzzling in all this, as it was earlier, is whether and how these traditions, as we can isolate them in the book of Joshua, correlate with the discoveries of archaeology. At present, it is probably most accurate to say simply: they don't (see below). What is clear, even now, is that the Joshua traditions we have do not reflect the initial processes by which Israel entered Canaan. What archaeology may be able to tell us, some distant day, is whether some stage of the process from fringe dwellers (hilltop villages) to central occupiers and controllers of the land (kingdoms) might be reflected in the traditions we have, associated now with the name of Joshua. At the moment, it is a question that we need to ask but cannot answer. Everything we know indicates clearly that the Israel imagined for

Joshua's time did not sweep into the land in a military campaign. What then generated these memories attributed to Joshua's day? We do not know. We are entitled to wonder whether there may be echoes here of the moves from the fringes to the towns.

FOCUS ON GOD'S DOING

The crossing of the Jordan is clearly portrayed as God's doing (Josh 3–4). So is most of the story of the capture of Jericho (Josh 6), but not all. The failure of the first attack on Ai puts it in the class of God's doing (Josh 7); not so the portrayal of the successful capture of the town (the name of Ai in Hebrew consistently has the definite article; literally: "the ruin"). The defeat of the coalition of five kings is equally God's doing (Josh 10:1–11); the defeat of the northern coalition is in the same category (Josh 11:1–9).

Crossing of the Jordan: Joshua 3–4

The account of Israel's crossing of the Jordan is a complex text (see Campbell and O'Brien, *Unfolding the Deuteronomistic History,* 112–17). Once it is looked at in any detail and allowance is made for a number of liturgical annotations, its possibility as a text reflecting a liturgical ceremony becomes clear.

That the people should sanctify themselves on the eve of the crossing (Josh 3:5) is entirely appropriate for a liturgical ceremony of major significance. The people are to follow the ark of the covenant of the LORD, maintaining "a space between you and it, a distance of about two thousand cubits; do not come any nearer to it" (Josh 3:4). The spaciousness of the spectacle can be imagined when we remember that a cubit was reckoned at about eighteen inches, so that two thousand cubits was about three thousand feet or about one kilometer. This is an immensely stately procession, led by the priests carrying the ark of God's covenant; as a matter of liturgical spectacle, Westminster or Rome would not have done better.

Bearers for the twelve stones were to be selected (3:12). Any liturgist knows the value of selecting people and preparing them for their roles in advance. When the soles of the priests' feet touched the waters of the Jordan, the river flow was to stop (3:13). Any liturgist knows the value of informing people of what lies ahead. Of course, the waters do not stop for the celebration of a liturgy; liturgy is about remembrance not reenactment. Were it reenactment, as they were nailed to the cross parish liturgy leaders would today find Good Friday ceremonies unduly painful.

The priests, with the ark, were to stand in the middle of the Jordan while all Israel crossed over — keeping the specified distance would imply a kilometer or so upstream and downstream of the stationary ark. At some point in the ceremony, each of two teams of twelve bearers picked up twelve stones from the bed of the river. For a less ornate liturgy, one or other of the teams of bearers would have sufficed. One set of twelve stones was to be placed in the middle of the Jordan (4:9); the other set of twelve was to be placed in Gilgal, where Israel had camped that night (4:3, 20). Two little catechetical instructions were associated with the sets of stones. The set in the middle of the river served to recall that "the waters of the Jordan were cut off" (4:6–7); the set at the Gilgal encampment recalled that "Israel crossed over the Jordan here on dry ground" (4:22; see 4:21–24).

In contrast to all this liturgical splendor, in the middle of the text it is also reported that "the Reubenites, the Gadites, and the half-tribe of Manasseh crossed over armed before the Israelites, as Moses had ordered them. About forty thousand armed for war crossed over before the LORD to the plains of Jericho for battle" (4:12–13). Stately processional liturgy and military order of battle are not normally confused; here the text combines them.

It is a stark reminder that people in Israel had at least two sets of traditions about this aspect of their past: those focusing primarily on what God did for them; those focusing primarily on what they did for themselves.

Gateway liturgy. From the biblical text and the findings of archaeology we know that the crossing of the Jordan, so splendidly depicted in Joshua 3–4, was not the way that the people of Israel in their beginnings entered the land. This knowledge is of some help to us in situating the liturgy portrayed for us in the text. It must go back to a period when Israel could think of itself as having entered the land in this way, therefore to a time when the awareness of its role as the dominant element in the land was alive for Israel. It is appropriate to call the ceremony of the Jordan crossing a "gateway liturgy." Precisely as liturgy, it would be a mistake to see it as celebrating a gateway into the land, a traditional memory of how Israel had entered the land in the past; as liturgy, put as universally as possible, it is a gateway into life, into new forms of life that hold the same sorts of possibilities that entry into a new land might have held.

As liturgy, it conveys to its participants the need of a crossing to be made. In that, it is similar to the remembrance of Jacob's crossing of the Jabbok (Gen 32). It need not be a territorial boundary that had to be crossed at some time in the past. As liturgy, it can have served for those times when the nation, community, or individual faced boundaries to be crossed, transitions to be made. Of course, it could have been the celebration liturgically of what was believed to have happened in the past; it is unlikely that such a past did not have its resonances in the present. Notable is the role of God in it all; the unfolding of the action is minutely accompanied by the instructions of God. It would be most appropriate, within a deuteronomic context, to celebrate liturgically the total involvement of God in the life of the individual, community, or nation. As the Shema (Deut 6:4–9) brought God into the totality of an individual Israelite's life and Jerusalem as sole place of worship brought God into the center of Israel's life, so such an entry into the land surrounded Israel by the reality of God.

What situations might have been appropriate for such a liturgy? The response can only be: many. Fundamentally, such a liturgy would be suitable for the celebration of what was held as past or what was hoped for as future. The occasions could indeed have been many. In the background would surely have been the belief that something like it reflected the way that, so long ago, Israel had entered the land.

Capture of Jericho: Joshua 6

The text on the capture of Jericho has a complexity all of its own. It starts with siege, it ends with extermination, and in between it celebrates wonder. It starts with a siege and the reference to king and soldiers (6:1–2); neither are mentioned in the rest of the chapter.

It ends with the issues of extermination (6:17–19, 21–26 [mixed]). In between, two portrayals coexist, each with marches around the city and a final shout — in one case very noisy with trumpet-blowing priests and armed men and in the other very silent with neither sound nor word, and in both cases the final shout. The wonder: when the shout was raised (either at Joshua's command [v. 16] or after the sound of the trumpet [v. 20]), "the wall fell down flat" (6:20). To add to the complexity, the Greek version of the chapter is substantially shorter than the Hebrew Masoretic text (see Nelson, *Joshua*, 83–86). The differences do not alter the observations made here.

Joshua 6:1–2, the siege and the reference to its king and soldiers, focuses primarily on Israel's doing (even though the LORD hands over Jericho to Joshua); these two verses, therefore, belong with the focus on Israel's doing (see the preceding section). Joshua 6:17–19, 21–26, with the issues of people, treasure, Rahab and family, and the curse, belongs in the "absolutely appalling" section. It is the celebration of the wonder that belongs here.

The LORD gives instructions to Joshua: for each of six days, circle the city once, with all the warriors preceding seven priests preceding the ark; on the seventh day, circle the city seven times, and at the sound of a long blast from the ram's horn or trumpet, the people shall shout, the wall will fall down, and in they go (6:3–5). Joshua then spoke to the priests and they/he (note two traditions: Kethib, they; Qere, he) spoke to the people (6:6–7). The procession sets off as instructed (6:8–9).

Duplication is present from the outset but does not become troubling until the seventh day (see v. 20). In 6:5, there is to be a blast from the horn or trumpet and "they" (the people presumably) are to shout. In 6:10, the people are to keep silence; only when Joshua tells them should they shout. In v. 5, the horn or trumpet gives the signal; in v. 10, Joshua gives the command. In 6:16, the two are smoothly harmonized; the trumpets sound and Joshua gives the word. The harmonization breaks down in 6:20; duplication triumphs. In v. 20 the Hebrew text has the report that "the people shouted" (presumably in response to Joshua's command in v. 16); the Greek does not have this clause. Verse 20 then goes on to have the trumpets sound (again) and, at the sound of the trumpets (not Joshua's voice), the people "raised a great shout" (again!). The wall falls and the people rush in.

Duplication is likely, with noise in one case and silence in the other; the issue is not very important. It is more important to recognize the possibilities for a liturgical celebration or a well-told story. The storytelling aspect is clear. In hushed suspense, the story is told of how the people walked around "the place" on six days and now seven times on the seventh; on the seventh circuit of that seventh day, the wall of the impregnable city falls in memory to the joyous sound of a single silence-breaking shout. Equally, a liturgy can be enacted with the noisy trumpet-blowing procession around the city, color and noise and splendor in plenty. The reality of the liturgical possibility is enhanced for us by the awareness that "such circulatory marches often formed part of the ceremonies at the installation of kings" (Boling, *Joshua*, 206). There is a duplication in the text: on the one hand, a noisy group with its armed men and its trumpet-blowing priests and its final triumphant shout; on the other, the circuits of the doomed city in hushed silence, followed by a mighty shout. A single liturgy is possible, involving both; equally possible is a liturgy for the noisy group and a story for the silent circuits. A decision between them is not needed (for further detail, see *Unfolding the Deuteronomistic History*, 119–23).

Most important, of course, is the recognition that both liturgy and story celebrate the wonder achieved by the LORD, the God of Israel. No matter what some may say about earthquakes blocking the flow of the Jordan and weakening the city wall, the reality is simple: a people's shout, no matter how mighty, does not collapse a city wall. Only God does that. Such a liturgy or such a story focuses primarily on God's action. As we have seen, the sortie of the spies implies a focus on Israel's action; in contrast, the chapters on the Jordan crossing and the Jericho capture focus primarily on God's action. The extermination issue completes the text of Jericho's capture, and we will deal with it in due course.

The focus in the texts concerning the Jordan and Jericho can be clearly seen to be primarily on God's positive action. Where the Jordan crossing is concerned, the tone is set by the two catechetical instructions: the waters of the Jordan were stopped before the ark; as we left Egypt, so we entered the land, on dry ground between parted waters. Only God can part the waters. Where the capture of Jericho is concerned, the means of capture speaks for itself. Only God can collapse the wall at a people's shout.

Importantly, while the focus of the texts may be primarily on God's action, nevertheless Israel's cooperation is required. It may seem too obvious to be said, but God's action does not replace Israel's participation. In the context of Israel's battle with Amalek (Exod 17:8–13), there is a comment from Reformed circles: "In vain shall Moses be upon the hill, if Joshua be not in the valley" (see Childs, *Exodus,* 317). In the context of Israel's entering Canaan, God opened the way but Israel had to cross the river; God collapsed the wall but Israel had to enter the city.

Empowerment liturgy/story. Whether the Jericho episode was told in story or enacted in liturgy, it could have functioned to empower hearers or participants with faith in what God could do through them, no matter how inadequate the means available to them. By contrast, the David and Goliath story could have empowered hearers who needed courage even when the means available to them were adequate, as a sling was in David's case. In the case of Jericho, a people's shout was scarcely adequate means to bring down a city's walls. The celebration of the memory might well have been a source of empowerment in people's lives or in their time.

APPENDIX TO JERICHO
Failure at Ai: Joshua 7

The text on the failure of the first attack on Ai (Josh 7) is something of a fish out of water. It is a text for a story, not for a liturgy. It is a story of Israel's failure, not of a successful Jordan crossing or city capture. It emphasizes the focus on God's doing. If Israel's obedience is withheld, God's action is withheld and the operation is a failure. It is, as it were, a negative focus on God's action, viewed through the lens of the failure of human cooperation. It is a reflection, in story form, on the theology of the ban at Jericho. According to the rules enunciated for Jericho (see 6:18–19, 24), Achan's action was indeed a breach of the ban; in stark contrast, it was not a breach of the ban according to the rules enunciated for Ai (see 8:2). The point of the story in chapter 7 is to emphasize the understanding that, in the light of the ban, God's action on Israel's behalf was dependent on Israel's not profiting from it.

The theme of the text is broached from the outset: "the Israelites broke faith in regard to the devoted things" (7:1). It is all there: Achan took some of the devoted things (Jericho rules) and God's anger burned against Israel. What can be affirmed in a sentence or two is then unfolded in story form.

The story opens with a reconnaissance expedition to spy out Ai. The report of the reconnaissance: the defenders are so few, two or three companies will do; no more are needed. So three companies are dispatched and are soundly defeated. Victory was expected; defeat resulted.

Joshua and the elders are portrayed in full prayer and penance for the rest of the day. Joshua puts the whole campaign in context: "Ah, Lord GOD! why have you brought this people across the Jordan at all" (7:7). God's reply, in the story: "Israel has sinned . . . they have taken some of the devoted things; . . . I will be with you no more unless you destroy the devoted things from among you" (7:12). The focus is on God, but Israel's cooperation is required.

Joshua is given instructions for a major search, involving Israel by its tribes, a search such as was instituted when Saul was missing on the occasion of Israel's selection of its first king (1 Sam 10:20–24). Joshua carried out his instructions. Achan was identified, confessed, and then he and his family and even their livestock were stoned to death and the remains burned and covered by a great heap of stones (7:20–26).

The successful attack follows in Joshua 8. It has been treated earlier because the focus is primarily on Israel's action. However, the juxtaposition of the two chapters, of failure and success, is not merely a matter of literary bridging; it is also indicative of how closely the two issues are interwoven. The attempt is made here to keep faith with this aspect by the use of "primarily" to modify the focus on either the action of God or of Israel. While the twin focuses are held together closely in the twin chapters narrating failure and success regarding

Ai, they are also present and closely interwoven in the texts where one focus is primary. The focus primarily on God's action appears to have been dominant in a particular context, perhaps liturgical. In another context, the campaign for example, it appears to have been important to focus primarily on the action of Israel, without relinquishing awareness of God in it all.

~MODERN FAITH~

What attracts me to these texts is the opportunity to watch theologians in ancient Israel exploring the ways in which God's action in the human sphere can be portrayed. For myself, I am in print saying that "as a rule, I don't ask God to do anything that I would not ask of a good friend" (*God First Loved Us*, 60). Friends can support us, encourage us, challenge us, remonstrate with us, hang in with us, be there for us, so many things. But there are areas where friends cannot replace us. As the saying goes: we die alone; no one can die for us. Many are the things in life that we have to do for ourselves, where no one can replace us — not even God.

I certainly would not ask a good friend to stop the Jordan's flow or to collapse the Jericho wall. I doubt that I would dare ask God either. Israel's liturgies celebrated both, but not without Israel's cooperation, Israel's participation. Israel had to cross and enter the land, an act that required courage (emphasized by Joshua's plea in the Achan affair). Israel had to march around the city and shout on signal, before entering the city.

As touched on earlier, the observation that is surely primary for modern faith is that there was more going on in the traditions of the book of Joshua than the conquest of a land and the massacre of the innocent locals. Two realities are dominant in the popular view of the text. To put it brutally: one (the conquest) probably should not have happened, at least in the way it is portrayed; the other (the massacre) certainly did not happen. Unfolding these, first, Israel is in possession of the land. There may be argument over the precise understanding of "Israel" in early times. There may be argument over what is understood as the limits of "the land." To the best of my knowledge, however, there is no argument over Israel's ultimate presence and possession. It was a fact; it did happen (for further reflection, see below). Second, in the text, Israel eliminated the locals. The Jericho text spells it out: "The city and all that is in it shall be devoted to the LORD for destruction" (Josh 6:17). Worse is that this massacre is portrayed as universal and as God's command: "So Joshua defeated the whole land . . . he left no one remaining, but utterly destroyed all that breathed, as the LORD God of Israel commanded" (Josh 10:40). To the best of my knowledge, there is no argument over the fact that this massacre never happened. There are too many texts that follow trying to account for the peoples that remained. If the massacre had occurred, there would have been no need for such texts. Only one conclusion can be reached. By and large, the massacre never happened.

We are still left with an uncomfortable claim in Joshua. The claim: God gave them the land. The discomfort: God had no right to do so, because others were already there. Such sensitivity is relatively recent. In earlier times, title to property and land could be simple: if I could take it and hold it, it was mine. However, today's readers have to live with relatively recent sensitivities, at least in theory if not always in political practice. Furthermore, we somehow hope that God's morals are above the transience of human perception and human moral development. All this raises problems that cannot be adequately addressed here.

Another source of discomfort demands acknowledgment even if no resolution is at hand. Correlation is as yet not possible between these Joshua texts about Israel's entry into the land and what we know archaeologically about the entry into the land of the people who were to become Israel. The villages described by Finkelstein and others (see above) are in the hills, ranging widely from north to south. The substantial texts in Joshua 2–11 begin in the Jordan valley, around Jericho and Gilgal, and deal largely with towns. Whether these conquest traditions reflected aspects of the transition from the hills to the towns we simply do not know. Perhaps future exploration will shed light on today's ignorance.

What modern faith may legitimately rejoice in is that there is more to the book of Joshua than widespread conquest and killing. Above all, there is the interplay in these traditions between what we believe

God does for us and what we believe we can do for ourselves. In the texts just considered, the focus is primarily on what God has done for Israel in the past.

Because of that "in the past," these liturgies open up a territory we have to leave largely unvisited here; it is the territory of future and fulfillment. The gateways to its avenues may at least be signaled. The procession to the Jordan stopped its flow; the shout at Jericho collapsed its wall. The waters of the Jordan parted again for Elisha to cross over (2 Kgs 2:14); symbolic or not, I know of no other case. Many a town was besieged; I know of none where the wall collapsed. Liturgies are about remembrance, not reenactment. We are not told how Israel experienced such memories. Isaiah once sang of future hope:

> Was it not you who dried up the sea, . . .
> Who made the depth of the sea a way
>   For the redeemed to cross over?
> So the ransomed of the LORD shall return,
>   And come to Zion with singing . . .
>   (Isa 51:10–11)

Alas, as we know all too well, it did not happen. The final great prophecies of Isaiah are superbly expressive of hope and equally superbly unfulfilled, at least in any literal sense. Did the continued unfolding of experience give a continued deepening and revelatory richness to Israel's understanding of its God? Should it do so for us today? Does that continued deepening include an awareness of the areas of life where God may be expected to act and an awareness of the areas of life where God does not act?

Israel's theologians are massively discreet. They theologize by juxtaposing matters. They seldom theorize; they seldom hold discourse. Sometimes pointers may be found in their texts. Often, users of the texts are left to their own reflections, left to formulate their own theological articulations.

THE ABSOLUTELY APPALLING

"Absolutely appalling" is an understatement, unfortunately; it is not an exaggeration. The texts involved may be brief, but we need to be conscious of their horror. The leit-motiv of 10:28–41 is: "he struck it with the edge of the sword, and every person in it; he left no one remaining in it" (10:30). With regret, this is ethnic cleansing with a vengeance. In today's world, it would bring those responsible before international courts of law; in the text of Joshua, the primary collaborator is God.

Readers may be relieved by the awareness that the horror never happened. Alternatively, readers may be even more deeply pained that theologians long ago thought fit to have God involved with horrors that they then knew full well had not happened. The matter needs exploration.

As noted earlier, this is not the place to explore the editorial levels involved. It is the place to confess with sorrow that some of the apparent fanaticism evident in limited areas of Deuteronomy is mirrored by equivalent fanaticism in limited areas of Joshua 1–12. Such confession is a delicate task. The danger is omnipresent of bringing a modern sensitivity to bear on the interpretation of an ancient text. We may shrink from the horrors of ethnic cleansing. We need to be aware of the convictions of an ancient time; we need also to be aware of the realities of our own time.

The first chapter of Amos is a good example of the ancient world's outrage at the use of excessive violence. Damascus threshed with sledges of iron; Gaza carried entire communities into exile; Edom cast off all pity; the Ammonites savaged pregnant women in a mere border dispute. In eighth-century Israel, excess of violence was condemned. Of course, as all Bible readers know, the concept of the ban (Hebrew: *herem*) was part of Israel's theological inheritance, shared as far as we know with the rest of the ancient Near East. It is portrayed as part of Israel's convictions in the early stages of its presence in the land. The ban, a complex concept, purportedly demonstrated that action was taken solely on behalf of God; to ensure purity of motive, everything was destroyed, people and livestock together; occasionally some booty was allowed. The human motivation of profit was allegedly removed; the action was undertaken for the sake of God alone. It appears to have been an understanding shared in the ancient Near Eastern world. The clearest and nearest example in Israel's area comes to us from the stele of King Mesha of Moab. It dates from late in his reign, probably between the years 840 and 820 BCE. According to Mesha, Omri king of Israel had humbled Moab for many years, for Chemosh, god of Moab, was angry at his land. In his stele, Mesha affirms how, at the orders of Chemosh, he took Nebo from Israel and slaughtered all those there, "for I had devoted it to destruction [the language of *herem*] to Ashtar-Chemosh" (line 17). Other examples can be cited from the ancient Near East.

This understanding of the ban — total destruction expressing dedication to God — is its basic and fundamental meaning. Modifications were apparently possible. In the case of Ai, for example, "its spoil and its livestock you may take as booty for yourselves" (Josh 8:2; not so for Achan in the preceding chapter who took cash and a cloak). At another stage, the verb came simply to mean total destruction (see, for example, Isa 34:2; 37:11; Jer 25:9; 50:21, 26; 51:3). All three meanings may be visible in Joshua 2–11.

We moderns would be well advised to refrain from any stance of superior sensitivity. Modern times have, in a century or so, seen the transition from war involving professional armies to war involving entire nations to war involving tribe and race (ethnic cleansing, genocide). It is not so long ago that Prussian Field Marshal von Moltke could write, "War is part of God's order.... In it, Man's most noble virtues are displayed — courage and self-denial, devotion to duty, willingness to sacrifice oneself, and to risk life itself" (quoted from Davies, *Europe*, 875). Times have changed; perceptions have changed. The modern world lives under threat of global annihilation. The modern world lives too close to the fate of Irish, Armenians, Gypsies, and Jews. The modern world is too familiar with the conflicts of Northern Ireland, Kosovo (however we name it), and the atrocities of Africa (whether Biafra, Rwanda, Sudan, Ethiopia, or others) and the many more we might name. Outsiders may not see God's approval involved; those concerned may see it differently.

In the rare art of biblical interpretation, few areas are as delicate and fraught with potential error as the attempt to date levels of editing. Nevertheless, if we make the assumption — and it may be a rash one — that those involved in such editing were aware of the efforts of others in the area, a possible sequence emerges in the editing of these Joshua texts. After all, you do not marry those who are dead; the dead are not left behind as faith temptation or military training for the living.

In Joshua's farewell address (Josh 23), Joshua adjures those he is leaving behind not to mix "with these nations left here among you, or make mention of the names of their gods" (23:7) and not to "intermarry with them" (23:12). Had Israel killed them all, these admonitions would have been quite unnecessary. At the beginning of the book of Judges, theologians in Israel pondered the impact of the peoples in whose midst they lived in those early days. At one level, they were deemed to be there in order to test Israel's faith and commitment. Would Israel, in the land, "take care to walk in the way of the LORD" (Judg 2:22)? The surrounding peoples were there "for the testing of Israel, to know whether Israel would obey the commandments of the LORD" (Judg 3:4). Had these surrounding peoples all been killed, as in the extermination texts of Joshua, they would hardly have performed these functions. Worse perhaps is the view that the locals were left so that "successive generations of Israelites might know war, to teach those who had no experience of it" (Judg 3:2).

Potentially, there are four levels of theological editing right here: (1) aspects of polytheism and intermarriage, (2) testing in faith and commitment, (3) testing in obedience to the commandments, and finally (4) training in the practice of war. Establishing a sequence here is highly uncertain. What can be said with certainty is that all four of these approaches would be fatuously wrong if the locals had been killed off already. It is likely therefore that the extermination texts of Joshua are to be situated chronologically later than the texts just discussed.

Joshua 23 is attributed to late levels of editing in the Deuteronomistic History (see Rudolf Smend ["Gesetz"]; Campbell and O'Brien [*Unfolding*]; perhaps also Judges 3:4 [5–6], with its emphasis on obedience to the commandments). If interfaith marriage and worship are placed ahead of faith testing and military training, the extermination levels in Joshua are late indeed. "Late" should not be thought of as the equivalent of "fallible" or "second-rate." At the very least, what "late" means in this context is "at a very considerable distance from the events reported" and even more "steeped in the crisis of exile or of post-exilic existence." What this may mean invites reflection.

What is to be said here is in no way a justification of the extermination theology of the book of Joshua. It is an attempt to understand how it might be possible for serious theological endeavor to be so appallingly wrong.

George Steiner has made a number of observations that evoke measured reflection. Central to these is the claim that the reality of monotheism "tore up the human psyche by its most ancient roots. The break has never really knit.... No fiercer exigence has ever pressed on the human spirit, with its compulsive, organically determined bias towards image, towards figured presence.... Historically, the requirements of absolute monotheism proved all but intolerable" (*Bluebeard's Castle*, 37–39). In the era of exile and post-exilic aftermath, Israel faced the real possibility that its fidelity to its core — its God — might cause it to cease to exist, might be the cause of its national death. Historically, from the judges to the exile, the requirements of absolute monotheism had indeed proved all but intolerable in Israel. Is it unthinkable that in such a period, under such existential stress, theologians might have reflected back as far as their national beginnings and pondered whether the price of their survival as a monotheistic people was not, perhaps, the initial elimination of the peoples around them worshiping other gods? Confronted with an attacker, few today would resist reacting. Might some in post-exilic Israel have entertained the awful thought of the obligation to eliminate the toxins from around them? We must surely judge the thought to be appallingly wrong. It may be that we should be slow self-righteously to judge the thinkers as pariahs.

As Jewish and Christian martyrs have been witness over the centuries, it is a heroic and noble act to die for one's faith. It is the opposite of heroic and noble to cause other peoples to lose their lives so that one's own faith may survive.

Whatever of the uncertainty of all this interpretation, we owe it to our forebears to ponder their texts and treat them with respect. To do this adequately, it is important to recognize the multiple strands that make up the traditions in the first part of the book of Joshua. We have grouped these strands into three categories: (1) where the text makes the claim that God played a principal role in Israel's occupation of the land; (2) where the text bears witness to a campaign on the part of Israel to achieve its occupation of the land; (3) where the text contains passages that can only be described as absolutely appalling, reporting the total extermination of the local inhabitants.

Surprisingly, there is no trace of this concern for the extermination of the local peoples in Joshua 1. Although the chapter lays out something of a program for the book, it makes no mention of the fate of the locals. The concern does not occur in Joshua 2–5 either. It first surfaces in Joshua 6, the capture of Jericho, where it occupies three verses (vv. 17–19), between Joshua's command to the people to shout (v. 16) and the report of the people's shout (v. 20). The extermination concern is continued in vv. 21 and 24. Joshua's curse on the city is a separate matter (see Sweeney, "Literary Function"). Joshua 7, the Achan story, is not about extermination but about the observance of the ban and the impact on Israel's campaign of the neglect of its God. In Joshua 8, the extermination concern receives four and a half verses (vv. 2a and 24–27), dealing with people not property. It comes to the fore, alas, in some fourteen verses in Joshua 10 (vv. 28–41). In the northern campaign, one should reckon with some three verses (11:11–12, 14). Summed up at its most favorable: three fragments and a paragraph. That is bad enough, but that is all — apart from the framing verses. At less than thirty verses, it is about a chapter's worth, yet it has come to dominate the overall popular impression of the book of Joshua.

Two things are worth insisting on: first, it is minimal in textual extent; second, it never happened in fact. A further question is inevitable: Where did it come from? The quick answer is that we cannot be sure. There are certain detailed codes by which we can trace traditions; with that, we can often be fairly sure. In general terms, the detailed code consists of language, phrases, ideas, and their expression. Not infrequently, instead of anything as demonstrable as the code of language, phrases, ideas, etc., there can be a certain spiritual fascination that may help us identify where material has come from. In such cases, however, we may suspect but we can seldom be sure.

In this case of what we have been calling the "extermination level," the detailed code includes several phrases. One such phrase is "with the sword" (overall, it occurs in thirty-three verses; a third of them are here); another is "every person" (*kol ha-nephesh;* twelve verses, half of them here); a third is "no one remaining" (= survivor; twenty-eight verses, a quarter of them here). The cluster of these three phrases together is only to be found here in Joshua 10:28–40. It is surprising, however, how many of the single phrases are used in contexts of total destruction.

The spiritual fascination, in this case akin to fanaticism, is to be found in several places in Deuteronomy. Two are well known for their extremism: Deuteronomy 13:15–16 (destroy the town) and Deuteronomy 21:18–21 (destroy the adolescent). The judgment of the rabbis on both passages is delightfully discreet and thoroughly unambiguous. Note the following: regarding Deuteronomy 13: "The destruction of a whole community because of idolatry (verses 13ff.) never occurred nor will it ever occur. The sole purpose of the warning is that it might be studied and that one might receive reward for such study" (with reference to the *Tosefta* [San. 14:1]). One aspect of such study would be presumably to affirm that it has never occurred and will never occur. Regarding Deuteronomy 21: "(A tradition says that this law was never operative.) If so, why was it written in the Torah? To study (more) and to obtain reward therefrom" (with reference to the *Talmud* [San. 71a]; both quotations are from Plaut, *Torah,* 1435, 1489).

A clause occurs in Deuteronomy that points to a recurrence of this concern in the book of Deuteronomy; the clause is "so shall you purge the evil from your midst" (Deut 13:6 [Heb.; NRSV, 13:5]; 17:7; 19:19; 21:21; 22:21, 24; 24:7). The fanaticism here is akin to that of Joshua 10:28–40. The absence of the clause from Joshua 10:28–40 may well be due to the fact that those being slaughtered were outsiders, not to be described as "from your midst." To suspect this connection is reasonable; to demonstrate it is not possible.

The issue of monotheism has been discussed earlier. It is important to be aware of it here. It is equally important to be aware of the place of monotheism in the theology of Deuteronomy. The Shema is the great commandment: "Hear, O Israel: The LORD is our God, the LORD alone" (Deut 6:4). The centralization of worship in deuteronomic Israel contributed to the assurance of monotheism. So important was it that the deuteronomic reform was ready radically to upset the social organization of Israel to achieve it. The book of Deuteronomy and the book of Joshua are, of course, closely associated.

Deuteronomy is in many ways one of the great humanitarian books of the Older Testament. What is such fanaticism doing in such a book? It has been said that "great wits are sure to madness near allied, and thin partitions do their bounds divide" (Dryden). Might it be true that impossible ideals risk being to fanaticism near allied?

Deuteronomy apart, righteousness runs risks with which, unfortunately, history is all too full. Two quotes from the Psalms will do for now. The first comes from the psalm some might term "the song of the righteous prig":

> I will not set before my eyes
>   anything that is base.
> I hate the work of those who fall away;
>   it shall not cling to me.
> Perverseness of heart shall be far from me;
>   I will know nothing of evil....
> Morning by morning I will destroy
>   all the wicked in the land,
> cutting off all evildoers
>   from the city of the LORD.
>   (Ps 101:3–4, 8)

Rather more surprising, at the end of a lovely evocation of creation, is:

> Let sinners be consumed from the earth,
>   and let the wicked be no more.
> Bless the LORD, O my soul. (Ps 104:35)

History suggests such aberration is regrettably widespread among human society; witch hunts and the Inquisition are only a beginning.

Before leaving these absolutely appalling extermination levels in Joshua, we need to recall where they occur: as insertions in the Jericho story and the story of Achan, prior to the capture of Ai, and in the dense little text of 10:28–40 (a six-town run around southern Judah, including Makkedah, Libnah, Lachish, Eglon, Hebron, and Debir, but not counting Gezer [whose king and his army figured as wiped out assisting Lachish]). It is worth noting that three of these kings — of Lachish, Eglon, and Hebron — are reported to have participated in the coalition of five assembled by the king of Jerusalem (see 10:3–5). According to the report in 10:16–27, they perished together, captured by Joshua in the cave at Makkedah. This, of course, contradicts the list that follows immediately in 10:28–40. It is one more piece of evidence that the extermination portrayed in 10:28–40 could not be taken as reality. The five at Makkedah or the six in the list are small beer in comparison with the thirty or so in Joshua 12.

~MODERN FAITH~

From the point of view of modern faith, perhaps the overwhelming result of attending to the "absolutely appalling" is the realization that it never happened. The extent of text is minimal. The concern articulated is surprisingly late. The drive motivating this concern may well be associated with monotheism.

Being restricted in extent, late in origin, and of possibly monotheistic inspiration may diminish something of the horror felt at the extermination issue; they do not alter the fact that such texts are absolutely appalling. It is worth remembering that although the events are portrayed as belonging to an early stage of Israel's presence in the land, the texts come from a late stage in Israel's story, when it was most probably outside the land and wondering why.

APPENDIX:
Archaeology and the Book of Joshua

Claims have been made that archaeology proves the Bible true. Alas, what the Bible claimed to be true was not examined. The claim was reduced to a narrow selection of unrepresentative verses. The meaning of the whole was not examined. Alas, when fuller and more professional archaeological techniques were brought to bear, earlier claims were discredited.

Attempts have been made to portray the book of Joshua as the account of Israel's conquest of the land; failing that, the reflection of Israel's infiltration into the land; failing that, the result of peasant revolt within the land. At present, the most likely account of Israel's presence in the land begins with some three hundred highland village sites reported by Israel Finkelstein (see *Bible Unearthed*, 97–118). In my judgment, it is also hugely to be regretted that, early in his chapter, Finkelstein after adverting to multiple evidence in the biblical text should continue "as archaeology suggests" and "once again archaeology can provide some surprising answers." All archaeologists know that, of itself, archaeology suggests nothing and, of itself, provides no answers. Archaeological results are mute until interpreted. The interpretation of archaeological discoveries can certainly suggest and can certainly provide some surprising answers. The interpretation of archaeological discoveries, like the interpretation of biblical text, is necessarily a subjective enterprise. Subjectivity needs to be respected; subjectivity needs also to be recognized and given due weight.

I do not expect archaeologists to be exegetes of biblical text; I do regret that some of them belittle the biblical text when they are ignorant of modern research regarding it. Exegetes are greatly helped and enlightened by soundly interpreted archaeological discovery. Without it, exegetes should still be able to express appropriate caution regarding realms of myth, legend, and unwise exaggeration. In the interpretation of the book of Joshua, unwise exaggeration was all too easily given credence.

Where the book of Joshua is concerned, I have elsewhere quoted William Dever, no mean authority, well informed, highly respected, and a fully professional archaeologist, to the effect that:

> Today, on the basis of the evidence...all archaeologists and virtually all biblical scholars have abandoned the older conquest model or even "peaceful infiltration" and peasants' revolt models, for "indigenous origins" and /or "symbiosis" models in attempting to explain the emergence of early Israel in Canaan. (*Biblical Writers*, 41)

A couple of years later, Dever authoritatively claimed that:

> We must confront the fact that the external material evidence supports almost nothing of the biblical account of a large-scale, concerted Israelite military invasion of Canaan. (*Early Israelites*, 71)

No informed scholar would disagree. A few moments of form-critical reflection makes quite clear that the text is a mixture of liturgies, stories, and reports. The reports are mainly toward the end of Joshua 1–12; the appallingly nasty bits are mainly in the reports. There is hope yet. It would be a grave disservice to those who have preserved the book over the centuries not to take on the task of probing beyond the extermination level to explore the other perspectives also preserved in the book.

SUMMARY

As we have seen, when exploring modern faith in relation to biblical text a couple of principles come into play. One was expressed in *Rethinking the Pentateuch*: there is "a shift from the Pentateuch as a record of Israel's *remembering its past* to the Pentateuch as a record of *Israel's pondering its present*" (9). This applies to much of the Pentateuch and elsewhere too in the Older Testament. Its corollary — that revelation comes not only from the past but also from the present — undermines the understanding of revelation as coming exclusively *from above and from the past,* an understanding that still influences many. As we ponder our lives and remember our past, in all the rich variety it involves (family, schooling, religion, culture), we come to a deeper understanding of ourselves and our world and a correspondingly deeper insight into our understanding of our God. That is surely an aspect of revelation, not the whole but an aspect — coming *from below and from the present.* These two thoughts have borne repeating from time to time in the unfolding of this book.

Two concerns are probably primary for us in the study of the book of Joshua. First, it is almost disconcerting to realize how late it was taking its place in Israel's literature. Second, the still-unanswered question is still to be asked: What is the primary message of the book? Lurking behind both concerns are the questions: What does this book tell us about ancient Israel and about ourselves? What does it tell us about our God?

My scholarly life has been intimately associated with the books of Samuel. I cheerfully assert that some of their traditions belong in the tenth century. It is widely accepted that the book of Deuteronomy belongs in the latter part of the seventh century and the present form of Joshua 1–12 depends on Deuteronomy. No one denies that traditions in Deuteronomy may be older than the seventh century. Nevertheless, in the chronology of composition Deuteronomy and Joshua are later than Samuel (Judges may be left aside). Logic places Moses and Joshua earlier than Samuel, Saul, and David. The chronology of composition may not do so.

The details need not be discussed here. What emerges clearly from the basic assertion is that, while some of the traditions in the book of Joshua may perhaps go back to the time of Israel's early presence in the land, they most certainly need not be so early, and in all probability a considerable majority of them is not so early. Liturgy remembers; it is not contemporaneous reporting. Sophisticated storytelling is seldom contemporary with the events it tells of. The "absolutely appalling" has been clearly shown to be chronologically late.

What purpose, then, was served by these liturgies and this sophisticated storytelling? For the purposes of discussion, the crossing of the Jordan and the capture of Jericho may be treated as liturgies. The message would not differ were they to be treated as stories for the telling. The texts concerning Ai, failure and success there, reflect the telling of stories. It is difficult to imagine them as liturgies.

The crossing of the Jordan (Josh 3–4) probably reflects a process of understanding of Israel's identity and destiny as a people. The process is, to a degree, mirrored in the two little catechetical instructions (Josh 4:6–7 and 4:22–24). The first is a simple remembrance that the flow of the Jordan was stopped to allow Israel to enter the land. A positivist might want to argue over whether the river flow actually stopped or not. A theologian, please God, would be looking to the symbolic meaning of the affirmation of such a stoppage. Israel's presence in the land had to do with Israel's relationship to God; the presence was the result of Israel's entry into the land, an entry facilitated by the stopping of the Jordan. Only God stops the river's flow in front of the ark. Of course, the river's flow has on a very few occasions in recorded history been stopped by the collapse of its banks. Such a stoppage is quite clearly not what the text envisages, not what the liturgy remembers. Israel owes its presence in the land to its God. In the liturgy, acknowledgment can be made and thanks can be given. It does not report the past for its own sake; it remembers the past for a fuller understanding of the present.

The capture of Jericho evokes a strand of theology in ancient Israel that is found in Deuteronomy 6:10–12. "The LORD your God has brought you into...a land with fine, large cities that you did not build...take care that you do not forget the LORD." Only God collapses city walls at a people's shout. Israel did not build Jericho. God gave it to them. The goodness of life in the land should not lead them to forget their God. Whether it is Hosea (they did not know that it was my doing, see Hos 2:8) or Proverbs (not riches lest I deny you, see Prov 30:7–9), affluent ease can lead too easily to the denial of God. The liturgy associated with Jericho does not report the past for its own sake; it remembers the past for a fuller understanding of the present.

The story of the failure at Ai may have many meanings. The nature of Achan's breach points to the independence of the story from the chapter that follows. Achan took from among the spoil a beautiful mantle, a couple of hundred shekels of silver, and a bar of gold (Josh 7:21). According to the instructions inserted into chapter 8, this was permitted. "Only its spoil and its livestock you may take as booty for yourselves" (8:2a). We may jest that poor Achan found himself in the wrong chapter. It is also of the essence of the Achan story that the town of Ai should be lightly defended (7:3, "they are so few"). In the following chapter, of course, Joshua's exploit in the capture of the town would be greatly diminished if the defenders could be rated as feeble, counted as few.

One message of the Achan story is surely: do not ignore God. The task is not difficult; Joshua and his troops can comfortably achieve it. In their confidence, Achan, a bit player in the scene, ignored God. Confidence in what you can do does not require that you have God do it for you; the next chapter makes that clear. Confidence in what you can do does suggest awareness of the reality and guidance of God. A story from the past has a point to make about the present.

The story of the success at Ai, equally, may have many meanings, especially when — as treated here — the text is evidently a base from which storytelling may be launched. One aspect is surely the exaltation of Joshua. The man is a top commander. Great generalship outlining the strategy; supremely competent execution of it; superb timing in the breaking out of the ambush; a thoroughly convincing victory satisfactorily finished off. Great stuff. Alongside this is the other aspect, that great generalship goes along with an honest relationship with God. So the awareness is there that God gave Ai into Joshua's hands and God gave Joshua the strategy, even if rather truncatedly (v. 2b). When the strategy is being unfolded, God gets a mention (vv. 7–8). At the key turning point in the battle, God is listed as giving Joshua the nod. The action is Joshua's throughout; this is something that Joshua and the troops with him can do. Awareness of God is never very far from it all.

In terms of this first part of the book of Joshua, it is important to be aware of what it does not portray. The first part of the book is *not* about Israel's occupation of the land of Canaan. The first chapter may give the impression that it will be about the occupation of the land; but the following chapters do not bear this out. The first chapter opens with wide-angle vision: "every place that the sole of your foot will tread upon I have given to you" (Josh 1:3). But, in the narratives apart from the reports, the sole of Joshua's foot does not tread very widely. The first part of the book ends, "So Joshua took the whole land" (Josh 11:23). Religious leaders, like politicians and spin doctors, have the bad habit of talking up events in ways that do not always tally with reality. Religious literature can fall into the same traps. The book of Joshua is a case in point.

Liturgies take Israel across the Jordan and into Jericho. An attack on Ai fails; an attack on Ai succeeds. Negotiations with Gibeon succeed beyond expectations — from the Gibeonite point of view. That is about as far as the narratives go, and that is not very far. The reports provide a lightning tour of southern Judah (six towns) and report on one battle in the north (in association with Hazor). These reports have the same ring of authenticity to them that, for example, British Prime Minister Neville Chamberlin's "I bring peace in our time" did on the eve of World War II, one of the two bloodiest and most beastly conflicts in human history. Of course, the second part of the book (esp. Josh 13–22) gives the impression of occupation of the whole land, because the whole land is distributed to Israel's tribes. The distribution is portrayed as sacral, largely by lot. The chronological periods reflected need not concern us here. It is widely recognized that they do not reflect Israel's early presence in the land.

Beyond some faith-inspired claims in scattered verses, the book of Joshua does not attempt a portrayal of widespread occupation; therefore it is not contradicted by recent archaeology. Recent archaeology may impose a welcome restraint on the folly of some faith-inspired claims, above all in the area of archaeology proving the Bible true.

On the other hand, the book of Joshua has not been "proved wrong" by archaeology. Superficial readings of the book may have been proved superficial. What archaeology has not yet given to the community of biblical scholarship is an understanding of what processes and what stages in these processes the book of Joshua may reflect and may derive from. As archaeology develops, these understandings may emerge. On the other hand, it is also possible that they remain shrouded in the uncertainties of the distant past. A full understanding of the book of Joshua is not given us primarily by the archaeologist's spade or camel-hair brush. Such understanding can only come, primarily, from careful attention to the text of the book, the literary forms involved, and the layers of editing that can be perceived.

Finally, and perhaps painfully, it is important to recognize that, for all its superb qualities, its exalted ideals, and its extensive theological impact, the book of Deuteronomy and the deuteronomic movement advocated a vision that failed. Josiah endorsed its vision but, in the service of that vision, died in battle rather too abruptly. His successors as king certainly did not, probably could not, commit to the vision. For whatever reasons, the deuteronomic vision did not generate an institutional legacy in the national politics and religious practices of its time. Some of that vision flowed over to the book of Joshua. Often in the book of Joshua, the deuteronomic portrayal of the past reflected the deuteronomic vision for seventh-century Israel, particularly those aspects that were most distant from reality.

Part Three

The Books of Samuel and Reality

The David of later times had reached legendary status.

*The David of the books of Samuel
is definitely down-to-earth and real.*

Chapter Five

Israel's Traditions
about King David

INTRODUCTION

The issue of biblical honesty needs examination. In their useful book *The Bible Unearthed,* Israel Finkelstein and Neil Silberman not infrequently decry as legendary fantasies the biblical narratives portraying the grand empire of David and Solomon (see, for example, 158, 162). As they are well aware, the Bible has its share of "mythmaking and heroic hyperbole" (152). Without any question, the Solomonic texts are an odd lot (fundamentally 1 Kgs 3–11), very different from the much more extensive texts regarding David. These Solomonic texts are particularly prone to their share of the "mythmaking and heroic hyperbole" that can be found in the Bible — or the self-inflation expected from petty kings, major rulers, or politicians.

That a respected scholar such as Israel Finkelstein should feel the need to write about these views in a popular book is indicative that they are held by a significant sector of his expected readership. This should not be surprising. Israel's prophets, for example, speak in down-to-earth terms of the injustice and infidelity they see in the society around them and of the disaster that not setting these right will cause. They go on to speak in far from down-to-earth terms of the future that God will bring about, where Israel will be God's wife in righteousness and in justice (Hos 2:16), where justice and peace will kiss (Ps 85:10). Most understandable. If God is great, surely the future with God will be great. Alas, the promises of the far from down-to-earth future remain unfulfilled — unless they are transformed and, as for many Christians, fulfilled in the coming of the crucified Jesus Christ. It depends totally on the understanding

245

of greatness. Is it associated with finery and royal palaces (see Matt 11:8–10)? Or is it associated with homelessness and crucifixion (see Matt 8:20)? The Bible associates greatness with David and Solomon. I find remarkable the honesty and down-to-earth quality of most of the biblical narratives about King David. For me, it can often serve as a paradigm of God's dealings with human life.

A trap for young players, always, and all too often for pious Bible readers too, is to take the spin doctors of life or politics at face value. Their presence is found in politics and life (especially for the "feel-good" spinners); they are found in the Bible. There will always be passages from the biblical equivalent of the spin doctors. For David: "The LORD gave victory to David wherever he went. So David reigned over all Israel; and David administered justice and equity to all his people" (2 Sam 8:14–15). The rebellious Absalom and his supporters would disagree with the "justice and equity" bit. For Solomon: "God gave Solomon very great wisdom, discernment, and breadth of understanding as vast as the sand on the seashore, so that Solomon's wisdom surpassed the wisdom of all the people of the east, and all the wisdom of Egypt" (1 Kgs 5:9–10 [Heb.; NRSV, 4:29–30]). This great wisdom, God's gift, did not prevent Solomon from finishing his life in serious idolatry (1 Kgs 11:1–8).

Monotheism, as George Steiner proposed (above), turns out to be at the core of it all. In life, it is the core of it all. Of the two great kings at the start of Israel's monarchy, Solomon ended up an idolater and David remained a monotheist. The story of Israel's kings (1–2 Kings) judges its kings by one primary criterion: Did they do what was right in the eyes of God? "What was right" meant monotheism (see the tables at the end of Campbell and O'Brien, *Unfolding the Deuteronomistic History,* 478–82; for deuteronomists, Jeroboam's sin was idolatry). That "what was right" meant monotheism is hardly surprising, because most of the history came from the deuteronomists, disciples of the book of Deuteronomy. That is what centralization in Jerusalem was all about. For Deuteronomy, monotheism was central: "Hear, O Israel: The LORD is our God, the LORD alone" (Deut 6:4). It is a valid test. Solomon failed it. Most of Israel's kings failed it. Most of us fail it. David passed it. David failed in many ways; on this test, however, he passed. ("Most of us fail it": we do not worship

Baal; all too often, though, we set our priorities around money and job, security, status, power, and the like.)

The biblical spin doctors had a ball with Solomon; the legendary gives spin doctors joy. It was not at all unknown in the ancient Near East of the time. The biblical narratives on David are surprisingly down-to-earth. Sometimes the legendary intrudes, but seldom. Many of the texts on David provide food for thought on how God is believed present in human lives. In this context, a sentence from Finkelstein and Silberman, the *Bible Unearthed* that worries me is "At the end of 2 Samuel, the pious David is shown establishing a great empire" (167). I am puzzled by this, because there is nothing of the kind at the end of 2 Samuel. Hyperbole is present in 2 Samuel 8. Even there, as Baruch Halpern points out, situating it alongside ancient Near Eastern display inscriptions (i.e., as state-of-the-art for royal propaganda): "If we take the text at its face value, rather than investing ourselves in its apparatus of implication, the picture is relatively modest.... They [the authors of the text] suggested, implied, insinuated that David's achievements were a great deal more extensive than in reality they were. But they did not openly prevaricate..." (*Secret Demons*, 195, 207).

Legendary status certainly gathered around David in the Deuteronomistic History, primarily reflecting his monotheism, his fidelity to *yhwh,* rather than other aspects of his reign. Examination of the Davidic texts will be valuable here.

GOD PROPOSES, LIFE DISPOSES:
David and the Books of Samuel

Preliminary: The emergence of monarchy

Before we can look at texts on David as king, we need to have a monarchy in Israel so that David can be its king. The biblical text on the emergence of monarchy in ancient Israel (esp. 1 Sam 8–10) is a fascinating test case for the approach to biblical narrative. There are three quite clear stances with regard to kingship: (1) a request is made by the elders on grounds of internal justice; (2) a gift is made by God on grounds of external defense; (3) a critical attack is leveled against kingship as apostasy and infidelity. As an approach to biblical text, are readers invited to reflect on these three and perhaps choose among them or are readers informed as to what took place at the time?

The first stance is to be found in 1 Samuel 8. Samuel has appointed his sons judges over Israel (8:1). What the nature of the office was, whether administrative or judicial, we do not know. What right Samuel might have been thought to have had enabling him to make such appointments we do not know. It does not matter very much. What matters is that the sons are portrayed as unjust; "they took bribes and perverted justice" (8:3). Consequently, all the elders of Israel ask Samuel for a king (8:5). The selection of Israel's first king is reported in 1 Samuel 10:17–24. The second stance is to be found in 1 Samuel 9. The day before Samuel's encounter with Saul, God had revealed to Samuel that "tomorrow . . . I will send to you a man from the land of Benjamin, and you shall anoint him to be ruler over my people Israel. He shall save my people from the hand of the Philistines; for I have seen the suffering of my people because their outcry has come to me" (9:15–16). It is not: I have heard their cry for justice; saving Israel from the Philistines excludes harmonization. The third stance is spread over both 1 Samuel 8 and 1 Samuel 10:17–24. "They have not rejected you, but they have rejected me from being king over them . . . forsaking me and serving other gods" (8:7–8). "I brought up Israel out of Egypt . . . but today you have rejected your God" (10:18–19).

Much can be said about these texts (see Campbell, *1 Samuel,* and Campbell and O'Brien, *Unfolding the Deuteronomistic History,* 233–45). Our focus here will be simply on the three stances. The plea for a king in terms of justice (first stance) is complicated by the role added later of defense: "that our king may govern us and go out before us and fight our battles" (8:20). With that extension, the first stance is verging on blending with the second; it makes space for the military achievement in chapter 11. It is not necessary to discuss it in detail here.

Harmonization, informing users as to what took place at the time, has been tried but is inappropriate and almost impossible without

distorting the meaning of the texts. In my view, the biblical juxtaposition of such tension-laden texts constitutes an invitation to
reflection. Kyle McCarter adopting the position of not welcome but
indulged, speaks of divine sanction given "even if only in a back-
handed way" (*I Samuel*, 162 [an exotic backhander!]). Ralph Klein
proposes that "this *request* for a king was sinful to Dtr.... [But] kingship was Yahweh's gift to a highly undeserving Israel" (*1 Samuel*, 79
[a split decision!]). Walter Brueggemann speaks of a "permitted-but-
disapproved" status, leaving the monarchy "theologically doubtful"
(*Samuel*, 66 [a most unusually ambivalent position for the God
of Israel to take]). And these commentators are only dealing with
1 Samuel 8 and 10! The God portrayed in the Older Testament
seldom settles for such half measures. Regrettably, 1 Samuel 9's presentation of the divinely initiated gift of a king, made by God to
Israel, for Israel's defense, is left out of the picture.

Invitation to reflection would include both Israel's needs (justice
and defense) and the risks involved (trust in royal power rather than
in divine protection or some other form of social organization). There
may be more. Two needs are evident, justice and defense. Two origins
are evident, request by the elders and gift by God. One concern is
voiced that in some way the adoption of a king involves the rejection
of God. There is abundant material for reflection. There is room for
choosing the most suitable attitude to secular power.

In my judgment, the biblical text not infrequently juxtaposes con-
flicting traditions and leaves their evaluation up to the reflection of
its users. Here, as often, the biblical text amalgamates rather than
adjudicates, inviting users to reflection.

Prelude: The case of Saul

The little collection focused on King Saul can be said to be both a gem
and an anomaly. Its opening verse (13:1) is to a degree symbolic of
the collection as a whole: it is both typical and atypical. Typical: most
accounts of the kings of Israel and Judah begin by saying, "And X
was Y years old when he began to reign, and he reigned for Z years."
Atypical: the account for Saul begins, "Saul was ... years old when he
began to reign; and he reigned ... two years over Israel" (NRSV). The
figure for his age is lacking; the length of his reign may be deficient.

Considerable discussion focuses on the verse. The anomaly extends to the collection as a whole: of course, the collection is about Saul; at the same time, the collection is not primarily about Saul — no exploit of Saul's is narrated and the role of God's representative in rejecting and selecting kings is central: Saul is rejected.

In the account of Israel's kings (Samuel–Kings), three chapters at most are given to Saul, about forty to David, and some eight to Solomon (with 1 Kgs 1–2 put in the "betwixt and between" basket). The contents of the three chapters are quickly summarized. The first lists preparations for battle, with Saul's Israelites hopelessly outnumbered by the Philistines. In the middle of the anxiety, with Saul at Gilgal and his forces trembling with fear, Samuel does not show up as he had promised (10:8); so Saul, as his people were deserting, offered sacrifice to entreat the LORD. Immediately, Samuel arrives, berates Saul, and announces that his time as king is over and God has chosen another to be ruler over God's people (13:13–14). Samuel then stalks off, leaving Saul with Jonathan. The last part of the chapter reflects the dismal situation of Saul's forces in confrontation with the Philistines.

The second chapter (1 Sam 14) may involve multiple traditions (see 13:3–4) but the present text portrays a victory by Jonathan, almost canceled out by Saul's ineptitude. At the end of the chapter (14:47–52), there is a summary of Saul's reign that is at odds with the image of Saul given us. It lists his victories: against Moab, Ammon, Edom, the kings of Zobah (an Aramaean kingdom), and the Philistines, "wherever he turned he routed them" (14:47) — even the Amalekites. According to the final verse, "there was hard fighting against the Philistines all the days of Saul" (14:52). We know next to nothing of all this successful military activity (except perhaps the highly contrived story of the campaign against the Amalekites in chapter 15). The summary includes Saul's three sons, his two daughters, his wife, and Abner, his army commander. From the narrative's point of view, the story of Saul is ended here (1 Sam 14). The story of David takes over with 1 Samuel 15. Naturally, the story of David inevitably includes a great deal of the activity of Saul. Some eighteen chapters later, in 1 Samuel 31, still as king, Saul loses his three sons in battle with the Philistines and takes his own life. But these are chapters in the story of David. It is difficult, obviously, to agree with Diana Edelman that 1 Samuel 8–2 Samuel 1 constitute "the narrative of Saul's career" (*King Saul,* 11).

The third of the three chapters (1 Sam 15) outlines Saul's formal and definitive dismissal; it clears the way for David. Ordered by Samuel to annihilate the Amalekites, flocks and all, Saul and the people complied where the "despised and worthless" were concerned, but they spared Agag, the Amalekite king, and the best of the livestock, "all that was valuable" (15:8–9). Indignant, Samuel dismissed Saul with the famous words, "obedience is better than sacrifice" (15:22). Samuel then slaughtered King Agag in the Gilgal sanctuary and returned home to Ramah, never to see Saul again. The chapter ends: "And the LORD was sorry that he had made Saul king over Israel" (15:35). According to the same verse, Samuel grieved over Saul. With Saul rejected, David is needed.

Something of the anomaly in the collection can be gauged by contrasting the dismal situation portrayed in chapter 13 with the triumphant note struck in the summary, 1 Samuel 14:47–52. It is as if chapter 13 was formulated by Saul's foes and the summary by his friends. The events, whatever they were, remain the same. In this, the little collection is not dissimilar from the much larger body of tradition that concerns David. David's friends had one view of the relevant material: "the LORD was with him" (1 Sam 16:14). David's foes had an opposite view of the same material, articulated by Shimei ben Gera of the family of the house of Saul: "Murderer! Scoundrel! The LORD has avenged on you all the blood of the house of Saul, in whose place you have reigned; and the LORD has given the kingdom into the hand of your son Absalom. See, disaster has overtaken you; for you are a man of blood" (2 Sam 16:7–8 [translation adjusted; NRSV misplaces the "all"]).

From 1 Samuel 16 to 2 Samuel 8, the traditions we have are substantially from David's friends; from 2 Samuel 11 to 2 Samuel 20, it is not easy to tell; 2 Samuel 21–24 is a separate collection in its own right (see Campbell, *2 Samuel,* esp. 184–210, and Campbell, "2 Samuel 21–24"). In the cases of both Saul and David, the traditions may be touched by the legendary here and there. They are not greatly distanced from the reality they claim to reflect. They are not the pretensions of despots. Beyond a couple of Solomonic verses and some Solomonic overkill, they are not based in the unreal realm of boastful dreams about long past founders.

THE STORIES OF DAVID'S
CLIMB TO POWER
(1 Sam 16–2 Sam 8)

The text from 1 Samuel 16 to 2 Samuel 5 is basically made up of stories of David on the run. "David the bandit" is a bit rough, but maybe not too inaccurate. Much depends on where one stands. In recent years, few but the far right would have called Che Guevara a bandit. The dividing line between freedom fighter and bandit may often depend on where the observer is positioned. David becomes king of Judah in 2 Samuel 2 and king of both Judah and Israel at the beginning of 2 Samuel 5. The remaining text (2 Sam 5:6–8:18) is fundamentally concerned with David's establishment in power in Jerusalem.

There can be little doubt that David, initially, was a highly successful guerrilla leader, on the run from King Saul, and with his eye on the top political job in Judah, namely, king. What is of interest is the reality that the stories are exactly what would be expected of the exploits of a guerrilla leader on the run. The text in 1 Samuel 16–31 is largely about the doings of David, even though Saul is intimately involved. The down-to-earth and far-from-legendary quality of it is the overall overwhelming impression. The text in 2 Samuel 2–4 is largely about the doings of others, even though David may benefit from what occurs.

David: Presence at Saul's court

When the narrative focus shifts from Saul as king to David as king-to-be, the first move has to be from the rural Bethlehem, where David had been, to the royal court, which was still where Saul was. Two traditions start the process. In one of these, David is recruited as lyre-player to soothe Saul in troubled periods; in the other, David comes to Saul's attention by distinguishing himself in battle with a Philistine champion. Once at Saul's court, David needs to make his presence felt. He is singled out to marry Merab, Saul's first daughter, but then passed over in favor of the another, Adriel the Meholathite. Saul's younger daughter, Michal, remedies this by falling in love with David. Saul settles on bridal compensation for the marriage of merely one hundred Philistine foreskins, thinking (according to the text) that getting them would cost David his life. It does not. David collects two hundred instead. A legendary touch, perhaps; hardly a particularly ennobling one. The marriage goes ahead; so does David's presence at the court. Saul seeks to kill his potential rival. Saul's son, the crown prince Jonathan, successfully intercedes for him. When Saul finally moves to eliminate his rival, it is Saul's daughter Michal who tips David off and helps him elude Saul's surveillance. David departs the court definitively.

The transfer of narrative focus from Saul to David is attributed first to God. Closure for Saul, regarding God's favor, is portrayed with the statement: "The LORD was sorry that he had made Saul king over Israel" (15:35). Samuel — in the text dismissing Saul but grieving for him — is sent to Bethlehem to anoint David: I have rejected Saul from being king; go to Jesse the Bethlehemite, "for I have provided for myself a king among his sons" (16:1). As Samuel retires from the scene, his job done, the narrator takes over with a faith-affirmation that determines the point of view from which the narrator will regard the traditions to follow. The faith-affirmation: "Now the spirit of the LORD departed from Saul, and an evil spirit from the LORD tormented him" (16:14). One might be tempted to attribute this to straightforward observation and the limited medical knowledge of the time. However, the straightforward observation is given to Saul's courtiers in the next verse: "See now, an evil spirit from God is tormenting you" (16:15).

From this beginning forward, the narrative is clear in presenting David as favored by God. At the same time, this divine favor is kept by the narrative to the interpretative framework. It does not intrude into the content of the traditions themselves. In this, the narrative is true to the central tenet of Davidic faith: leave nothing to God except total trust. It is never expressly articulated; it is frequently practiced in the narrative traditions.

Samuel may have done God's bidding in anointing David in the privacy of the family circle; in the narrative, it is not mentioned again until David's coronation over all Israel (2 Sam 5:2). The text we have is put together by someone believing in God's commitment to David; the traditions put together in this way tell it without God's express involvement.

So it is as lyre-player that David moves from Bethlehem to Saul's court, with military duty as Saul's armor-bearer. In this capacity, one tradition has him at Saul's side on the battlefield when the Philistine champion appears. In this tradition, David acts as a man of faith (see 1 Sam 17:32–37). Ignoring the transfer to Saul's court, another tradition has David come from Bethlehem with supplies for his brothers, arriving at the battlefield just as the Philistine champion appears. In this tradition, David acts as a man of ambition (see 1 Sam 17:26–27). In the first tradition, David's success against the Philistine launches David's military career and ignites Saul's jealousy. In the second, it brings David to the court of Saul, enabling David's continued success and Saul's smoldering jealousy.

The narrator's interpretation of the events is given in 18:12–14: the LORD was with David. Those well disposed to David will agree; those ill-disposed to David will not.

With David now present at the royal court (miserable though it may have been, as courts go — see 1 Sam 22:6) and successful as a military commander, his preeminent status is to be signaled by marriage to one of the two royal princesses. The first does not come off; the second does. David's departure from Saul's court is imminent, and with it the rift between the two, Saul as king and David as rival, becomes public. But before that, the narrative gives David support from both Saul's son and daughter, Jonathan and Michal.

God's will may have been expressed in Samuel's anointing of David as replacement king. The narrator may have been correct in claiming that the LORD was with David. The happenings that bring David to court and have him leave it are portrayed on a totally secular level: skill with the lyre, skill on the battlefield, and skill in winning the hearts of influential friends. Nothing unexpected here.

Tradition has long seen David's combat with Goliath as a striking example of God's intervention on behalf of the underdog. This can be a gross misunderstanding. Full discussion would be out of place here (but see my *1 Samuel,* 167–93); two points will be enough. First, there is *no evidence* that David was small. Second, there is *good evidence* that the sling was an effective military weapon.

Point One: there is *no evidence* that David was small. Some seven pointers are relevant; five are available to English-language readers and two require knowledge of Hebrew. First, the youngest child need be neither youthful nor small. The youngest must be younger than the siblings; the youngest may be the biggest. Second, Saul was a big man and king; it is most unlikely that he would have allowed as his armor-bearer anyone who was physically unimpressive. Third, a small (presumably uncultured) shepherd boy is unlikely to be seriously considered for marriage to a king's daughter (17:25). Fourth, David's description of himself as killer of lions and bears reveals him as fast and tough, with excellent reflexes (17:34–35). Fifth, Jonathan swapped his gear with David (18:4), and Saul's eldest son and crown prince was hardly a little chap, especially when his father was reckoned as head and shoulders above the rest (see 1 Sam 10:23). Sixth, the Hebrew word *na'ar* has a wide range of meanings, including an infant (1 Sam 1:22; 4:21), young soldiers who can have sexual intercourse or kill (1 Sam 21:5–6 [Heb.; NRSV, 21:4–5]; 2 Sam 2:14–16), or the national director of public works (1 Kgs 11:28). The core semantic field for the meaning of the word seems to be dependence, whether in the family or in service. Its meaning on Saul's lips regarding David is clear: David is a recent recruit and the Philistine is a hardened veteran (1 Sam 17:33). Finally, seventh, the same word, *na'ar,* is used for all Jesse's sons (1 Sam 16:11; as later for David's sons [2 Sam 13:32]); the three eldest of Jesse's sons were in Saul's army on the field of battle.

Point Two: there is *good evidence* that the sling was an effective military weapon. Moderns need to be aware that a slingshot is different from a sling. Slingshots are for kids; slings were for killing. Two pieces of information are relevant here. First, the unerring accuracy of the slinger, vaunted in the case of seven hundred picked men from Benjamin (Judg 20:16). Second, the inclusion of sling-stones among a list of standard military supplies, such as shields, spears, helmets, coats of mail, and bows (2 Chr 26:16).

Conclusion: David was the right man, in the right place, at the right time, and with the right weapon. As long as the Philistine's shield was with his "shield-bearer" (17:7), the poor man was a sitting duck, the perfect target. Far from having no real hope in force of arms, David had a sling; with a little lateral thinking, the sling can be recognized as the perfect weapon in the circumstances. At the right range, David was invincible and the Philistine was dead. As a novelist, Joseph Heller gives the scene a full chapter for its retelling. "Frankly, the way I saw it, Goliath didn't stand a chance.... I took dead aim at the dark hole of the open mouth ... and I knew in my bones that there really was no way I could possibly miss. I missed. I caught him in the forehead instead, above the left eye" (*God Knows*, 64, 74). Heller also knew what David could do if he did miss; he could run for the hills (66).

There are legendary aspects, of course; legendary accretions are to be expected. The description of the grizzled veteran is a natural spot for such accretions. The forty days, morning and evening, of Goliath's speechifying (17:16) is surely a candidate for such an accretion. The name Goliath, occurring only twice in the chapter (17:4, 23; "the Philistine" occurs twenty-seven times), may be another accretion, transferred from Elhanan's exploit (2 Sam 21:19). The speeches could be adjusted at any time.

Where this episode is concerned, David needed to be confident, aggressive, and tough. From all we know of David, he was exactly that. He also needed a steady nerve; trust in God could contribute to that, as could ambition. All in all, nothing unusual here.

David: Beyond Saul's court

The material here stretches from 1 Samuel 19:18 to 26:25, so a little more than seven chapters; the traditions are of quite diverse kinds. As the most extensive block of traditions prior to David's assumption of kingship, these traditions show something of where the man was coming from and how he rose to power.

They begin with the affirmation of prophetic and political support for David (the prophet Samuel in 19:18–24 and the crown prince

Jonathan in 20:1–42); the former is suspect and the latter possible. There follow the moves that lead David to Adullam and his resources there. Two triads cluster the traditions that follow. In the first, at Nob Saul slaughters priests, at Keilah David delivers a town and Saul hopes to trap David, and in the mountains Saul is in hot pursuit of David. In the second, two stories of David's sparing Saul flank the story of David in Carmel being persuaded to spare Nabal. Only then does David leave Judah behind him.

The note of Davidic propaganda runs strongly through these traditions. It is scarcely the honorable propaganda that might be expected from a later time, when David was legend and model. As propaganda, it is no longer needed once its goal has been achieved. Similarly, the need to denigrate Saul is unlikely to be long-lasting, probably not more than a generation or two. As defense of David (classical: apologia; cf. McCarter, "Apology"), the need might be longer lived. Artful arrangement introduces a complicating factor of the potential difference in time between a tradition's origin and its use in a more extended composition. Such dating is seldom simple.

After being let down from Michal's window and escaping Saul's watchers in Jerusalem, David's first stop is reputedly with Samuel at Ramah. While association with Samuel bodes well for David, the passage's authenticity has to be highly suspect. First, it is substantially not an affirmation about David but an explanation for the saying, "Is Saul also among the prophets?" (19:24) — differently explained in 1 Sam 10:12. Second, it is in tension with the earlier claim that "Samuel did not see Saul again until the day of his death" (1 Sam 15:35). Third, there is strong evidence for revision and rewriting in a couple of the Samuel–Saul texts, 1 Samuel 9–10 and 15 (see Campbell, *1 Samuel*, 104–10, 151–61; also Campbell, *Of Prophets and Kings*). Finally, the three waves of messengers falling into frenzy, followed by Saul himself, has unmistakable parallels with the passage where Elijah sits on the top of a hill and three waves of soldiers are sent to capture him (2 Kgs 1:9–15). The message is clear: prophets outrank kings. David has Samuel on his side.

The tradition of Jonathan's friendship and support is more likely to have roots in past reality. It portrays a rift between Saul and David that cannot be bridged; Saul has even hurled his spear at his own son (1 Sam 20:33). The propaganda value of the tradition is huge; Saul's son and successor is committed to David as king-to-be. Saul to Jonathan: "For as long as the son of Jesses lives . . . neither you nor your kingdom shall be established" (1 Sam 20:31); Jonathan to David: "The LORD shall be between me and you, and between my descendants and your descendants, forever" (1 Sam 20:42).

The next two traditions are a mixed bag. The tradition of David with Ahimelech, priest of Nob, presents David as an undeniable liar. According to David, the young men, to rendezvous with him, were on a secret mission for the king and had kept themselves from women. Of course, there was no secret mission for the king; David was on the run from the king. Just as untrue, there were no young men. In due course, David's lie will cost Ahimelech his life and the lives of eighty-five fellow priests (1 Sam 22:6–23). It is not pretty. Perhaps David's people reported it because it led Saul into murderous sacrilege. Later generations are unlikely to have invented it.

The tradition of David saving his skin at the court of Achish, king of Gath, where he will later be welcome, is a different kettle of fish. It speaks of David's prowess and reputation; it speaks of David's cleverness in feigning madness. Some have worried that it sits uncomfortably with David's later service under Achish (1 Sam 27:1–7; also 1 Sam 29:6–10). A storyteller wanting to use both traditions would have had no trouble bridging the gap, having Achish warned to be on his guard because in the past David had proved a clever dissembler. The later episode with Achish will have its value as propaganda. While it has the potential to be turned against David — he worked for the Philistines — the present text portrays David favorably. The complex of associations with Achish at Gath make later invention unlikely.

Associated with the Adullam cave, a cluster of three little traditions wraps up this introductory material preceding the two triads mentioned above. First, David attracts followers, "his brothers and all his father's house . . . " and, as translated by the NRSV, those "in distress, . . . in debt, . . . discontented" gathered to him (1 Sam 22:1–2). The designation of his followers demands attention. If it is read negatively, for example as "outlaws and malcontents" (McCarter), it can reflect badly on David's endeavors; propagandists would not touch it and later legends would not endorse it. When the contexts where the terms occur are examined, the distress, debt, and discontent does not originate from within the "malcontents" but is imposed on them from the outside. Today, we might more accurately say oppressed, disadvantaged, and marginalized. Having the support of his brothers and his family establishment can be expected to reflect to David's credit.

A tradition has David place his father and mother under the protection of the king of Moab for the duration of his struggle. They are not heard of again in the text. Two elements attract my attention. First, David is portrayed dealing with the king. I doubt that Ruth's ancestry would have cut much ice after so many generations. More likely, in my judgment, is the value for David's reputation if he is seen dealing with kings as equals (note, at the court of Achish: "Is not this David, the king of the land?" [1 Sam 21:11, NRSV]). The value is there for propagandists, loyal apologists, and later generations. Second, David's parents are placed in safety for the duration. A longish campaign is in view, here at the outset; later, in relation to the outcome, a long civil war is reported (2 Sam 3:1). This is no short-lived or spontaneous protest; it was planned.

A final note can wrap matters up here. According to the text, David went further "into the land of Judah" on the advice of "the prophet Gad" (1 Sam 22:5). No "prophetic" role is claimed; no consultation with God is mentioned. In 2 Samuel 24, the prophet Gad functions in accordance with "the word of the LORD" (see 2 Sam 24:11–14); here nothing of the kind is recorded. Similarly, nothing of a prophetic nature is recorded for the prophet Nathan in 1 Kings 1. Were Gad and Nathan capable of prophetic function on occasion, but at other times loyal adviser and smart strategist (Gad) or good friend and smart politician (Nathan)? To what extent has the figure of the early prophets been influenced by later editors? "Instead of being the odd one out, it is a possibility that he [Gad] more closely resembles the average figure of these early prophets, before the creation of the Prophetic Record" (Campbell, *Of Prophets and Kings*, 114). It is unlikely that the text is a late creation.

With David and his men firmly within the land of Judah, the action-centered traditions fall into two groups of three, two triads. The first triad portrays Saul as aggressor — at Nob, at Keilah, and in the wilderness of Maon. The second triad portrays David as savior, sparing life when it is in his power to kill — with Saul in the cave, with Nabal at Carmel, and with Saul again in camp at Hachilah. This is probably skillful organization of material to denigrate Saul and to enhance the image of David.

The first triad begins with the episode at Nob. It denigrates Saul to great effect. The speech given to Saul, holding court under the tamarisk tree, reveals a threatened man by whose admission his own son supports his rival, David. Saul is then guilty of the sacrilege of slaughtering eighty-five of Israel's priests for a crime of which they are innocent. David is reported saying to Abiathar, "I am responsible" (1 Sam 22:22); apparently, David's original lie pales into insignificance alongside Saul's massacre. David's loss (his lie) is outweighed by David's gain (the support from Abiathar). The sacrilege is made clear when Saul's troops are reported to refuse his orders. "But the servants of the king would not raise their hand to attack the priests of the LORD" (1 Sam 22:17). Doeg the Edomite, their commander and a foreigner, is portrayed obeying Saul. The king's troops refuse; their foreign commander obeys. The narrative does not explain how one man could execute eighty-five. Beyond that, he (no name given; it could be Doeg, it could be Saul) put the city to the sword, Nob, described as "the city of the priests"; "men and women, children and infants, oxen, donkeys, and sheep, he put to the sword" (1 Sam 22:19).

Saul's son, his crown prince and eldest son, is against him; Saul's troops are against him; only Doeg, the foreigner, is for him. The scandal of murderous sacrilege is against him. As propaganda, this could hardly be improved on.

The second story in the triad relates to Keilah, described as a walled town with "gates and bars" (1 Sam 23:7). Again, the propaganda value is high. David is portrayed as saving Keilah from Philistine oppression — how symbolic! David does so with the repeated backing of the LORD, despite the misgivings of his men (1 Sam 23:2–4). The NRSV has "Thus David rescued the inhabitants of Keilah"; the Hebrew has literally "saved" and the NRSV renders it as "rescued." There is nothing wrong with the translation; no propagandist, however, would have settled for it.

According to the text, when Saul heard David and his men were inside a walled town, he moved at once to spring the trap on his rival. Inside, David "saved" while outside Saul "plotted evil" (23:9). A further note is added, however, which propagandists might invoke as evidence of God's support of David, alerting him to danger. Alternatively, it is on record as evidence of a certain popular resistance to David. The question: will the people of Keilah surrender David and his men to Saul. The oracular response: "They will surrender you" (1 Sam 23:10–12).

This ambiguity continues, with the tradition of Jonathan's loyalty to David, on the one hand, balanced by the tradition of the loyalty of Ziphites to Saul (1 Sam 23:15–24). This latter tradition paves the way for chapter 26.

The final story in the first triad is the thriller of the mountainside chase in the wilderness of Maon. David and his men were on one side of the mountain, Saul and his men on the other. David was on the run; Saul was closing in. Only a Philistine raid elsewhere that needed Saul's urgent attention allowed David to escape. The tradition portrays a political power struggle, pure and simple; surprisingly, the text does not involve God. In the military measures taken, the structures of kingly power are rudimentary; both leaders are present.

The second triad opens with the story of Saul easing nature in a cave, with David and his men in the back of it — a clear case of the king being caught with his pants down (1 Sam 24:1–22). Once again, undignified for a more exalted view of royalty. The first part of the text, with Saul and the cave, could be a storyteller's delight, with options to exercise and expansion to decide on. Close attention to the text reveals the preservation of pointers to three options: (1) David himself never intended to kill Saul, but merely snipped his cloak; (2) urged by his men, David moved to kill Saul, but changed his mind; (3) urged by his men to let them kill Saul, David refused and reproached them. Expansion in some form is needed, with Saul's troops waiting outside the cave and Saul asking, "Is this your voice, my son David" (24:17 [Heb.; NRSV, 24:16]). A storyteller could easily have the troops held back. An option that would take care of both issues would have David leave the cave by a second opening. No smart guerrilla leader would risk having his men trapped in a cave with only one entrance! Safely out of sight, David can call to Saul (see Campbell, "Diachrony and Synchrony," 226–28).

Skirting such detail, we may focus here on the conversation reported between Saul and David. David eloquently pleads his innocence. "May the LORD therefore be judge . . . and vindicate me against you" (1 Sam 24:16 [Heb.; NRSV, 1 Sam 24:15]). The response given Saul is astonishing: "You are more righteous than I. . . . Now I know that you shall surely be king" (1 Sam 24:18, 21 [Heb.; NRSV, 1 Sam 24:17, 20]). From David's point of view, the text is brilliant. For all that, it does not lose sight of its context: Saul went to his house; David and his troops went up to "the stronghold." This is in the wilds of Judah, with David pitted against Saul. Later, in the wilds of Transjordan, Absalom will be pitted against David. Even the relationships are paralleled. David to Saul, "my father" (1 Sam 24:12 [Heb.; NRSV, 1 Sam 24:11]); Saul to David, "my son" (1 Sam 24:17 [Heb.; NRSV, 1 Sam 24:16]). David and Absalom are of course father and son.

The Carmel story, with Nabal, Abigail, and David, not only has David win as wife a woman portrayed as beautiful, intelligent, and articulate and have the LORD strike dead a man, her husband, portrayed as surly, mean, and hostile to David. The story goes further and has David prevented from bloodshed, above all through Abigail's speech. The speech given Abigail is beautifully crafted: when David becomes king, there will be no cause for grief, no reproach over the shedding of innocent blood (1 Sam 25:30–31). It is reaffirmed in David's response (1 Sam 25:32–34).

Finally, in Saul's camp by night, on the hill of Hachilah, David is presented standing over the sleeping Saul, refusing to have him killed, but instead removing the king's spear from beside him. Again the exchange between the two men. Again astonishing words given to Saul: "I have done wrong; come back, my son David, for I will never harm you again . . . ; I have been a fool, and have made a great mistake" (1 Sam 26:21). No propagandist could have asked for more, created more.

However, both 1 Samuel 24 and 26 pose problems for a propagandist and pose problems for anyone attempting to date these two chapters. The basic problem is simple: David is spoken of highly, but so is Saul. Saul is presented in remarkably noble terms. "You are more righteous than I" (1 Sam 24:17); "May the LORD reward you with good for what you have done to me this day" (1 Sam 24:19). These are not the words of an average politician about his rival. Saul again: "I have done wrong; come back, my son David, for I will never harm you again.... I have been a fool, and have made a great mistake" (1 Sam 26:21). In what circumstances would it have been appropriate to praise David and praise Saul simultaneously? That is precisely what these two chapters do.

A few chapters later, Joab and Abner will do battle, representing two kings. Here the two men, Saul and David, are presented representing themselves. It may be high-flown rhetoric; nevertheless, it is a raw and down-to-earth power struggle.

David: Beyond Judah

First Samuel 27–31 presents the traditions of David in self-imposed exile from Judah. It is not necessary to repeat here what has been said above. The ambiguity is patent. Supporters of David can delight in its propaganda value; opponents of David can harbor their suspicions.

From the point of view of David's supporters, he was forced out of Judah by Saul's hostility, he successfully raided enemy settlements in the area, and he was forced to absent himself from the battle in which Saul and his sons died. Could David and his force have turned the tide of battle in Saul's favor? The Philistine commanders are reported to have thought so. From the point of view of David's foes, he abandoned Judah as a rebel, he sold himself as a vassal to the Philistines, and he abandoned Saul to Philistine defeat.

The last episode, the battle of Gilboa, could be built up on the analogy of King Josiah seeking to prevent the Egyptian forces uniting with the Assyrians against Babylon. Josiah did not achieve his aim and died; David might have achieved victory and Saul would have lived. As to the reality, they probably did not know then; we certainly do not know now.

David: Achieving royal power

The opening chapters of 2 Samuel present the traditions of David's rise to power, first as king over Judah, then over Israel as well. Once again, it is not necessary to repeat here what has been said above. The ambiguity is patent. Supporters of David can delight in the propaganda value; opponents of David can harbor their suspicions.

David accepted responsibility for what happened at Nob (1 Sam 23:22). Was David responsible for the deaths of the Amalekite (2 Sam 1) or Ishbaal (2 Sam 4)? The text is emphatic that he was not. Opponents of David harbor their suspicions; it was all too convenient. God is not invoked. The battle between the forces of Joab and the forces of Abner (2 Sam 2:12–32) is a single episode from the "long war between the house of Saul and the house of David" (2 Sam 3:1). What it brings to the fore is the reality that neither side in the conflict — whether northern with a base at Mahanaim or southern with a base at Hebron — wielded significant power. Both sides were scrapping with relatively limited forces over a relatively miserable bit of local territory. The Bible makes no attempt to hide it.

The book of Chronicles provides a quite different picture of the transfer of power to David. Among other things, it reports significant support for David at Ziklag, at the stronghold, and on the eve of the battle of Gilboa (see 1 Chr 12). Just as 2 Samuel 21–24 reveals to us how much we do not know of some of the events and structures associated with David, so 1 Chronicles 10–12 is a reminder of how little we know with certainty about the transfer of power from Saul to David. Cases can be made, hypotheses can be proposed; certainty remains out of reach.

David and Jerusalem: 2 Samuel 5

The text has the capture of Jerusalem as the first thing David does after his coronation in Hebron. Given the importance of Jerusalem as David's capital city throughout his career, the "city of David" (2 Sam 5:7), it is surprising how little we know about the city's capture. No numbers, no strategy, no details beyond David's advice using two Hebrew words that, in the context, we can only grasp through conjecture (5:8; NRSV, "let him get up the water shaft"; see commentaries).

The biblical text gives more information on the capture of Jericho or Ai than it does on the capture of Jerusalem. Yet, where David is concerned, Jerusalem outranks them both. If nothing is said, perhaps nothing was there to be said.

The question of God's role in David's success, whether cause or consequence, is left open. The Hebrew of 5:10 has "And David became greater and greater and the LORD, the God of hosts, was with him." Some translations respect this, staying with "and"; others resolve the issue (cf. the NRSV: "for the LORD . . . was with him").

The notice of David's palace is given one verse. The initiative is attributed to King Hiram of Tyre; there are chronological problems. It is worth noting that the palace built for David is reported to have been replaced by Solomon in the next generation; little has changed till now! It is probably unfair to note that the biblical text gives seven verses to these matters (2 Sam 5:6–12) and Stoebe's 1994 commentary devotes seventeen pages to it.

The children are unlikely to be legendary, especially in the light of their names. The children born to David before the occupation of Jerusalem were Amnon, Chileab, Absalom, Adonijah, Shephatiah, and Ithream (see 2 Sam 3:2–5). Of these, two have names compounded with the element "-jah," denoting *yhwh*. The sons born to David in Jerusalem have the names Shammua, Shobab, Nathan, Solomon, Ibhar, Elishua, Nepheg, Japhia, Elishama, Eliada, and Eliphelet (see 2 Sam 5:13–16). Four of these are compounded with the element "Eli-," reflecting the name of El, God of Jerusalem. To the best of our knowledge, the god El was easily assimilated to the God *yhwh*. Two of Saul's sons (Ishbaal and Meribaal) have names compounded with the element "-baal," reflecting the name of the god Baal. Later Israelite tradition substituted "-boshet" (shame) for "-baal" (so, Ishboshet and Mephiboshet) but opposition between *yhwh* and Baal does not seem to have been definitively established before Elijah's time, a century later (see 1 Kgs 18:17–40). It is unlikely that Saul was indulging in religious infidelity.

The chapter wraps up with the reports of two victories over the Philistines (2 Sam 5:17–21, 22–25); while the possession of Jerusalem may be understood, there is no mention of it in either passage. The first has the Philistines hear that David has been anointed king over Israel and has David leave for "the stronghold" from which he goes up to attack the Philistines at Baal-perazim. If the stronghold is Adullam — as is probable — south of Jerusalem and on the fringe of Judah, then David has outflanked the Philistines and the attack is presumably from the rear. The second reports a Philistine flight from Geba (uncertain) to Gezer, both north of Jerusalem. Neither account is embroidered; no attempt is made in the text to expand David's successes against the Philistines beyond these two victories. Domination of the Philistines is not mentioned; the legendary has no place. Commentators may seek to heighten the significance of these two accounts; it is interesting that the text does not.

The Ark and Jerusalem: 2 Samuel 6

David is commonly credited with a stroke of genius in bringing the ark of God to Jerusalem, so uniting religious Israel on his new capital. Such a reading ignores the nuances of the text.

The text clearly gives the initiative to David. Equally clearly, the text gives control to God. In itself, such divine control is in David's favor; God controlled the movement of the ark that brought it to David's new capital. God's control is narrated in two stages. First, approaching the city, God strikes Uzzah dead. The attempts to discover a reason for God's anger are futile, running contrary to the text, which does not give a reason for it. God struck him dead — that is enough; God stopped the procession — that is the point. That is all and that is enough. David's reaction is understandable, but the narrative's emphasis on it is surprising. Three verbs and three verses: David was angry, David was afraid, David was unwilling (6:8–10). This is definitely not the stuff of legend. Having stopped the procession, God then starts it again. God gives the green light, blessing Obed-edom and his household, the foreigner to whose house the ark had been diverted, specifically "because of the ark of God" (6:11–12). The narrative has David, recognizing the theological green light, resume his initiative of bringing the ark to his city, Jerusalem.

While the move is immensely favorable to David, the narrative hardly originated in Davidic circles, much less those of David's foes. Devotees of the ark seem the most likely source. Had it involved the legendary later David, the narrative would surely have been differently told.

The sharp exchange with Michal has nothing to do with the attitude of an aristocratic princess toward David's lack of dancing decorum (6:20–23). David's "uncovering himself... as any vulgar fellow might" (6:20) would have been frowned on by any self-respecting woman at the time. Saul, "coming from the field behind the oxen" (1 Sam 11:5), may have been at best the son of a wealthy farmer. He may have been styled king of Israel; aristocrat he surely was not. If a class-conscious "establishment" had existed in early Israel (and to the best of our knowledge it did not), it would probably have looked down on King Saul as little more than a "jumped-up plough boy." Michal was his daughter; "aristocrat" she was not. Ignored by David she certainly was.

David's dynasty and Jerusalem: 2 Samuel 7

Most kings like the idea of keeping the kingdom in the family; not all achieve it. God's promise of a dynasty is cause for royal trumpeting. The literature around 2 Samuel 7 and the promise of a Davidic dynasty is massive. The reworking of the biblical text has been considerable. As far as we can see, the original formulation of the promise was probably modest enough (see, for example, Campbell, *Of Prophets and Kings*, 72–81). What is of particular interest in this context is that, in its original form, it would appear that God's word from the prophet Nathan was a rejection of David's proposal to build a temple. Divine rejection of royal piety is hardly characteristic of legend.

2 Samuel 8: The summary

The last word on this chapter can be taken from Baruch Halpern, from a book that is certainly not characterized by excessive deference to David. As quoted earlier, Halpern comments: "If we take the text at its face value, rather than investing ourselves in its apparatus of implication, the picture is relatively modest.... They [the authors of the text] suggested, implied, insinuated that David's achievements were a great deal more extensive than in reality they were. But they did not openly prevaricate..." (*Secret Demons,* 195, 207). Conclusion: the chapter is par for the course among royal inscriptions; it is not unduly into the legendary class.

When looking at a text like 2 Samuel 8, it does no harm to remember the couple of chapters associated with Saul's reign. Inspection of 1 Samuel 13:1–14:46 leaves the impression of poor Saul as pretty much a loser. To the contrary, 14:47–52 rates Saul highly: "he fought against all his enemies on every side...wherever he turned he routed them" (14:47). Then as now, what one wrote depended on where one stood. For all the mystique, kings are politicians.

In 2 Samuel 8, the claim made regarding the Philistines is very limited (see 8:1). Booty from Edom and Moab, Ammonites, Philistines, and Amalek, as well as Hadadezer is rolled up into a single verse (8:12). Some boasting is likely where the last named is concerned (8:3–10; also 2 Sam 10). In Halpern's words, invoking the model of Tiglath-Pileser, "David made no gains in Syria. But, brilliantly, the author of 2 Sam. 8 leads the uninformed reader to believe that he did....It is, again, precisely the method of royal inscriptions to aggrandize accomplishments in the subtext, without prevaricating at the literal level" (*Secret Demons,* 192–94).

Background: 2 Samuel 9–10

I stand by my judgment that 2 Samuel 9–10 are to be considered anticipatory appendices to the stories of David's middle years, 2 Samuel 11–20 (see Campbell, *2 Samuel,* 87–96).

Where the episode with Mephibosheth is concerned, similar information is presented by both 2 Samuel 16:1–4 and 19:18, 25–31 (Heb.; NRSV, 19:17, 24–30) within the Stories of David's Middle Years and by 2 Samuel 21:1–14 (see v. 7) within the Special Collection. The differences are subtle but present; "in all probability, three independent traditions are involved, reflecting different aspects of the same event" (Campbell, *2 Samuel,* 89).

Where the military campaigns of 2 Samuel 10 are concerned, they provide a context for the siege of Rabbah in what follows. It is doubtful whether such a context needed to be provided, but it is there. Leonhard Rost regarded 2 Samuel 10 as a separate source and comments: "The style is simple, concise and terse; the action pushes continually forward; there are speeches only at decisive points.... It is quite clear that it was a soldier who wrote the report, perhaps even a general" (*Succession*, 62, 64). Its trustworthiness as history has to be in doubt.

~MODERN FAITH~

A movement is afoot at the moment to use archaeological results to downplay the Bible's portrayal, above all, of David and Solomon and the claims made about them. Much of this is welcome if it brings legendary hype closer to biblical reality. At the same time, the old adage "once bitten, twice shy" plays here. Many from around my generation still remember the claims of a not-too-distant past that heralded triumphantly the archaeological evidence that proved the Bible true. In due course, humble pie was on the menu because both archaeological evidence and Bible had been misread. Bitten! Confronted with claims now that archaeology proves the Bible incorrect, those whose memories are tender will understandably be doubly shy of being bitten a second time. Passionate conviction carried people away the first time, proving the Bible right when it was wrong; it is understandable to fear that passionate conviction may carry people away in the opposite direction the second time, proving the Bible wrong when it was right. The fear is heightened by examples where the Bible is manifestly misread by those who should know it better.

Biblical texts need interpretation; this book should be evidence of that. Archaeological evidence needs interpretation; archaeologists are well aware of that. Biblical legends and later legends have inflated the images of David and Solomon and their impact on their times. Bringing these legends back into line with the bulk of biblical text about Israel's early monarchy is obviously desirable. Any contribution from archaeology in this regard is valuable and beneficial. At the same time, it is unbalanced to seize on legendary inflation to facilitate biblical deflation. Biblical text, soberly understood, proves often enough to be remarkably sober. Some sobriety all round does no harm.

In the past, parts of the Bible were claimed as true — in the light of outmoded interpretation and inadequate archaeological excavation. More recently, parts of the Bible are claimed as untrue — in the light of outmoded legend and incomplete archaeological information. Perhaps the future holds a more balanced outcome. Perhaps!

From the point of view of modern faith, it is worth being aware that contemporary references to Saul, David, and Solomon — and others around that time — are not to be found in the nonbiblical documents currently available. Some overclaim is visible in some of the biblical text, especially regarding Solomon. Some overclaim has been hyped into legendary images of David and Solomon. Close reading of the Davidic biblical narrative shows it to be surprisingly down-to-earth and unpretentious.

The nonbiblical documents currently available do not have references to the time of David and Solomon. Currently, such references begin around the mid-ninth century. Four come to mind: "Ahab, the Israelite" mentioned in the monolith of Shalmaneser, c. 852 (*ANET*, 279); "Jehu, son of Omri" mentioned in the same Shalmaneser's Black Obelisk, c. 840 (*ANET*, 280–81); "the house of David" mentioned in the Tell Dan stele, c. 835 (*IEJ*, 45:1–18); Omri and son mentioned in the Mesha stele, c. 830 (*ANET*, 320). Before this mid-ninth-century period, there has to be time for Saul, David, and Solomon, as well as Jeroboam and others. It is quite a squeeze. Our concern here, however, is not so much with chronology as with the quality, above all, of the Davidic texts. Are they the exaggerated legend of later years or are they surprisingly sober in what they portray?

For me, one of the surprisingly sober aspects of the early Davidic texts is that David is anointed as replacement for Saul in 1 Samuel 16 and finally replaces Saul in 2 Samuel 5, some twenty-one chapters later. The struggle has gone on between Saul and David for some sixteen chapters; another couple of chapters have seen David assuming kingship over Judah; finally almost three more are needed for David to assume the crown that was Saul's. What is the understanding of God's action in Israel underlying such a presentation of the tradition? It is likely that the anointing texts for Saul, David, and Jehu are later additions to the earlier traditions (for one view, see Campbell, *Of Prophets and Kings*). The texts in 1 Samuel 10 and 15 show evidence of overwriting; the anointing in 1 Samuel 16 is unmentioned in the traditions that follow (perhaps hinted at in 2 Sam 5:2). There is a

perception being expressed that what the political process brought
about was in line with God's will. Furthermore, this divine will was
mediated through the prophets (Samuel and Elijah/Elisha/disciple);
but, surprisingly, this divine will was brought about by the political
process first and foremost.

Akin to this is the interpretation of the text's claim that *yhwh* was
with David (esp., 1 Sam 17:37; 18:12, 14, 28; 20:13). The question
for interpretation: was *yhwh* with David because he was successful,
or was David successful because *yhwh* was with him? The statement
in the description of David, "and the LORD is with him," need imply
no more than that David handled himself well (1 Sam 16:18); it may
fit with what follows but need not derive from it. A good example of
the text's openness is 1 Sam 18:14; the literal Hebrew reads: "And
David was successful in all his doings and *yhwh* was with him." As is
so often the case, the "and" linking the two clauses has its meaning
determined by the context. The question for interpretation, therefore,
remains open. For some, David's success is evidence of God's being
with him. For others, God's being with him brought about David's
success. The text leaves the question unanswered. We moderns might
be cautious about leaping in where ancients feared to tread.

Associated with this is the portrayal of David's faith: leave nothing to God but trust. Facing the Philistine, David had a weapon that
gave him the edge in the combat — a sling. According to one version of the tradition, faith in God impelled David (1 Sam 17:37); in
the same tradition, however, David's confidence is attributed to experience (1 Sam 17:34–35). Experience, of course, can generate trust
in God, trust in one's own abilities, or trust in both. According to
the alternative tradition, personal ambition compelled David (1 Sam
17:25–27). Ambition, of course, can coexist with faith and trust.
The text, holding both, is superbly ambiguous. Legendary adulation
would be unlikely to tolerate such ambiguity.

Another striking aspect of these texts of David's climb to power
is the ordinariness of day-to-day life in their portrayal of David's
activities. The story now in 2 Samuel 23:13–17 of David pouring out
"to the LORD" the water brought him in his thirst by three warriors
who risked their lives to get it from the well in Bethlehem is the stuff
of legend. It is surprising that almost nothing of the kind found its

way into the 1 Samuel traditions of David's time as a guerrilla leader. There is next to nothing legendary about the text of David's climb to power; its context is the unadorned politics of the time.

THE STORIES OF DAVID'S MIDDLE YEARS (2 Sam 11–20)

The bulk of the stories of David's climb to power were marked overwhelmingly by their down-to-earth and far-from-legendary quality. Close attention to the stories of David's middle years (2 Sam 11–20) will reveal that they are not so different, given the difference in their context — the rise toward power on the one hand and the exercise of power on the other. The "small highland village that controlled a sparsely settled hinterland" that Finkelstein and Silberman spoke of describing tenth-century Jerusalem (see above) is exactly the right setting for these stories. "Dynastic intrigues" do not play a major role in the misnamed "Court History"; the open rebellion of a discontented son (Absalom) certainly does. How David handles himself in the exercise of power is the focus of these stories. Where they came from and when still has scholars pondering.

Monarchies vary enormously, from the model of Vienna or Versailles and the luxury of the oriental potentate to much more modest operations. David's was distinctly modest. Monarchs have "top of the pile" status (at least publicly), displayed in various ways, assured by access to wealth, supported by control of armed force.

The text of 2 Samuel 11–20 portrays David's as a modest monarchy. Display is not particularly visible. David has wealthy friends in Transjordan, but access to wealth at home is not flaunted. Military power is there, although whether it is portrayed as effectively in Joab's hands is an open question. Also an open question is whether this military power is portrayed as going much beyond the sort of forces available to David as a guerrilla leader. Good guerrilla tactics avoid frontal battles. As king, David's forces are portrayed in active warfare, but certainly not on any grand imperial scale. The text refrains from the grandiose; so should its interpreters.

By common consensus, the text of 2 Samuel 11–20 is in a class apart from all other biblical literature. By common experience, it is a conundrum to its serious interpreters. Passages that appear markedly unfavorable to David are balanced with passages that are markedly favorable to David. Questions such as where the text came from, coupled with when and why it might have been composed, have scholars pondering. So far, no consensus has emerged.

Attempts to account for the favorable/unfavorable aspects by appeal to different origins (e.g., a base-text and further editing) have not been convincing. In what follows, it will be important to be aware of the ordinariness of the portrayal of David's kingdom, the light-and-dark ambiguity of the stories, and the moments where decisions would have benefited from wise advice. Basically, the text has four blocks of narrative, one of sexual lapse and three of political lapses. They can be categorized by reference to Bathsheba, Amnon, Absalom, and Sheba ben Bichri (2 Sam 20).

In none of them is the drift of the story unambiguous. Can a focus be found in the risks of royalty? It would be possible to highlight sex in the case of Bathsheba, imprudence in the case of Amnon, and sentiment in the case of Absalom; in the case of Sheba, it is a short sharp lesson in raw power. Murkier depths abound. Paltry rather than palatial; neither fabled nor legendary. Where might such stories have come from?

David: His sexual lapse

Bathsheba–David

The massive unanswered question is why such a story was ever told. There is nothing like it in the rest of biblical literature. There is nothing like it in the whole of Western literature, outside dramatic or novelistic fiction. Why was it told? Where did it come from?

David had many wives. Second Samuel 3:2–5 gives the names of half a dozen sons and their mothers; 2 Samuel 5:13–16 notes only "more concubines and wives; and more sons and daughters," listing the names of eleven offspring (sons). We have the *stories* of only two of his wives, both married to other men — Abigail to Nabal and Bathsheba to Uriah. Both women's husbands died conveniently. According to the text, God ended Nabal's life and Joab ended Uriah's. In Abigail's case (1 Sam 25), the story is clearly favorable to David. In Bathsheba's case (2 Sam 11–12), the story is basically unfavorable to David, despite the mention of David's prompt repentance before Nathan and God's love for Solomon (Jedidiah, 12:25).

Leaving Joab in the shadows — which is where he flourishes — none of the other three characters in the story is free of puzzle. Bathsheba, despite views to the contrary, is portrayed as squeaky clean. She is the model of a pious Israelite woman, purifying herself after her period (2 Sam 11:4). She is described as very beautiful; nothing in the text suggests immodesty. She was washing (English translations often have "bathing"; the Hebrew can mean either, more often washing [e.g., 2 Sam 12:20]); in the cramped conditions of David's Jerusalem, a cloth and basin are more likely than a bath. Her house was close enough to the king's house for her to be seen from the royal roof; proper kings do not live cheek by jowl with commoners. The puzzling feature: Why did she tell David, "I am pregnant"?

At first sight, Uriah is a pious and right-minded soldier who refuses to enjoy the pleasures of leave while the ark and the army are in the open field. The ark did not always go out with the army; puzzling is why David, as supreme commander, would have ordered what was improper and why Uriah disobeyed orders. Adding to the puzzle is why Uriah slept with the royal staff so that everybody knew he had not gone home. Did David have him killed to get him out of the way or because he knew too much?

It is often taken for granted that David was besotted with Bathsheba. This is possible, but most uncertain. The text portrays a one-night stand. Seeing her from his roof, David did not know who she was. He had inquiries made; informed of her identity, he sent messengers to get her. Between their night together and the announcement of her pregnancy, the text does not mention any contact. What was the point of summoning Uriah, her husband, back from the front and sending him to his house? The text does not disclose whether Uriah's return home was ordered by David because he did not love Bathsheba and needed a cover for her embarrassing pregnancy or whether it was a short-term measure to gain David some time because he did love her and needed time to think or, worse, because he might have wanted her to be available in the future — sometime, for something, perhaps. Similarly, we have to wonder whether Uriah's death was ordered to make Bathsheba available for David to marry or because Uriah knew enough about what had happened to embarrass David? Questions abound; answers are few.

God could conveniently be called on to dispose of Nabal. In this story, however, God most inconveniently called on Nathan to get involved. Any properly protected king would have kept the prophet at bay. Where does this story come from and why was it told?

Wise counsel might have been sought at a couple of points. Should David have gone out with the army? Probably not. The army did not need him and a two-year absence from the capital would have been unwise. The military forces evident in later Davidic texts suggest David would not have had the capacity to mount a full-scale siege, Assyrian or Roman style. Intercepting and interdicting foraging parties would have been enough to starve the townsfolk into submission. Joab was right to bring in David at the end; before that, he was probably not needed.

Wise counsel was certainly needed when the message arrived that Bathsheba was pregnant. A number of options were open. Among them, have her eliminated; it could have been easily done. Have her go to the country and keep quiet; it would require her cooperation. Have Uriah come home on leave and sleep with her; it would have required cooperation from them both. Short-term measures would have invited long-term difficulties. Wise counsel was needed.

Counsel might have been advisable as to whether it was wise to take the air on the roof late in the afternoon. Counsel might have been advisable as to whether it was wise for the king to consort with a woman who was the wife of one of his soldiers, possibly daughter of another of his soldiers (see 2 Sam 23:34) and granddaughter of one of the most respected counselors of the realm (see 2 Sam 16:23). Alas, kings and presidents seldom seek advice on these issues.

David: His political lapses

Amnon–Tamar–Absalom

The story of Amnon's death is a sad and sordid history. It includes his rape of his half-sister Tamar, David's inaction, and Absalom's murder of his brother at a sheep-shearing party. It also includes Absalom's flight into exile, David's leaving him there too long, and David's bringing his son home and reconciling with him too late. It is a lot to cram into one story, but that is probably where it belongs (2 Sam 13–14). Amnon's rape of Tamar incurred Absalom's anger, David's inaction led to Absalom having Amnon killed, which led in turn into Absalom's exile, and David's reconciling with him too late. It is a sad and sordid story.

At a benign and surface level, it is a story of royal folly; at another level, it is quite possibly a story of ruthless malevolence. For King David to send Tamar to Amnon without an escort was an act of remarkable imprudence. For David to do nothing about Amnon's rape of his sister Tamar was equally an act of singular imprudence. To dither about Absalom, whether to keep him in exile for the murder of his brother and whether to reconcile with him when he'd been brought home, was again an act of extreme political imprudence. If this seems harsh, it is reckoning with the story at a benign and surface level; at a deeper level, alas, the possibilities are darker, much darker.

The darker level is almost unthinkable, but only almost. It is the appalling thought: Did David organize this, starting with the rape? Four moments in the story need attention. First, in the story, Jonadab knows Amnon is ailing and Absalom knows Amnon is aroused; does David know nothing? Second, when the story has David aware of what Amnon has done, the story has David do nothing; his two eldest sons will settle the matter between them. Third, the story spends four verses on David's allowing Amnon to go to Absalom's sheep-shearing party, where Absalom will have him killed (2 Sam 13:23–29). Why does the story have the four-verse exchange between David and Absalom? Finally, when the story has the matter settled and Amnon dead, Jonadab reappears on the scene and implies that he has known all along (2 Sam 13:32–35). The story does not have David speak so much as a word of reproach.

Is it conceivable that the story has David send Tamar to her fate in order to find out which of these sons has the steel to be king, the steel that the next story — perhaps — will show David himself to lack?

It may be regrettable, but perhaps the strongest argument for declining such a dark interpretation of the narrative is the extraordinary ineptitude attributed to David in his dealing with Absalom. Could vicious political ruthlessness and unbelievable political ineptitude be combined in the one man or was ineptitude dominant in both episodes? According to the narrative, Absalom fled to Geshur, east of the Sea of Galilee; David left him there for three years (2 Sam 13:38). If Absalom is in line to be David's successor, the king's choices are clear: bring him home or banish him for life — settle the matter. The narrative has David make no choice. Joab makes his first appearance as a powerbroker at David's court. Joab organizes Absalom's return and after his return to Jerusalem, nothing happens for a further two years (2 Sam 14:28). The story has Absalom put the king's choices to Joab: let him accept me or execute me (2 Sam 14:32). Unfortunately, after five years, it was too late for reconciliation. Father and son kissed; Absalom began organizing his coup.

Counsel was advisable regarding Amnon's request for a visit from Tamar. "By all means, my lord the king, send the princess but escorted by a burly bodyguard with orders not let her out of his sight." Counsel was advisable regarding the rape. "Deal with it, my lord the king; bad blood between those two will be bad for the kingdom." Counsel was advisable regarding the invitation to the feast. "It might be wise to be present, my lord the king, lest things get out of hand." Finally, counsel was advisable regarding the murder. "Pardon him or banish him, my lord the king. Uncertainty will breed instability." Wise counsel was needed; none was taken.

Absalom–David

The story of Absalom's revolt is the most fascinating of all. The political implications are never far from sight, but the foreground is filled with a surprising mass of detail. The detail hardly fits with any exalted picture of the anointed king. David's feet are firmly on the ground. There is little difference in degree between these stories of royal flight and those of the guerrilla leader.

According to the text, Absalom spent four years organizing his rebellion throughout all Israel; apparently David knew nothing about it. The rebellion died when Absalom died, courtesy of Joab; politics played their role. Joab made himself responsible for putting down Sheba's revolt. Power is seldom separated from politics.

When he heard the news, David is reported to have immediately abandoned the allegedly impregnable Jerusalem. He had left Keilah, his decision influenced by a divine oracle. Despite both Zadok and Abiathar being in town, the decision-making in this narrative will be without the influence of oracles from God. Prayer will have its place (2 Sam 15:31); God's role will be acknowledged (2 Sam 17:14). For all that, in the narrative, decisions will be made without oracular influence. Wise counsel and good decisions go hand-in-hand. Decisions will be important in the story; perhaps oracles would be a distraction.

The narrative's start is decidedly gloomy: open rebellion and abandonment of the city. The exchange with Ittai the Gittite (a foreigner from Gath) offers a couple of glimmers of light, soft and dim, but a lighter tone. David is portrayed as certainly generous, probably confident; he can say to Ittai, "Go back." Ittai, who has not been around long enough to develop a compelling loyalty, probably sees David as a winner; he will stay. There may also be an indication here of the size of the forces involved. Ittai commands six hundred Gittites. When the order of battle is organized, and the army divided into three groups, one third under Joab, one third under Joab's brother Abishai, and one third is under Ittai's command (18:2). Ittai may well have had more than his own six hundred in his group; in all probability, however, the numbers were not large.

The next encounter is vintage David. The two priest figures, Abiathar and Zadok, show up with the ark of God's covenant. David sends them back into Jerusalem. "If God favors me, I will be back; if not, God's will be done." Then David adds: "You two go back into the city, with your two sons. I will wait at the fords of the wilderness until word comes from you." The details are not given; the storyteller can fill them in. But the drift is clear. David has total trust in God and promptly sets up a communications network. When the time comes, it will work extremely well.

Having set up his communications network, David turns to prayer. "O LORD, I pray you, turn the counsel of Ahithophel into foolishness." When the time comes, this too will work extremely well (see 2 Sam 17:14).

Next, the narrative has David meet Hushai. He too is sent into Jerusalem to be David's counter-intelligence agent. What he learns can be reported to David through the communications network that has just been set up. That too, as we will learn, worked extremely well. David may be on the run; he is portrayed remaining a very competent operator. As Hushai entered Jerusalem, the narrative has Absalom enter the city too (2 Sam 15:37). In this narrative, nothing happens by chance.

Two more vignettes are given of David on the mountain before the narrative moves its focus back to Jerusalem. In the first, Ziba servant of Mephibosheth, Jonathan's surviving son, shows up with supplies for David and the allegation that Mephibosheth is waiting in Jerusalem for Saul's kingdom to be handed back to him (2 Sam 16:3). David reaches a quick decision: "All that belonged to Mephibosheth is now yours."

To balance that image of David acting in kingly fashion, the next vignette has one of Saul's supporters, Shimei ben Gera, scream at David all that David's enemies believed about him: "Murderer... Scoundrel...Man of blood" (2 Sam 16:7–8). Abishai, soldier to the core, wants to take the man's head off. David's command: "Let him alone.... The LORD has bidden him" (2 Sam 16:11–12). Shimei is very nasty to David; David, on the other hand, is very nice to Shimei — and deeply respectful of God. It is typical of Davidic tradition; back both sides and be good to God. Shimei gives expression to what we might otherwise never have known: how David was viewed by his opposition. Tradition gives expression to an almost fatalistic piety on David's part.

David and those with him continued to toil up the hill. Shimei kept pace, continuing to curse and hurl stones at David and his entourage. It is hard to conjure up anything less kingly.

The narrative takes us back to Jerusalem and into the midst of Absalom's counselors. Ahithophel's first recommendation is politically astute and brutally ruthless: let all Israel see you taking your father's women sexually. His second suggestion is equally wise: let me strike down David now before he has a chance to regroup. Hushai, David's man, plays to Absalom's vanity: better to wait, mass the forces from all Israel, and have them led into battle by Absalom in person (2 Sam 17:7–14). Vanity wins and Hushai's advice is accepted. The news of Ahithophel's counsel is sent to David at the fords, and (perhaps just in case) he and his troops cross the river before the night ends.

The forces of both men were positioned across the Jordan, to the east, Gilead for Absalom and Mahanaim for David. Absalom gave Joab's job as army commander to Amasa, closely related to Joab; David's troop commanders were Joab, his brother Abishai, and Ittai the Gittite. Apart from Ittai, the army commanders come from a closely related group, almost family; again, it is a pointer to relatively primitive organization at David's court.

The narrative gives three verses to Absalom's defeat (2 Sam 18:6–8); the aftermath of defeat gets considerably more attention. The narrative gives seven verses to the death of Absalom (2 Sam 18:8–15), fourteen verses to the news being brought to David (2 Sam 18:19–32), and nine verses to David's reaction (2 Sam 19:1–9a [Heb.; NRSV, 2 Sam 18:33–19:8a]) — thirty in all.

The soldier who discovered the trapped Absalom did not kill him, earning Joab's angry reproach. Joab himself is reported to have thrust three spears into the still living Absalom; ten of Joab's elite bodyguard surrounded Absalom, "struck him and killed him" (2 Sam 18:15). Clearly, Joab had no doubts as to what had to be done; equally clearly, responsibility was not to be pinned on him.

The narrative had David say, "My own son seeks my life" (2 Sam 16:11). In the past David had appeared to dither over Absalom. Now dithering is no longer possible; battle is about to be joined. Three options are in the narrative context. Kill him (Uriah's fate), confine him (effectively Mephibosheth's situation), banish him (Absalom earlier). To do nothing is not an option. Effectively, David does nothing.

The narrative does not help its users in reaching a decision. In the case of Uriah, David had been ruthless. In the case of Amnon, it is possible that David was either ruthlessly callous or sentimentally foolish. In the case of Joab, to come, David is ruthless, sacking him from his army command. The political necessity for Joab's dismissal is clear; blame for Absalom's killing is not mentioned. Joab, in due course, outmaneuvers his king. What is the case here? Is David royally ruthless, but well protected on the PR front — Absalom is popular? Or is David unroyally sentimental — Absalom is his eldest surviving son? The narrative leaves us in the dark.

The narrative has David being emphatic but vague about Absalom: "Deal gently for my sake" (2 Sam 18:5; colloquially, "Go easy on the boy"). "Take Absalom alive; do not kill him" would have been more appropriate, but it is not what the narrative reports. Did David anticipate what would happen on the battlefield and protect himself? Worse perhaps, did David order the killing and cover for himself? Joab's language was quite clear: "Why then did you not strike him there to the ground?" (2 Sam 18:11). The reluctant soldier's quote from David is not so clear: "For my sake protect the young man." The first messenger is discreet (2 Sam 18:29); the second messenger's circumlocution accurately reflects the political situation.

Shortly, Joab will be replaced as army commander; the killing of Absalom will not be mentioned. Later, Davidic tradition blames Joab for the deaths of Abner and Amasa; the death of Absalom is not mentioned (1 Kgs 2:5). Abimelech is reported to have killed his seventy brothers, the sons of Jerubbaal (Judg 9:1–5). Baasha is reported to have wiped out "all the house of Jeroboam" (1 Kgs 15:29). Zimri, another army commander, did the same to Baasha's sons (1 Kgs 16:11). Jehu had the seventy sons of Ahab killed (2 Kgs 10:1–11). The political logic is unambiguous. On the surface, David's action is unambiguous; below the surface, ambiguity is king.

There is more to be said, but as interpreters of the text we might be well advised to leave the matter where the narrative leaves it — in the shadows of uncertainty. Either way, ruthless or sentimental, David does not come out of it very well. Another question remains unasked and unanswered: Where was Joab in all of this? He killed Abner. He smoothed the way for Uriah's killing. He facilitated Absalom's return. He killed Absalom. He will kill Amasa. For all his kingly charisma, does David wield the scepter while Joab wields the power? Is politics always symbiotic?

Back in the days while Ishbaal was still alive and David was king of Judah only, a long war was waged between north and south, Ishbaal's people and David's people, whatever these groupings might mean to historians. Now, with Absalom dead and David in Transjordan, these issues recur. The debate occupied all of seven verses at the start (2 Sam 19:10–16; Heb.; NRSV, 2 Sam 19:9–15) and a further four verses at the end (2 Sam 19:41–44; Heb.; NRSV, 19:40–43). In these few verses, the issues are debated that affect the organization of the state in Israel and Judah. The debate as reported is remarkably superficial; the state is remarkably unstable. The most sophisticated text we have of the period is surprisingly narrow in its focus; quite frankly, we are not given the big picture. Say the people of Judah: "David's our kin and Amasa has got Joab's job" (2 Sam 19:13–15; NRSV, 19:12–14). Say the people of Israel to the people of Judah: "We are bigger than you" (2 Sam 19:44a; Heb.; NRSV, 19:43a). Outcome: "The words of the people of Judah were fiercer than the words of the people of Israel" (2 Sam 19:44b; Heb.; NRSV, 2 Sam 19:43b). Hardly what we might call the cream of elevated political discourse.

In between these two passages of apparently national interest, the text has David deal with limited issues of local politics. Shimei shows up, a committed follower of Saul who nevertheless knows a winner when he sees one. David reconciles with him. Mephibosheth shows up to plead his cause against Ziba. Who knows where truth lies? David divides the property between them. The eighty-year-old Barzillai, one of David's wealthy east-of-Jordan supporters, begs off going to Jerusalem. David makes sure of his loyalty and lets him go. These are the minor issues of pork-barrel politics. Yet the narrative puts them front and center.

Joab–Sheba–David

On a surface level, the final episode in this extraordinary narrative concerns the rebellion of Sheba ben Bichri, a Benjaminite who rallies "all the people of Israel" to withdraw from David. Behind the narrative of the rebellion is the narrative of power in the kingdom and who wields it. Joab went out soldier and returns commander.

To be sure of the allegiance of Judah, David had appointed Amasa as army chief (2 Sam 19:14–15; Heb.; NRSV, 2 Sam 19:13–14).

Amasa was given three days to rally the troops from Judah and failed to keep the deadline; why, the narrative does not say. David gave the top job to Abishai, Joab's brother. Heading out against Sheba, they met Amasa at Gibeon, a few miles north of Jerusalem. Joab killed him, took command of the army, and duly put an end to Sheba's rebellion. The narrative ends: "Joab returned to Jerusalem to the king." What the king thought about it is left to the reader's imagination.

The list of David's officials — Joab, Benaiah, Adoram, Jehoshaphat, Sheva, Zadok and Abiathar, and Ira the Jairite — puts a clear full stop at the end of the narrative. End of story it may be; unduly impressive it is not.

Conclusion

These stories of David's middle years revolve around the strengths and weaknesses of one man. There is no indication in them of the organizational complexity of developed royal power. These stories are not alien to an early David's environment.

Wise counsel was needed at many points along the way of the narrative of Absalom's rebellion. Should the royal party abandon the allegedly impregnable Jerusalem? Should priestly support, Abiathar and Zadok, accompany David or wait for his return to Jerusalem, meanwhile masterminding his communications network? Should David keep Hushai with him for wise advice or infiltrate him as counter-intelligence agent among Absalom's advisors? Ziba could be important; what is to be done about him? Shimei is obnoxious, but he is a Saul supporter; kill him or leave him? What is to be done about Absalom and how is it to be portrayed publicly? There are issues to be settled with Shimei and Mephibosheth. More important, there is the matter of wider allegiance to be settled. Finally, what should David do about Joab, now that he has murdered Amasa, David's choice for army chief? Does David take the advice later given Solomon and kill him or does David accept the compromised symbiotic balance of military and political power? Wise counsel was needed at many points along the way.

It is hard to imagine this narrative coming from a Davidic court. A court in the northern kingdom would have badly needed wise counsel.

Such a source is possible. The court of Jeroboam, first of the northern kings, has to be a contender.

The Special Collection (2 Samuel 21–24)

These four chapters constitute a carefully coordinated collection at the end of 2 Samuel, organized concentrically, comprising some six Davidic traditions, four apparently from early in his public career and two songs from much later. The fascination of the four earlier traditions is that they reveal how little we actually know of David's doings where we thought we were well informed. These chapters are as it were a "third wave," differing from the adulation of David's climb to power and equally from the reserve of David's middle years (David's exercise of power). They do not, however, radically change the judgments expressed above; we need not, therefore, deal with them in detail here (for full discussion, see Campbell, "2 Samuel 21–24").

~MODERN FAITH~

If the presumption has been out there of a vast Davidic empire, it needs to be cut back in line with reality. Most of the biblical text about David hews close to reality. There are interpretative statements of the "God was with him" kind; these are clearly faith statements. Friends accept them; foes dispute them. The picture of David's day-to-day activity is remarkably restrained. That, of course, is much less the case for the much smaller amount of text (some nine chapters) devoted to Solomon, especially where his wisdom, his temple, and his visit from the queen of Sheba are concerned. The legendary quality of some of the material is scarcely concealed; it wasn't concealed in the inscriptions of contemporaries either. Legends in their own lifetimes — or rather, in their own inscriptions! The extent of Solomon's idolatry is not concealed; it is given a full chapter. Only two verses give him sovereignty from the Euphrates in the far north to the Egyptian border in the far south (1 Kgs 5:1, 4 [Heb.; NRSV, 4:21, 24]), both clearly in the realm of legendary or political hyperbole. There is not a word in the text about the exercise of such sovereignty.

These stories of David's middle years (2 Sam 11–20) are pretty much unique in Western European literature. Who else but David would sustain interest in the relatively trivial details of his trudging across the Jordan and his traipsing back to recover the kingdom he should never have lost in the first place? Over the centuries of biblical tradition, David has become an unquestionably legendary figure. In the book of Kings, David has become the figure of the model king against whom others may be measured. Of all the Bible's kings, David is the most idolized, the most exalted. Even in these far-from-legendary texts, David is king and enjoys something of the majesty that goes with this position. The majesty is worth highlighting, for the text itself is far from majestic. Stripped of finer points, these stories concern two rapes, two murders, and two rebellions, ending in two killings (of the two rebels). The narrative is closer to misery than majesty. There is a mystery in all this, for such can be human life at its best and at its worst — exalted and flawed. There is majesty in the dignity of the king. There is misery in the fragility of flawed situations. There is grandeur; there is pettiness. These stories put all this under the microscope, exploring human behavior with analytical precision. They make no judgments; they leave little untouched.

For all the mystery — royalty, rape, murder, rebellion — the majesty and misery, what fascinates me about these stories is how they portray the working out of God's will in ways that do not bypass human dispositions (alternatively expressed: how these stories present human dispositions in all their detail and yet see in them the working out of God's will). As presented in the total context, it is God's will that David remain king. It is said in the text that God defeated the good counsel of Ahithophel in order to bring ruin on Absalom (2 Sam 17:14); neither David nor Absalom would have been aware of that. Hushai was given a delicate task; he insinuated himself into the inner circle and played on Absalom's vanity, knowing that David needed time. From his point of view, he played a risky hand and played it well (see 2 Sam 15:34). The narrator would surely have agreed and, at the same time, claims it was ordained by God (2 Sam 17:14). In the utter mystery of the transcendent God, why not? In the utter mystery of the transcendent God, David had to trust Hushai's instincts and Hushai had to run his risks. David's faith leaves nothing to God but trust.

David did not leave things for God to do for him; he did them for himself. Some of what he did he rightly regarded as evil ("I have sinned"). He may be portrayed as fragile and flawed, deeply flawed; for all that, he is portrayed as God's instrument. Remarkable and rather encouraging for the rest of us.

David's model status in parts of the book of Kings probably reflects the fact that he stuck to *yhwh;* he didn't go after distractions. Solomon became a senile idolater. David may have been a senile sinner; idolater he was not. The way David's life unfolded — harassed by Saul in the first place, troubled by Amnon and Absalom later, at the height of his power seriously threatened by Absalom — he could be forgiven for not claiming God was with him. That was left to narrators. The whisper of God was not easily heard. As for us, so for David, other goals and other gods could have been tempting. Yet, apparently, David stuck to *yhwh;* he didn't go after distractions, go after other gods. David is not the product of legendary dreamings. Solomon "in all his glory" may have been; David wasn't. For me, there is a fascination here: a world where the whisper of God is not easily heard; a faith that is not distracted from that whisper. A world where what I do I do and what God does God does and, in faith, I trust there is interpenetration and intersection.

SUMMARY

As we have seen repeatedly, when exploring modern faith in relation to biblical text a couple of principles come into play. One was expressed in *Rethinking the Pentateuch:* there is "a shift from the Pentateuch as a record of Israel's *remembering its past* to the Pentateuch as a record of Israel's *pondering its present*" (9). This applies to much of the Pentateuch and elsewhere too in the Older Testament. The second principle impacts solidly on the understanding of revelation as coming exclusively *from above and from the past,* an understanding that still influences many. As we ponder our lives and remember our past, in all the rich variety it involves (family, schooling, religion, culture), we come to a deeper understanding of ourselves and our world and a correspondingly deeper insight into our understanding of our God. That is surely an aspect of revelation, not the whole but an aspect — coming *from below and from the present.* These two thoughts have been repeated from time to time in the unfolding of this book.

Faith has to accommodate itself to fact. God does not square the circle; Genesis does not determine the age of the universe. Were the Davidic traditions clearly post-exilic, I have no doubt that faith would and should find its way to build on that fact.

As regards any Solomonic temple in Jerusalem, archaeologists have nothing to go on and can expect nothing. It is highly likely that King Herod, preparing the podium for his temple, leveled everything in sight. We text people are in a similar situation. We have almost no text that we can trust from the time of Solomon: 1 Kings 3–4 does not offer much; 1 Kings 6–8 is entirely concerned with the temple; 1 Kings 9 is reporting about Solomon rather than offering text purported to be from him; 1 Kings 10 reports the visit of the queen of Sheba; with 1 Kings 11, Solomon is heading steeply downhill. Finkelstein describes Solomon, a tad minimalistically, as "the son of a local chief of a small isolated highland polity" (*David and Solomon,* 172). While the text about Solomon might strongly disagree, textually there is nothing from Solomon comparable with what we have from David that might dispute this.

From David we have extensive text. Does it smack of the late and legendary? Not really. The stories of David's climb to power are exactly what we would expect of a guerrilla leader seeking to overcome the existing authorities. Propaganda, of course; highly exaggerated, not really. The stories of David's middle years are almost boring in their attention to local detail and are remarkable in their unwavering scrutiny of human behavior. Were they otherwise, faith would surely accommodate to the fact. But because they are not, faith does not have to. As noted earlier, some four of Israel's kings are mentioned in extrabiblical documents around the mid-ninth century. Somewhere in the preceding century or so, there needs to be space for Saul, David, Solomon, Rehoboam, and Jeroboam at least. To all appearances, there is plenty of room.

Conclusion

When we look back over where we have been in these reflections, two things emerge: first, we can see easily enough why what our forebears did in the interpretation of text we can no longer do; second, we can see what we can do ourselves and how we can be encouraged by it.

Apparently primeval texts (Gen 1–11) become more interesting when we realize they may not be about events that never happened but about our lives that do. Ancestral texts (Gen 12–36) are amalgamated rather than evaluated. They may have begun with concerns for origins; in the text we have now, they tend to reflect what the present brings to bear on understanding those origins. The question the wise do not answer: Is it the legends that shape our present, or is it our present that shapes the legends? The wise know that it is both, so they do not answer.

Sinai may benefit from not being a way station leading to the land. Focus on the meaning of what is actually there in the text may be more profitable than projecting thoughts about what we think should be there. An uncertain sanctuary structure would, of necessity, have had to belong to a distant past. God's presence is a matter of the present.

The book of Joshua, interpreted as conquest and extermination, has always been an embarrassment. It is a relief to recognize how much of the book is concerned with more important issues and to be able to relegate conquest and ethnic cleansing to the more appropriate back seat where, in the book, they belong.

David is a legendary figure in biblical tradition, model king, author of psalms, and the like. It is refreshing to find the stories of David's time to be so far from legendary. The experience of recent generations has given us a nose for propaganda and brought home to us the value of information from both sides of any issue. The stories of David's climb to power give us David's side. Within the stories of David's middle years, the voice of Shimei ben Gera gives us a protest from Saul's side. In these same stories of David's middle years we see human behavior put under the magnifying glass. The texts are unlikely to be far from the times.

The Bible is not the voice of God subtly echoing into human space. It is a voice of many sounds, an echo chamber in human space where the voices can be heard of those living in the presence of God and pondering their experience. The pondering is preserved for us that we may the better live in the presence of God and ponder for ourselves.

A final reflection is in place. It has been eye-opening to look closely at Davidic texts and discover how down-to-earth they are. It can be a release to discover just how complex the book of Joshua is, not to be reduced to a simple and brutal expropriation of others' land. It can be freeing to recognize that the early texts of Genesis (Gen 1–11) are most faithfully read as studies in human living (the Garden, the flood, etc.). It is probably pretty problem-free to see in Israel's ancestors the legendary figures whose legends played their role in the shaping of Israel's identity. It may not be so liberating at all to realize that any reliable historical image of Moses and the Exodus can hardly be recovered beneath the legendary traditions that have grown around it and obscured it. It may not be so immediately liberating to realize that the portrayal of Israel's experience at Mount Sinai, as we have it in the present biblical text, is probably a chronologically late construction (i.e., it did not happen the way it is told). Where does all this leave us with our Bible?

For me, the Bible (Older Testament, at least) reflects the endeavor of believing people to understand and express their experience of God. To call the outcome "mixed" is an understatement. Some of it is very good; some of it is ordinary; some of it is awful. Some of it speaks to us of God; some of it is what we might expect to hear God saying to us. This, for me, is word of God. The Bible, as a whole, is for me more honestly named word of God's people. From this "word of God's people" we distill what is for us "word of God." Much depends, of course, on how "word of God" is understood.

In these texts that we have been examining, what we have seen is a glimpse of the possibility that the image we now have of Israel's origins is one that evolved relatively late in Israel's story. The Sinai texts are perhaps the biggest shock, suggesting a move from origin toward end. The reality that all was not as it seems (more precisely: as the text has it seem) results from phenomena in the text that are inescapable: (1) all-Israel is portrayed as present there at Sinai, and scholars know that all-Israel was not; (2) two powerful forces of tradition (nonpriestly and priestly) are present there and only one itinerary going there is preserved; (3) immense energy is involved in composing the text of the sanctuary there and yet the Israel-of-the-sanctuary does not move further.

The ancestral texts are open to the kind of move that the Sinai texts suggest. The "humanity" texts, above all Garden and flood, do not report the history of the past but reflect on the experience of the present. They are open to a late shaping of Israel's story. The book of Joshua and the books of Samuel do not stand in the way. The book of Joshua is an enigma, but it is not reporting the traditions of all-Israel's conquest of Canaan. The books of Samuel are a portrayal of David that does not rise above the down-to-earth and ordinary. Alongside the slow process of deepening understanding runs the reality of flesh-and-blood Israel — from its early kings to its pre-exilic prophets to all that follows — providing the raw material for reflection.

In this understanding, Israel's experience over the centuries has brought it to an understanding of itself and its relationship with its God and its world in ways that were previously not open to it. In the portrayal of its past, Israel treasures the outcome of reflections on its present. From these reflections comes revelation.

Out of all of this — Pentateuch, Joshua and Judges, Samuel and Kings, big prophetic books and smaller prophetic books, Psalms, Proverbs, and all that, to say nothing of the Newer Testament, gospels, letters, and all that — there is a sacred treasury that we name the Bible. In that treasury, generations have found words that inspire their faith in God; in that treasury, generations have found words that support and encourage their life with God.

With a different sequence from the Older Testament in the Greek (also English-language Bibles), the Hebrew Bible ends with the book of Chronicles and the decree of Cyrus, king of Persia, for the rebuilding of a temple in Jerusalem (2 Chr 36:22–23). Of course some prophecy and much more was written afterward; of course much of the work of compilation was done afterward, in what we call the post-exilic period. For all that, Chronicles is the story of the temple, and the temple dominates the Hebrew Bible's end. In the present text, God is portrayed at Sinai commanding the building of a demountable sanctuary in order to be present in Israel's midst (Exod 25:8). At the inauguration of Jerusalem's temple, God is portrayed saying that "my name ... my eyes and my heart will be there for all time" (1 Kgs 9:3). At the end of the Hebrew Bible, King Cyrus of Persia is reported proclaiming God's order to build a temple in Jerusalem (2 Chr 36:23). When we come to the Newer Testament, the focus is on the experience of Jesus, whether ending in the Gospels of Matthew and John (toward the close of the first century) or with the last words of longing in the book of Revelation, "Come, Lord Jesus!" (Rev 22:20). Both temple and Jesus speak of God here among us. Jews await the Messiah; Christians await that Coming. For Jews and Christians, there is faith in the God who is "utterly other" and who loves us; for Christians, there is as well faith in the God who is "utterly us" and who manifests that love. For both there is mystery and the shortness of life to ponder it in.

Love is a remarkably complex concept, a word that we use in a surprisingly wide range of contexts. We speak of loving sport or loving music. We speak of loving nature or loving our pets (whether cats, dogs, white rabbits, or whatever). We speak of loving people, our love for the poor, for the oppressed, and so on. Above all, we speak of loving those who love us — and even here the range is enormous. Parents love their children and children their parents; siblings love each other, usually; relatives can love each other; friends love each other. At the heart of it all is the love one has for one's beloved. We know about estrangement and hate; we know about the flaws and frailties of love. We also know what we mean by love, more or less. But what do we mean by God's love for us or by our love for God? Spirit to spirit, without direct sense experience, we are left with analogies; necessarily, analogies limp.

In Jewish and Christian faith, we believe in God's relationship to us and ours to God. With all due respect to others who think differently (for example, figures from Hobbes and Hume to Kant and Hegel), in such matters relationship precedes behavior. The core of religious faith is relationship with God; the morality of behavior, individual or social, ineluctably follows as a consequence of that relationship. We can safely speak of God's being committed to us; we may know ourselves as committed to God. Christians believe in the life, death, and resurrection of Jesus Christ, son of God and son of Mary. In John's Gospel, we find "No one has greater love than this, to lay down one's life for one's friends" (John 15:13). That is what Christians believe Jesus did, making God's love for human ordinariness so evident — in a way no words can. So, from the Newer Testament, "love" is an appropriate word. Hosea uses the word, in good company in the Older Testament: "as the LORD loves the people of Israel, though they turn to other gods" (Hos 3:1). So, from the Older Testament, "love" is an appropriate word. What does it mean for us in the reality of our lives?

When struggling to find language to speak of the God who is "utterly other" — where "transcendent" is the traditional theological term — technically we should often put a "more-than" or a "transcendently" in front of adjectives used about that utterly other God. ("Transcendently" [= beyond the limits of ordinary experience] is an awkward word, while "infinitely" is easier; but transcendently has the advantage of pointing to the heart of the matter.) We normally leave it unsaid; but it needs to be understood, because it is a strict requirement of the traditional treatment of analogy where God is concerned. When analogy is needed, the positive is emphasized, the negative eliminated, and then follows the move to the "more than" or the "transcendent" (Latin: *positive, negative, eminenter*). So if the language of "a personal God" is deemed by some to be problematic, tending to evoke all-too-human echoes, the language of a "more-than-personal" God can retain the values of the personal while insisting on openness to the transcendent. Classically, God's all-powerfulness is more than we can dream of; "more-than-almighty" reminds us of the human limits of our idea of almighty or all-powerful. Classically, the reality of God's being all-knowing is vastly more than we can imagine; "more-than-omniscient" reminds us of the human limits of our notions of knowledge. Perhaps "more-than-loving" should perform much the same role in the expression of God's love, God's commitment. "Love" is an appropriate word;

"more-than-loving" may be a useful reminder of the technically transcendent aspect, the limits of our human understanding of the possibilities of love. It could serve as an occasional qualifier: a loving God, emphatically less limited, speaking linguistically, if recognized as a more-than-loving God, a transcendently loving God. It is appropriate — right and good — to speak in faith of a loving God, of God's love for us. It makes greater sense if we realize that God's love, love attributed to God, is not restricted by the limits of what we understand as love. At a level of reflective depth in our theological understanding, awareness on our part that when we speak of a loving God what we necessarily mean is indeed a more-than-loving God, a transcendently loving God, leads to honest clarity. It enables awareness of a love that is truly God's.

Adequate words for the expression of that love are hard to come by. Thank God for wordless moments to treasure in our journeying. Faith in that love is a source of support and encouragement, of life-giving meaning and deep-seated joy.

Appendix

Favorites

Genesis 8:21

I will never again curse the ground because of humankind,
for the inclination of the human heart is evil from youth;
nor will I ever again destroy every living creature as I have done.

A somewhat jaundiced view of the human heart, but alas all too often all too accurate. "Never again" — theologically, it is like a second creation. What a wonderful acceptance of us as we are, whether made or emerged. With thinking like this, what need is there for a Fall to account for our troubled world?

Genesis 12:3

In you all the families of the earth
shall be blessed.

A magnificent pipe dream that has not and will not come to be. But what a human goal, what a vision of God!

Isaiah 19:24–25

On that day Israel will be the third with Egypt and Assyria,
a blessing in the midst of the earth,
whom the LORD of hosts has blessed, saying,
"Blessed be Egypt my people, and Assyria the work of my
*   hands,*
and Israel my heritage."

Amos affirmed Israel was special, "You only have I known of all the families of the earth" (3:2); the same Amos denied Israel was special,

295

"Did I not bring Israel up from the land of Egypt, and the Philistines from Caphtor [associated with the Aegean] and the Arameans from Kir [associated with Mesopotamia]?" (9:7). Deuteronomy described Israel as chosen by God "out of all the peoples on earth to be his people, his treasured possession" (7:6). Genesis, however, linked the ancestors and Israel with blessing for "all the families of the earth" (12:3). Isaiah could not have picked a more extraordinary threesome. Should faith set no limits to God's love?

Hosea 3:1

Just as the LORD *loves the people of Israel,*
though they turn to other gods.

I love them though they don't love me. That gives hope.

Isaiah 5:7

He expected justice, but saw bloodshed;
righteousness, but heard a cry!

God is seen to want a just world without oppression; if we don't work for that, we don't work for God.

Isaiah 43:4

You are precious in my sight,
and honored, and I love you.

A powerful transformation of redemption, accepting that we are deeply loved by our God.

Job 7:21

Why do you not pardon my transgression
and take away my iniquity?

Dare we deny God the right to forgive?

Isaiah 43:25

I, I am He [the One] who blots out your transgressions
for my own sake, and I will not remember your sins.

Our transgressions blotted out for God's own sake. Is there greater love than this?

Isaiah 54:10

For the mountains may depart and the hills be removed,
but my steadfast love shall not depart from you.

"Love is not love which alters when it alteration finds or bends with the remover to remove" (Shakespeare, Sonnet 116).

Jeremiah 2:13

They have forsaken me, the fountain of living water;
and dug out cisterns for themselves,
cracked cisterns that can hold no water.

The parched dry or the living green. We know them both. We choose.

Jeremiah 13:11

For as the loincloth clings to one's loins,
so I made the whole house of Israel
and the whole house of Judah
cling to me, says the LORD.

A loincloth clings close to the loins, next to the skin. What an image for the intimate closeness of God.

Ezekiel 37:14

I will put my spirit within you,
and you shall live.

The identity of God with life. God forbid that we should get it wrong.

Ezekiel 47:9

Everything will live
where the river goes.

Because, for Ezekiel, the water for the river flowed from the sanctuary. For later times, the river is symbolic of God's gift of life.

Micah 6:8

To do justice, and to love [faithful] kindness,
and to walk humbly with your God.

A one-sentence summary of life before God.

1 Kings 9:3

God says of the temple:

My eyes and my heart
will be there for all time.

We need symbols of God's presence in our midst.

Proverbs 8:30–31

Rejoicing in his inhabited world
and delighting in the human race

Joy and delight: an example for lives of religious faith, allowing due place for sorrow and grief.

Psalm 42:1

As a deer longs for flowing streams,
so my soul longs for you, O God.

Would I were in closer touch with my soul; as I long for those I love, so should I long for my God.

John 15:13 (The Death of Jesus)

No one has greater love than this,
to lay down one's life for one's friends.

I know no clearer statement of faith that Christ's cross was an expression of God's love.

1 Cor 1:23–24 (Christ Crucified)

Christ crucified,
a stumbling block to Jews and foolishness to Gentiles,
but to those who are called, both Jews and Greeks,
Christ the power of God and the wisdom of God.

Christ crucified: for Christians, the ultimate expression of God's love and God's commitment to human life; unbelievably absurd to think that the transcendent God should so care for us — unbelievably wonderful to believe.

Bibliography

ANET *Ancient Near Eastern Texts Relating to the Old Testament.* Ed. J. B. Pritchard. 3rd ed. Princeton, NJ: Princeton University Press, 1969.

Barnet, Sylvan, Morton Berman, and William Burto. *A Dictionary of Literary Terms.* London: Constable, 1964.

Boling, Robert G. *Joshua.* AB. Garden City, NY: Doubleday, 1982.

Brueggemann, Walter. *Genesis.* Interpretation. Atlanta: John Knox, 1982.

———. *First and Second Samuel.* Interpretation. Louisville: John Knox, 1990.

Campbell, Antony F., SJ. *Of Prophets and Kings: A Late Ninth-Century Document (1 Samuel 1–2 Kings 10).* CBQMS. Washington, DC: Catholic Biblical Association of America, 1986.

———. *The Study Companion to Old Testament Literature: An Approach to the Writings of Pre-Exilic and Exilic Israel.* Collegeville, MN: Liturgical Press, 1989, 1992.

———. *God First Loved Us: The Challenge of Accepting Unconditional Love.* Mahwah, NJ: Paulist Press, 2000.

———. *1 Samuel.* FOTL. Grand Rapids: Eerdmans, 2003.

———. *Joshua to Chronicles: An Introduction.* Louisville: Westminster John Knox, 2004.

———. "Diachrony and Synchrony: ISam 24 and 26." In *David und Saul im Widerstreit — Diachronie und Synchronie im Wettstreit: Beiträge zur Auslegung des ersten Samuelbuches,* ed. Walter Dietrich, 226–31. OBO. Fribourg, Switzerland: Academic Press, 2004.

———. *2 Samuel.* FOTL. Grand Rapids: Eerdmans, 2005.

———. *The Whisper of Spirit: A Believable God Today.* Grand Rapids, MI: Eerdmans, 2008.

―――. "2 Samuel 21–24: The Enigma Factor." Forthcoming in *For and Against David: Story and History in the Books of Samuel,* ed. G. Auld and E. Eynikel, 347–58. BETL 232. Leuven: Peeters.

Campbell, Antony F., SJ, and Mark A. O'Brien, OP. *Sources of the Pentateuch: Texts, Introductions, Annotations.* Minneapolis: Fortress, 1993.

―――. *Unfolding the Deuteronomistic History: Origins, Upgrades, Present Text.* Minneapolis: Fortress, 2000.

―――. *Rethinking the Pentateuch: Prolegomena to the Theology of Ancient Israel.* Louisville, KY: Westminster John Knox, 2005.

Carr, David M. *Writing on the Tablet of the Heart: Origins of Scripture and Literature.* New York: Oxford University Press, 2005.

Childs, Brevard S. *Exodus.* OTL. London: SCM, 1974.

Clendinnen, Inga. *Agamemnon's Kiss: Selected Essays.* Melbourne: Text Publishing, 2006.

Clifford, Richard J. *The Cosmic Mountain in Canaan and the Old Testament.* HSM 4. Cambridge, MA: Harvard University Press, 1972.

Collins, John J. *Introduction to the Hebrew Bible.* Minneapolis: Fortress, 2004.

Dalley, Stephanie. *Myths from Mesopotamia: Creation, the Flood, Gilgamesh and Others.* Oxford: Oxford University Press, 1989.

Davies, Norman. *Europe: A History.* Oxford: Oxford University Press, 1996.

Dever, William G. *What Did the Biblical Writers Know and When Did They Know It? What Archaeology Can Tell Us about the Reality of Ancient Israel.* Grand Rapids: Eerdmans, 2001.

―――. *Who Were the Early Israelites and Where Did They Come From?* Grand Rapids: Eerdmans, 2003.

Domning, Daryl P., with Foreword and Commentary by Monika K. Hellwig. *Original Selfishness: Original Sin and Evil in the Light of Evolution.* Aldershot, UK: Ashgate, 2006.

Dozeman, Thomas B., and Konrad Schmid, eds. *A Farewell to the Yahwist? The Composition of the Pentateuch in Recent European Interpretation.* SBL Symposium Series 34. Atlanta: Society of Biblical Literature, 2006.

Durham, John I. *Exodus.* WBC. Waco, TX: Word Books, 1987.

Edelman, Diana Vikander. *King Saul in the Historiography of Judah.* JSOTSup 121. Sheffield: Sheffield Academic Press, 1991.

Estés, Clarissa Pinkola. *Women Who Run with the Wolves: Contacting the Power of the Wild Woman.* London: Rider, 1992.

Exum, J. Cheryl. "Who's Afraid of 'The Endangered Ancestress'?" In *The New Literary Criticism and the Hebrew Bible,* ed. J. Cheryl Exum and David J. A. Clines, 91–113. JSOTSup 143. Sheffield: JSOT, 1993.

Finkelstein, Israel, and Neil Asher Silberman. *The Bible Unearthed: Archaeology's New Vision of Ancient Israel and the Origin of Its Sacred Texts.* New York: Free Press, 2001.

———. *David and Solomon: In Search of the Bible's Sacred Kings and the Roots of the Western Tradition.* New York: Free Press, 2006.

Flannery, Tim. *The Weather Makers: How Man Is Changing the Climate and What It Means for Life on Earth.* New York: Grove, 2005.

Frerichs, Ernest S., and Leonard H. Lesko, eds. *Exodus: The Egyptian Evidence.* Winona Lake, IN: Eisenbrauns, 1997.

Fretheim, Terence E. *Exodus.* Interpretation. Louisville, KY: John Knox, 1991.

Friedman, Thomas L. *The Lexus and the Olive Tree.* New York: Farrar, Straus and Giroux, 2000.

Fulghum, Robert. *It Was on Fire When I Lay Down on It.* New York: Villard, 1989.

Gunkel, Hermann. *Genesis.* Macon, GA: Mercer University Press, 1997. German original, 3rd ed., 1910.

Halpern, Baruch. *David's Secret Demons: Messiah, Murderer, Traitor, King.* Grand Rapids: Eerdmans, 2001.

Heidel, Alexander. *The Gilgamesh Epic and Old Testament Parallels.* 2nd ed. Chicago: University of Chicago Press, 1949.

Heller, Joseph. *God Knows.* New York: Knopf, 1984.

Jericke, Detlef. *Abraham in Mamre: Historische und Exegetische Studien zur Region von Hebron und zu Genesis 11,27–19,38.* Culture & History of the Ancient Near East 17. Leiden: Brill, 2003.

Kaiser, Otto. *Isaiah 13–39.* OTL. London: SCM, 1974.

———. *Isaiah 1–12.* OTL. 2nd ed. completely rewritten. London: SCM, 1983.

Kirk, G. S. *Myth: Its Meaning and Functions in Ancient and Other Cultures.* Cambridge: Cambridge University Press, 1971.

Klein, Ralph W. *1 Samuel.* WBC. Waco, TX: Word Books, 1983.

Knierim, Rolf P., and George W. Coats, *Numbers.* FOTL. Grand Rapids: Eerdmans, 2005.

Levine, Baruch A. *Numbers 1–20.* AB. New York: Doubleday, 1993.

Mayes, A. D. H. *Deuteronomy.* NCB. London: Oliphants, 1979.

Mays, James Luther. *Hosea.* OTL. London: SCM, 1969.

McCarter, P. Kyle, Jr. *I Samuel.* AB. Garden City, NY: Doubleday, 1980.

———. "The Apology of David." *JBL* 99 (1980): 489–504.

McCarthy, Dennis J. *Treaty and Covenant: A Study in Form in the Ancient Oriental Documents and in the Old Testament.* AnBib 21A; new edition completely revised. Rome: Biblical Institute Press, 1978.

McKenzie, John L. *Dictionary of the Bible.* New York: Macmillan, 1965.

Miller, Patrick D. *Deuteronomy.* Interpretation. Louisville: Westminster John Knox, 1990.

Miller, Patrick D., Jr., and J. J. M. Roberts. *The Hand of the Lord: A Reassessment of the "Ark Narrative" of 1 Samuel.* Baltimore: Johns Hopkins University Press, 1977.

Nelson, Richard D. *Joshua.* OTL. Louisville: Westminster John Knox, 1997.

———. *Deuteronomy.* OTL. Louisville: Westminster John Knox, 2002.

Noth, Martin. *Exodus.* OTL. London: SCM, 1962.

———. *Numbers.* OTL. London: SCM, 1968.

———. *A History of Pentateuchal Traditions.* Trans. B. W. Anderson, 1972. Reprinted: Chico, CA: Scholars Press, 1981; German original, 1948.

Plaut, W. Gunther, ed. *The Torah: A Modern Commentary.* New York: Union of American Hebrew Congregations, 1981.

Powell, Barry B. *Classical Myth.* 4th ed. Upper Saddle River, NJ: Pearson, 2004.

Propp, William H. C. *Exodus 1–18, 19–40.* AB. New York: Doubleday, 1999, 2006.

Pury, Albert de. "Le cycle de Jacob comme légende autonome des origines d'Israel." In *Congress Volume: Leuven 1989,* ed. J. A. Emerton, 78–96. Leiden: Brill, 1991.

Rad, Gerhard von. *Old Testament Theology.* Vol. 1: *The Theology of Israel's Historical Traditions.* Edinburgh: Oliver and Boyd, 1962.

———. *Deuteronomy.* OTL. London: SCM, 1966.

———. "The Form-Critical Problem of the Hexateuch." Pages 1–78 in *The Problem of the Hexateuch, and Other Essays.* Edinburgh: Oliver and Boyd, 1966.

Ratzinger, Joseph. *Introduction to Christianity.* London: Search, 1969.

Rofé, Alexander. "An Enquiry into the Betrothal of Rebekah." In *Die Hebräische Bibel und ihre zweifache Nachgeschichte,* ed. E. Blum, C. Macholz, and E. W. Stegemann, 27–39. Neukirchen-Vluyn: Neukirchener Verlag, 1990.

Rost, Leonhard. *The Succession to the Throne of David.* Sheffield: Almond, 1982. German original: 1926.

Sanford, John A. *The Man Who Wrestled with God: Light from the Old Testament on the Psychology of Individuation.* New York: Paulist, 1981.

Schmidt, Ludwig. *Das 4. Buch Mose Numeri: Kapital 10,11–36,13.* ATD. Göttingen: Vandenhoeck & Ruprecht, 2004.

Schniedewind, William M. *How the Bible Became a Book: The Textualization of Ancient Israel.* Cambridge: Cambridge University Press, 2004.

Schuster, Marguerite. *The Fall and Sin: What We Have Become as Sinners.* Grand Rapids: Eerdmans, 2004.

Seebass, Horst. *Numeri 10,11–22,1.* BKAT. Neukirchen-Vluyn: Neukirchener Verlag, 2003.

Skinner, John. *Genesis.* ICC. Edinburgh: T. & T. Clark, 1910.

Smend, Rudolf. "Das Gesetz und die Völker: Ein Beitrag zur deuteronomistischen Redaktionsgeschichte." In *Probleme biblischer Theologie: Gerhard von Rad zum 70. Geburtstag,* ed. H. W. Wolff, 494–509. Munich: Kaiser, 1971.

Steiner, George. *In Bluebeard's Castle: Some Notes towards the Redefinition of Culture.* New Haven, CT: Yale University Press, 1971.

Stoebe, Hans Joachim. *Das erste Buch Samuelis, Das zweite Buch Samuelis.* KAT. Gütersloh: Gütersloher Verlagshaus, 1973, 1994.

Sweeney, Marvin A. *The Twelve Prophets.* Vol. 1: *Hosea, Joel, Amos, Obadiah, Jonah.* Berit Olam. Collegeville, MN: Liturgical Press, 2000.

———. "On the Literary Function of the Notice Concerning Hiel's Re-Establishment of Jericho in 1 Kings 16.34." In *Seeing Signals, Reading Signs: The Art of Exegesis. Studies in Honour of Antony F. Campbell, SJ, for His Seventieth Birthday,* ed. M. A. O'Brien and H. N. Wallace, 104–15. London: T. & T. Clark, 2004.

Trible, Phyllis. *God and the Rhetoric of Sexuality.* OBT. Philadelphia: Fortress, 1978.

Van Seters, John. *Abraham in History and Tradition.* New Haven, CT: Yale University Press, 1975.

Vervenne, Marc. "The 'P' Tradition in the Pentateuch: Document and/or redaction. The 'Sea Narrative' (Ex 13,17–14:31) as Test Case." In *Pentateuchal and Deuteronomistic Studies: Papers Read at the XIIIth IOSOT Congress, Leuven, 1989,* ed. C. Brekelmans and J. Lust, 67–90. BETL 94. Leuven: Leuven University Press, 1990.

Ward, William. See under Frerichs and Lesko.

Wellhausen, Julius. *Die composition des Hexateuchs und der historischen Bücher des Alten Testaments.* Cited from the 4th unchanged printing, Berlin: de Gruyter, 1963. Originals, 1876–78.

Wenham, Gordon J. *Genesis 1–15.* WBC. Waco, TX: Word Books, 1987.

Westermann, Claus. *Genesis 1–11: A Commentary.* Minneapolis: Augsburg, 1984; German original, 1974.

———. *Genesis 12–36: A Commentary.* Minneapolis: Augsburg, 1985; German original, 1981.

———. *Genesis 37–50: A Commentary.* Minneapolis: Augsburg, 1986; German original, 1982.

Wolff, Hans Walter. *Hosea.* Hermeneia. Philadelphia: Fortress, 1974.

———. *Joel and Amos.* Hermeneia. Philadelphia: Fortress, 1977.